Son, I Like Your Dress

a memoir by

Meredith Guest

Son, I Like Your Dress, is an intimate, funny, excruciatingly honest account of a male-to-female transsexual who considers herself living proof that God does have a sense of humor - and a wicked one at that. It is rich with stories and infused with insights from a thoughtful person with an uncommon perspective.

Son, I Like Your Dress

A Memoir

By Meredith Guest

Lulu Press, 2015

First Printing: 2015

ISBN   978-1-312-85415-4

Please direct inquiries to:

mergguest@gmail.com
www.meredithguest.net

Your thoughts and comments are welcome.

Contents

"The stuff work of omnipotence" about her rising religious stardom; "I was the pin in [my mother's] lapel."

Dedication

This book is dedicated to my remarkable, beautiful, much beloved children, Caleb and Lia. You have always been gifts far beyond my deserving.

Acknowledgments

How does one acknowledge all the people who have played an important role in the unfolding of one's life, of the telling of one's story? It is, of course, impossible. I therefore, with regret and yet, relief, must limit myself to those who had a direct part in the making of this book. First and foremost, I wish to thank my life partner, Janet Johnson, who not only helped in ways beyond the telling but also suffered and sacrificed that it might be told at all. To her I owe a debt of eternal gratitude. To the SCRIBS writing group, Bob Canning, Vivien Straus, Jim Brumm, Lisa Consani, and Lori Delap who read, commented, critiqued and advised me. To David Dodd for unfailing encouragement and for putting me in touch with Heather McCloud who read and commented with great perception. And thanks to Diana Spaulding who read the manuscript and made even more helpful suggestions. To all these and countless more, I am indebted.

Prologue

My daughter, Lia, is sitting at the kitchen table, papers spread out in front of her, filling out an application for graduate school. "Mer, what year were you born?" she asks.

I look up from the onion I am chopping and intone in my finest southern drawl, "No self-respecting Southern woman reveals such delicate information." I go back to the onion. She keeps working on her papers. After a moment, I ask in my regular voice, "And besides, why does your school need to know the year I was born? The last time I checked twenty-six qualified you as an adult," after which I mumble, as if to myself but loud enough for her to hear, "evidence to the contrary notwithstanding."

She ignores the sarcasm. "You're my emergency contact."

"They need to know my birthday in order to contact me if you get a tummy ache?" I ask incredulously.

She cuts her eyes at me. "Mer..." she says, clearly exasperated.

"Okay, okay. 1948," I reveal.

Her expression of mock annoyance changes to one of genuine surprise. "Wow," she exhales, "that's a long time ago."

It is sobering to be confronted with the mortality of someone you love, someone who has been with you from your birth, someone you assumed would always be there, and without whom you cannot imagine your life.

I look up into her wide, clear, blue eyes and say evenly, "Tell me about it."

Because the story that follows is thematic rather than chronological, I have provided a timeline of my life to be found in the appendix. If you are the sort who likes things neat, tidy and well ordered, you may find it helpful in navigating places, events and people without losing your way nearly as often as I did.

Basically, there are three geographic periods:
1. **The Mississippi Period** – birth to 30. Includes marriage to Marsha, mother of our two children.
2. **The Maryland Period** – 30 to 38. All lived on Dayspring Farm. Includes birth of children, Caleb and Lia.
3. **The California Period** – 38 to present. I was almost 50 when I finally and fully came out and began living my life as a transwoman.

Some of the chapters/essays will include more than one period, since the themes – as befits a life – were not neat, tidy and well ordered.

separate (handwritten)
Too long! (handwritten)
spaces! (handwritten)
spaces! (handwritten)

A Note on Religion

→I am Christian. The way through my life has been guided by the teachings of Christianity. I do *not* believe Christianity is the only way; I'm not even sure it's the best way; it's just *my* way. Often and in many places, I edited out or tried to tone down the religious language so as not to provoke the anti-Christian sentiments some people who likely would read the story of a transsexual might have. Yet I hope you will understand that I cannot speak honestly or accurately about my life without reference to my faith. I am a Christian and that fact and my faith have been essential, powerful, and mostly positive parts of my journey.

Clearly, I am not a fundamentalist. I reject fundamentalism in all its manifestations, even those manifestations with whose basic message I tend to agree, e.g. gay rights fundamentalists, animal rights fundamentalists, environmental fundamentalists, health and wellness fundamentalists, dietary fundamentalists, etc. If there's one thing you can say about all fundamentalists, it is that they are always fundamentally wrong. Life is too complex and interesting to submit itself to the overly neat and rigid categories of fundamentalism, however well meaning.

Nor am I a biblical literalist. Biblical literalism is absurd. No one in their right mind takes the Bible literally when the writer of John refers to Jesus as "the Lamb of God." In addition to being absurd, it's tragic. As Marcus Borg and J.D. Crossan illuminate in their books on the Christian scriptures, imposing a modern world view on the Bible, a view that equates truth with facts, misses the whole point. The Bible is not a historical document, not in the modernist sense. It's not interested in history as we understand it. It's interested in who God is, who we are, how to live, and what it all means. If the authors of the Bible could hear how their writings are used in the churches that proclaim them, they would be mystified and appalled. They might also conclude – justifiably – that modern people are hopelessly dense when it comes to spiritual matters and nowhere would this be truer and more tragically apparent than in the churches.

I say this because at times I will employ overtly religious language. I do this with trepidation, because I know some will find it offensive. But I also do it intentionally, because I am not willing to cede the language of faith – or the Bible – to religious lackeys of the empire whose primary purpose is to pronounce divine sanction on the status quo, and if not sanction, then silence.

We are in a battle for language between those who imagine and aspire to a just and peaceful society and those who want to preserve the status quo. I hope in this work to recapture some of the lost ground, not just for religion and religious language, though that, too, but for all who imagine, long for and work to build a new heaven and a new earth regardless of what they call it.

Genesis

Sometimes I think my life could have begun like one of those good news/bad news jokes. The Doctor walks into the hospital waiting room and says, "Well, Mr. Guest, I have good news, and I have bad news. The good news is your wife just gave birth to the little girl you've always wanted. The bad news is she's male." So it was I lived the childhood of a boy named Hank. It wasn't a bad childhood; it just wasn't mine.

The End of Innocence

It is an old memory – over half a century now. I am on the playground of the elementary school that sits just next to the combined junior and senior highs and across the street from the public swimming pool where we – all the white kids, that is – virtually live throughout the oppressively hot Mississippi summers. I am standing with a friend. We are in second or third grade. Despite abundant evidence, I am not yet aware that I am a boy. I know because this memory and the one that follows both live inside me as the memories of a little girl, making them both unique and precious.

In the memory, my friend and I are watching the Brownies follow their leader like a row of ducklings to the Girl Scout hut that overlooks the Sunflower River, the town's low-tech sewage system. I sigh, "Don't you wish you could be a Brownie?" a wistfully rhetorical question, since to me the answer is perfectly obvious. I mean, who wouldn't want to wear one of those adorable little brown dresses, have the matching brown beanie bobby-pinned into their flowing locks, disappear into the inner sanctum of the Girl Scout hut and do whatever wondrous and magical things it is Brownies do?

My friend, however, does not share my dreamy reverie. He just turns and looks at me with what I remember as a mixture of incredulity and disgust. I was never the brightest crayon in the box, but I did not need to be "whopped upside the head with a two-by-four" as they are fond of saying in the South, to realize that there were some things best left unspoken, and so, with aching, secret yearning, I watched the Brownies until I was much too old to be one.

It was the end of innocence – and the beginning of a lie.

Goddess Worshiper

As a child, I watched girls a lot. In fact, I was a fan club of one for the entire female sex. For all my Christian upbringing, I was a Goddess worshiper from the start and every girl a priestess. I ogled them with sheer, desperate, aching adoration. I studied their faces like a sculptor studies a subject, their eyes, their noses turned ever so slightly upward in an obvious physiological proclamation of feminine superiority, their mouths, their lips, their delicate ears. I especially loved their hair, at all the ways they wore it, at the various devices they used to contain it, always in vain, because at least some of it invariably escaped into the wind to play about their faces, catching and reflecting the sunlight like the sea. And then they would reach up with their delicate fingers and tuck it deftly behind an ear in that simple, unconscious motion that to me symbolized femininity like a salute. I watched their fluid bodies skip, dance, spin and twirl like water over stones in a brook. I listened to their voices, high as bird-song, shrill as a hawk. I marveled at their clothes, so varied in form and fabric, color and pattern, their shoes – even their socks were a marvel to me. I was intrigued by everything about girls, though I admired them from afar, like a devotee who deigns himself unworthy to approach the divine beloved. While it is true I paid particular attention to those that most nearly embodied the cultural notions of beauty, I never made fun of girls, even girls whose failure to approximate those definitions made them objects of other's ridicule. Even though I was aware that some were more perfect than others, they were all more perfect than me.

First Love

My other memory as a girl is of a boy. I met him one summer in a church day camp called Vacation Bible School. Many a blissful summer was sullied by a week or – God forbid! – two of what could only be described as an ecclesiastical concentration camp.

Sequestered like a group of surly malcontents, we morosely endured hours of enigmatic stories from the Bible that rendered the imaginings of Walt Disney pale by comparison. For one brief, magical week, this cultic hell was broken by a boy named Tommy who lived in a distant land called Tutwiler. Tommy was visiting his grandparents, people I didn't know but who earned my eternal gratitude when they sent him as a ray of pure sunlight into that interminable period of summertime darkness. Sir Tommy of Tutwiler, my knight in shining armor, my first true love, my hero, my man.

I still remember his laugh, the way his eyes sparkled – they were green – the color of his hair, dark brown and shiny. I tried desperately to sit next to him during arts and crafts, one of the few times we were allowed to speak freely, but then, I could think of nothing to say. How does a girl speak words of love to a boy she knows sees her as a he? It was delicious agony, and I remember wondering where Tutwiler was and if I could ever think of a reason my parents might take me there. Then, as suddenly as he came into my life, he was gone forever.

Perhaps my subsequent loss of interest in men was, in part, because where I grew up one of the worst insults a person could hurl at another was to call him "Butcher." Now, if somebody called you Butcher in an insulting way, you'd probably be more inclined to question the person's sanity than to be offended. But in the particular Mississippi town where I grew up, there was a man whose mannerisms and bearing were so affected it was generally assumed that he must be gay. His last name was Butcher. And so, early on I knew that the very name of someone identified as gay was a curse, a taunt, an insult of the highest order, and I somehow recognized – even as a child – our consanguinity, our bond of blood, and knew if anyone ever discovered my true identity, I too would fall under his curse.

These and countless other prohibitions, individually as invisible as the dots of a pointillism, taken together created "No Trespassing" signs across the entire landscape of my identity, barring entry into all those places that felt like me.

What Did I Know and When Did I Know It

Perhaps the greatest gift of my transsexuality is that I had to search for answers to questions that most people have the luxury of never asking.

Despite the ambivalence, the confusion, the need to please and conform, I always knew I was not a boy. In my case, however, there was some fairly compelling evidence suggesting otherwise. But this evidence, this fleshy fact of physiology, no more make me feel like a boy than the loss of a man's penis and testicles would make him feel like a woman. Or, by the same token, if a woman one day woke up to discover a penis hanging between her legs and a hairy, boobless chest, it still wouldn't make her *feel* like a man. A penis may define you as a man in the eyes of others, but if you aren't one, it just makes you feel like a queer.

Nor is knowledge the same as awareness. I know that blood is coursing through my veins, but I am not aware of it. I know that I am right-handed but am conscious of that fact only when repairs on one of the countless things that are constantly breaking on this funky little piece of property requires me to use my left hand. I knew I was a girl, but hanging onto that when everyone else thought of me as a boy was like trying to hold onto a piece of soap in a tub of warm water with shampoo in my eyes. I'd have it – and then it would slip away.

For the bulk of my childhood, I lived in a kind of passive acquiescence haunted by a vague sense that something was not quite right; *I* was not quite right. I had these unnatural longings as real, persistent and hidden as the need to breathe, longings to wear dresses, have long hair, be a Brownie, get the ruffled nightgown on the cover of the J.C. Penny catalog from Santa, then crawl into my father's lap and cuddle. These longings rarely occupied the landscape of my consciousness. Rather they seeped through it like a subterranean spring, surfacing only occasionally, usually unseen or else mistaken for something else.

Shortly after I came out to my mother, she remarked that if this had been my older brother, Richard, it wouldn't have been so hard. "He was the one who never liked to get dirty, who always cared so much about how he looked. You…you were such a tomboy." I loved her for using the term reserved for boyish girls, and I too, have puzzled at how much I acted like a boy. But then, how and when might I have acted otherwise? I was given my father's name, swaddled in boy-blue minutes after my birth, treated in every respect like a boy, talked to like a boy, given boy toys, dressed in boy clothes, taught to do boy things, and on top of that, I was a pleaser. I was a lost cause from the start. Maybe if I'd had an older sister…but no. This was not something they would have wanted to see, and even confronted with evidence, their recognition would have quickly turned into denial just like it did for me when puberty began ratcheting things up.

During puberty, the passive acquiescence of childhood was inadequate to deal with what was no longer a vague sense of longing, but rather, a persistent urge driven by the dawning of sexuality. I don't know when, and I certainly don't know why – perhaps the hormonal brew coursing through my veins fermented in the vat of denial and emerged as some strange vintage – but at some point, putting on girl's clothes became erotically intoxicating. I became obsessed with it; in time, I would become addicted to it. Still, it started out innocently enough.

In sixth grade, I went through a period when I'd go into the guest bedroom, close the door, take one of Mom's dresses out of the cedar chest, put it on and call my classmate, Joyce. I'm not sure what we talked about; it was, after all, a long time ago, but, to the best of my recollection, I think we talked about the things girls usually talked about: Who liked who. How we felt about Mrs. Smith. What happened at recess. Who did what to who and how that made him/her feel. How we felt when he/she said this/that. Classic girl talk. Of course, I couldn't talk to Joyce about these things at school. I was, after all, impersonating a boy, and boys, that is boys who didn't get beat up, who didn't go to therapy in distant towns, who didn't raise eyebrows of suspicion, couldn't talk openly to a girl – and especially not about things like this. I was allowed to chase them, harass them, pull their hair, try to look up their dresses, but I could not have a simple, friendly conversation with one – at least, not in public. So I was forced to do it over the phone, dressed secretly in one of Mom's dresses. For her part, Joyce probably thought of me a lot like straight women think about gay men. As for me, I just wanted a friend who I could talk to, share experiences with and confide in. In other words, I just wanted to be a girl like all the other girls.

Over forty years later I would meet an eight-year-old who, though male, was living her life as a girl just like all the other girls. While I was certainly glad for her, the meeting filled me with a strange and peculiar sense of sadness, and suddenly the decades old memory of the phone calls to Joyce returned, and for the first time ever, I wondered, What happened after I hung up?

What did I do? Where did I go? How did I feel when I had to go back to being a boy? Did I cry? Was I depressed? I can't remember; yet I think the sadness evoked by the eight-year-old transgirl gives me a glimpse.

I imagine her – me – curled up on her bed, hugging her beloved white and black terrier. She is utterly and completely alone and knows it, feels it, suffers it, bears it. There is no one to talk to about what is going on inside her, no one to comfort her, to hold her, to tell her that she is okay. The thought of her there all alone breaks my heart. Oh God, how I wish I could fold time back on itself and be there in that room with that child and cradle her in my arms and tell her that there is nothing wrong with her, that it is all going to come out okay, that one day she will look back and realize it has been, in many ways, a gift.

Yet imagining her there all those years ago, I realize that the sadness is tempered by a steely determination. After all, she must have been a strong little thing; otherwise how would she have survived? And not just survive, she would, by God, live to be – and so she has. So, by God, she has.

Girl's Camp

The summer after sixth grade, neighbors up the street invited me to accompany them on a vacation to pick up their two daughters from camp and afterward, spend a week traveling and camping. It seems they wanted a boy along to help with the manly camping chores like collecting firewood and helping set up the tent, chores two belles-in-training could hardly be expected to do; they might, after all, break a nail. It was my first and only visit to an all-girl's camp.

I don't know what I expected, but when we arrived, the first thing I noticed was *not* the idyllic surroundings, the rustic log cabins nestled in the woods, the beautiful clear blue lake complete with diving platforms and a flotilla of canoes. No, what struck me speechless was that the place was crawling with – you guessed it – girls! They were everywhere, and I mean everywhere! James Audubon going to sleep and waking up in Bird Heaven could hardly have been more excited than me.

Of course, I had seen crowds of girls at school, but this was different. Here no boys contaminated the surroundings, sullied the view, spoiled the splendor of girls, nothing but girls. The place buzzed with a palpable force field of pure, unmixed, unadulterated girl energy. Had I been less shy – a LOT less shy – and prone to musical outbursts, I might have thrown my hand over my chest and belted out the old Ginger Rogers/Fred Astaire tune *Heaven, I'm in heaven!*

What I *did* do was, right there on the spot, without even thinking about it, hell, without even knowing I was doing it, execute a feat of great intellectual acuity: I performed a near perfect Aristotelian syllogism. In case you don't remember or don't know what a syllogism is, it is "a trio of propositions of which the third (the conclusion) follows from the conceded truth of the other two."

Aristotle's famous example goes like this: Man is a rational animal; Socrates is a man; therefore Socrates must be a rational animal. More likely you remember the mathematical formulation: if A=C and B=C, then A and B must be equal. In my case it went like this: Only girls can be at an all girls' camp; I am at an all girls' camp; therefore I must be a girl. It was perfect! It was foolproof! It was inarguable! In no time at all I would be running around with the other girls, screaming and chasing and diving into the lake clad in my adorable girl's bathing suit, and, of course, I'd magically have pigtails! (Hey, a little suspension of disbelief is a suitable reward for a twelve-year-old who has just performed a near perfect Aristotelian syllogism, don't you think?)

My few moments of overwhelming joy were short-lived, however. Soon the presence of a boy was noticed, and I was suddenly the object of unnerving, unwanted and unwelcome interest. Like a nail being struck by a hammer, I was impaled, crucified on the reality of what I was – a boy, an alien in this world of girls, an invader from the Other Galaxy. I pulled inside myself like a turtle and tried my best to become as small and inconspicuous as possible.

Also on that trip, I had my first experience of falling in love with a girl.

The older of the two girls was Nancy. She was probably only a year or so older than me, but, having left behind the childish things of elementary school for the sophistication of junior high, I was beneath her notice. I was, after all, only the help. Beth was about a year younger than me and whereas Nancy had short, curly blonde hair, Beth had thick, shiny, dark hair that fell in gentle waves to her shoulders.

One night Beth and I ended up sitting alone across from one another at a picnic table. Where the others were I have no idea. Between us a candle burned, and into its flame, Beth was feeding small twigs, which she watched with fascination alight and be consumed. With equal fascination I watched Beth. The soft glow of the candle illumined her face with a radiance that captivated me, and for the first time ever I noticed that Beth had the most beautiful brown eyes. I understand now where the idea of cupid comes from; for indeed, as if struck by an unseen arrow, I was instantly smitten. It was a wonderful sensation, rich, intoxicating and so powerful it has stayed vivid to me after all these years; and yet, as suddenly as it came, it was gone. Maybe my endocrine system, in a moment of curiosity, decided to dump a bunch of hormones, newly minted in my still developing testes, into my bloodstream to see what might happen and then, afterward, thought better of it.

By contrast, I also had my first and only experience of domestic violence on that trip. If my parents ever fought – and surely they did – I never heard it; and I never heard about it. For all I knew, they loved each other without conflict until the day Dad died. I was completely unprepared, therefore, when one night I was awakened by the sound of Beth and Nancy's father threatening their mother. I couldn't see them, but I could hear them plainly enough. "If you don't shut up," he growled with a malevolence I had never imagined possible coming from any adult I knew, "I am going to beat you..." whereupon she began to beg and plead with him like a small child. I waited to hear the blow, the sickening sound of fist on flesh, but none came. I think he walked away. Probably they had been drinking. I don't know, but it took me a long time to fall back to sleep. Afterward, nothing was ever said about it, and nothing was ever the same. Without being told, I knew that now I was expected to become part of the conspiracy of silence to which they were all party. Fortunately, it was at the very end of the trip. Terrible as it was, I certainly came home a wiser child with a new, more mature appreciation for my own parents.

At about the same period, my parents became close friends with a couple who had a boy several years younger than me named T.J. The adults were fond of going out together, and so, given that nothing so spoils a good meal as a child, they left T.J. in my care.

No sooner was the car out the driveway, than T.J. and I were pawing through my mother's clothes, filling bras with rolled up socks, donning dresses along with hats and gloves and heels. Once properly attired, we paraded around the house pretending to be our mothers. (Probably, had we taken to doing some of their cleaning chores, they'd have gladly provided us with our own wardrobes.)

On a couple of occasions, after playing for a while in maternal drag, we began to feel vaguely guilty, so we took off the girl clothes, put them carefully away and, as if to cleanse ourselves, re-attired in combat camos complete with army helmets and toy weapons. Fundamentalists might say that proof of our wickedness was that we did not have to be told that dressing as girls was an abomination. Of course, we didn't have to be told that Blacks were inferior to Whites or that a woman's place was in the home, either. (T.J. – perhaps in a dramatically desperate attempt to fully cleanse himself – went on to join the Marines and fight the godless communists in Vietnam. Talk about an abomination.)

If anyone ever suspected what was going on with T.J. and me, they never mentioned it, and I never confessed. God only knows what would have happened had I had an older sister. Nothing she owned would have been safe. I'd have been wearing her Kotex in my BVDs.

The summer before I started college, the summer when (God forgive me) I led the great youth revival, I was living with my best friend Marvin who had an older sister. One day, while washing off the ubiquitous sticky coating of Mississippi grime in their old claw-foot tub, I spied her madras two-piece swimsuit hanging on a towel rack. Hearing no one else in the house, I put it on. Admiring my skinny, firm body in the medicine cabinet mirror, I looked absolutely adorable – even a little sexy. It was terrifying and exhilarating, exquisite and excruciating, totally right and totally forbidden all in the same moment.

I had to go to the bathroom a lot that day, though I could scarcely enjoy myself, since Marvin's dad, a mountain of a man, had a way of busting into the bathroom without warning whenever nature called, and he was absolutely the last person in the world I wanted to catch me wearing a girl's two-piece – adorable or not.

From these auspicious beginnings, the cross-dressing waxed and waned, grew passionately hot and depressingly cold the older I got. Periods of guilt-ridden obsession would be followed by periods of hopeful remission to be followed by periods of guilt-ridden obsession to be followed by…well, you get the picture. On the surface, I appeared to be just another teenage boy ambling clumsily through life. Beneath the surface, I was a refugee struggling to survive in a psychic no man's land. With no one to turn to, living in arguably the most openly homophobic part of the country, utterly unaware that there was anyone else like me in the entire world, I expended an ever-increasing amount of energy hiding, repressing, sublimating and denying.

This struggle to find the Truth that the facts concealed felt a lot like swimming upstream. Due to a fluke of physiology, because I was male, I was thrown unceremoniously into the river leading to manhood. And it was a river, not a road or a path. On roads you have to propel yourself along, plus there are lots of alternate routes. While people choose to follow a different path, few question the direction in which their gender river flows. But I was like an anadromous fish, the kind that fights its way up raging rivers, hurls itself into the breathless air, breasts raging waterfalls, runs a gauntlet of hungry predators all in response to some desperate, frantic, mysterious urge.

From time to time, I would pause in this gargantuan struggle and resolve to stop this insanity, turn around and let myself be carried along by the river's inexorable flow. But no matter how hard I tried to make it work, no matter how many times I purged my secret collection of women's wear, make-up, curlers, fingernail polish, undergarments, I knew if I was ever going to find peace and my appointed destiny, I would have to work my way back upstream to some unknown place that lived in the dim recesses of my unconscious like a smell, a taste, the residue of a dream. And never for a minute did I doubt that in so doing something would have to die – and that something would almost surely have to be me.

The journey out of denial and into knowledge began in earnest one summer evening about a year before we moved from Dayspring Farm to California. It was one of those points in time that embody both alpha and omega – a beginning and an ending. The children and Marsha were once again visiting her parents back in Mississippi. In the wee hours of the morning while most of the world slept, I ventured forth from our house clad in forbidden attire and stealthily walked the two-tenths of a mile to a grassy meadow encircled by the ancient apple orchard. It was a winding gravel road that passed few other dwellings, and the dense, lush canopy of hardwoods sheltered me from the full moon's ethereal glow.

When finally I crept out onto it, the meadow was wrapped in the airy silence of deep night, and the bright summer moon cast my skirt-clad shadow clearly upon the fecund earth. Searching the edges of the forest like a prey animal searches for the predator, I ventured forth with the timidity of a field mouse. I don't know why; I don't know what moved or possessed me, but I removed my shoes and socks until my bare feet swam in the meadow's thick, dew-sodden grasses, and I began to dance.

It was as if, at the very last second, the young woman hidden deep inside me wrested free my body from the white-knuckled fear that had hitherto controlled me. In a moment of wild and ancient ecstasy, she transfused her blood into muscle, tendon, ligament, bone until my very flesh incandesced in a field of feminine phosphorescence.

People scoff at the ridiculous impossibility of the virgin birth. Not me. In that moon-drenched meadow, God made love to me. He ravaged me like a lover too long denied, filled me with his hot emission, and in my womb began to grow the child of our true union.

It would yet be many years before with labor, sweat, blood and tears, she was born, but the period of my gestation had nonetheless begun; and in that moonstruck meadow, I knew it.

Out of the Closet

We speak of coming out of the closet as if it were something that occurs at a given time and place like a coming of age ritual or, better still, a cotillion, one of those elaborate and expensive rituals reserved for girls of sufficient social standing, during which they are presented to proper society as ladies, suitable for breeding by males of means with desirable pedigrees. But the parade of petticoats that welcomes rich southern belles into adult society was denied me; though our lack of wealth and social standing were hardly the primary reasons. Even coming out to myself emerged slowly and painfully like a tooth, or, better still, a whole set of teeth. I have about as much idea of when I finally accepted myself as transsexual as I have about when I got my last molar – though I can assure you, it was considerably later.

After my exhilarating dance in the meadow, I had taken to embarking on short forays into public places with mixed results. Even under the best of circumstances, it's hard to pass for a woman when you're a forty year old, 6'2" male dressed like a woman – and I, by no means, represented the best of circumstances. After being chased from a mall by a group of laughing, pointing teenagers, I went back into hiding until we moved to California a year or so later. Once in the Golden State, it wasn't long before I discovered the Castro district in San Francisco – the Gay Mecca – where the only problem people had with me dressing as a woman was that I did it so badly. "Honey, that purse just does not go with those shoes, and, I mean, where *did* you find those shoes?"

One particularly memorable Sunday I joined thousands of other queerfolk for the annual Castro Street Fair, a huge street party where, dressed en-femme, I was, by comparison to the other revelers, about as exotic and interesting as a house sparrow, a *female* house sparrow at *(handwritten margin note top: "! ((— Interesting imagery / language !!!" with "A")*

that. Walking through the crowded streets, I realized that merely being around other people – even lots of other people – was not going to turn the penny. Eventually, I would either have to bite the bullet and join the human race as a transwoman or else suffer the lonely agony of a life lived in the closet.

While pondering this vexation, I noticed among the countless other discarded items on the litter-strewn street, a flier. Now this is a classic example of what someone I knew long ago called *The Staff Work of Omnipotence,* because there was nothing notable about this random piece of paper that should have attracted my attention; yet it did. To anyone else it was merely an announcement about a beginner's class for a gay square dancing club, but by this time I was familiar enough with God's peculiar sense of humor that I could hear the voice of the Almighty crooning in his best cowboy twang, "Hey, purty lady, how 'bout you and me go doe-see-doe?"

The evening of the first class, I dressed in a long denim skirt purloined in the recent separation from Marsha, *(handwritten margin: "??? when did this happen.")* along with my new, knee-high, black, fringed moccasins purchased just for the occasion. They had thin, flat soles, thus making me no taller and, being black, I fancied they even made my feet look smaller. I wore a white, western-style shirt beneath which I had a bra filled with boobs tediously constructed from large balloons filled with melted Crisco, which – I am both proud and mortified to admit – I designed, engineered and constructed myself.

So attired, I drove over an hour from my house to the city, whereupon I sat in my car paralyzed with fear. Peering out the car window through the open doorway of the community center, I could see a milling crowd waiting for the class to begin. Why was I so afraid? And here of all places. This was the same crowd of gay men and lesbians I had just spent an entire day with at the street fair without incident. Was I afraid they would reject me? Throw me out? Laugh at me? I knew they wouldn't. And yet, I couldn't move.

Of all the taboos passed down and practiced by humans throughout time, the bending of gender, especially from male to female, has got to be high on the list of the most forbidden. Like everyone, I knew this, and no one had to tell me that violating the sacred taboos is dangerous. Even the drive to the city dressed as a woman was fraught with peril. What if I was stopped by a highway patrolman or the car broke down? Even if I could pass as a woman – which wasn't likely – my driver's license clearly said "Male". What if I had a wreck and was injured? Not only would I have to suffer the consequences, but those family members and friends who would come to my aid would also come into the knowledge, the terrible, humiliating, secret knowledge of who and what I was. No mere mortal can set themselves up against the arcane power of such sacred taboos without feeling afraid.

I also didn't want to be seen as a fool, and yet, I felt foolish, and I knew I looked foolish. How could I not? I had committed myself to impersonating a man since I was seven and I was now in my mid-forties. Testosterone had had its way with me physically, mentally and emotionally. A skirt, fake boobs and too much makeup would not magically erase that no matter how much I wished they would or fantasized they might.

What I would learn – and this is true in varying degrees for everyone – was that you cannot live your truth, you cannot become your authentic self without violating taboos and risking being a fool; there's simply no way. And the price is always high, if not externally, then internally – and in the case of LGBT people, too often, both.

Just before the fear managed to pin me to the mat for yet one more humiliating defeat, I remembered an experience I had years earlier on a ropes course I did with my 4-6th grade students. It was without doubt one of the most memorable things I ever did with a class, since pants-pissing terror has a way of breaking down the customary distinctions between students and teacher. One particularly difficult element of the course required climbing a rope ladder straight up a redwood tree to some obscene height and then trying to walk a single strand of steel cable while holding onto a rope hanging downward from another cable far above. I managed to get myself to within reach of the bottommost cable when a surge of overwhelming panic seized me. After several agonizing minutes of icy paralysis, the woman below holding the belay line to which I was tethered (but had not yet tested) said almost quietly, "You don't have to go on if you don't want to, but before you come down, just push through your fear and take one more step."

That's what I was remembering as I sat in my car staring through the open doors where the first square dancing class was about to begin. As I reached for the key to crank the car and return home defeated and despondent, I heard a gentle voice inside my head say, "Just go through the door, and then, if you want to, you can turn around and leave, but just push through your fear enough to get through the door. That's all you have to do."

My heart racing, on the verge of hyperventilating, I summoned every ounce of courage I could and willed myself out of the car, up the sidewalk, past an ominous group of young males playing basketball on an outside court and through the open door.

No sooner had I crossed the threshold than an overly thin queen in his fifties looked up from his table and without even so much as a hello, got up, took me by the arm, led me to the edge of the dance floor and yelled into a waiting crowd of men, "I have a girl here." From that moment on, I didn't worry about how I looked, or what people thought, or what terrible thing might happen; I was waaay too busy trying to figure out which step came next.

9 space indentation is distracting,

Though I wrote an official coming out letter (a copy is in the appendix), there were countless more comings out. Like bee stings, none of them killed me, but all of them hurt. Besides my immediate family, there were, of course, friends, both new and old, my kids' friends, my kid's friends' parents, my partner's kids and some of their friends, and pretty soon, even my partner's kids' kids. Then there was the nice deputy sheriff who dropped by to tell me he had shut down the out-of-control party Lia threw when we were away for the weekend, my dentist and doctor, my kids' dentists and doctors, the high school vice-principal with a notably deficient sense of humor who suspended Caleb from his senior prom when, in a state of slobbery inebriation, he and an equally intoxicated friend left an incredibly stupid message on the school's answering machine, the emergency room nurse and then the physician who treated me for my very first urinary tract infection (I was very excited), the lab nurse who I could have kissed when she exasperatedly noted the doctor's mistake in ordering a prostate test, the bank teller, the clerks at Safeway, Noah's Bagels, See's Candy (you cannot make it through this without good chocolate) and on and on and on it goes. Furthermore, other people in my life were likewise required to come out to people in their lives about me, sometimes with the same stings of shame that I felt. While it's true you can't get the honey without risking the stings, still, it's hard to ask others to suffer for a reward they will scarcely enjoy.

Shortly after I had begun to bask in the warm glow of life outside the closet like a moth emerging from a prolonged stay in its chrysalis, my mother got dangerously ill. It seemed her body had come to the perverse conclusion that it needed to destroy its red blood cells. Maybe it just wanted to start over, who knows? Anyway, Amy, my younger sister, had already endured a two-week stint at the small rural hospital in Georgia close to where Mom lived, and Greg, my younger brother was on caretaker duty when they moved her to Emory University hospital in Atlanta. At the time, I was frantically racing the clock to become a successful novelist before all our money ran out. The clock won, hands down. (No pun intended.) Since as a writer, I was not gainfully employed in a real job, I was tapped to take over Mom's care when Greg needed to resume his life of worthwhile employment.

While I had come out to them in the safety of a letter, I knew it was only a matter of time before – to borrow from the Gospel of John – my word had to become flesh. But with Mom being seriously ill, this didn't seem like the time, so, sighing deeply, I told her I would come home one last time in the guise of her son. At least, I assured myself, she was no longer at Hospital-In-The-Sticks, Georgia, but rather, Emory University where the Sons of the Confederacy (my former playmates) were less apt to use me for target practice.

Since Mom was no more a fan of television than I, we had plenty of time between the pricks and proddings to talk with a candor that had been impossible before. As a child, I hadn't really trusted Mother. I always felt like she had a hidden agenda, that I was important to her primarily for the notoriety she derived from my rising religious stardom. As my therapist once put it: I was the pin in her lapel.

In the role of caregiver to my mother, I likewise became better acquainted with Meredith who was, as yet, still new to me. Lots of other people got to know her as well. I informed the doctors and the nurses that I was Mabel's transsexual son. (I yet lacked sufficient internal permission to identify myself as her daughter.) I told her closest friends as well as her minister who, having a gay brother, was about as accepting as his fundamentalist religion allowed. What I remember best, though, was the look on the men's faces when I revealed my transsexuality to them. Rather than the hatred I had always expected, they instead, looked as though they would at any second, turn and run screaming down the hospital corridor protectively clasping their beloved crotches. I told them, because I knew mother would need to talk about it, and – like the chivalrous boy I had been raised to be – I wanted to have at least opened the door for her. Perhaps I should have begun by assuring them that I was neither contagious nor interested in them.

For reasons as mysterious as it began, mother's body decided to cease its campaign against its red blood cells, and so, after about a week at home, she was sufficiently recovered for me to return to California and continue writing the great American novel. Even though I had worn a little make-up every day I was there, as well as clothes much more suited to a modern woman (i.e. jeans) I decided that she still needed to see me in a dress lest she begin to think it was all some sort of terribly confusing, drug-induced hallucination. So the day Greg came to take me to the airport, I put on a long gray dress and joined them without fanfare at the dining room table where they were going back over the doctor's complicated follow-up regimen one last time. After final warnings, instructions and reminders from Greg and me, Mom looked up and in her simple, earnest, Southern way, said, "Well, son, I like your dress." I knew at that moment if I ever wrote a memoir, that would have to be the title.

At the end of the novel *Transsister Radio*, the main character, Dana, a male-to-female transsexual finds a man and together they move away to live happily ever after. Whenever Jennifer Boylan, a well know trans author, wanted to foray out of her closet, her main concern was getting hit on by men. These writers describe my experiences and the experiences of the male-to-female transsexuals I know about as accurately as Cinderella and

Prince Charming living happily ever after in the castle describes most people's experience of marriage.

For one thing, when transwomen finally muster the courage to come out of the closet, they usually emerge dressed in attire appropriate to the generation of girls they missed being. So here is this hulking 200-pound, six-foot male, beard shadow visible under layers of the wrong shade foundation, long blonde wig askew, clad in a miniskirt, fishnets and go-go boots parading through the mall like either a clown or a hooker with no prospects. From the outside it looks ridiculous; from the inside it's an excruciatingly painful attempt to reclaim a lost childhood. By this time testosterone has done its work with machine-like precision, and the body in which she is destined to live out her days, regardless of the amount of blood, sweat, tears and money she invests in trying to remake it, can be altered just so much. And while life out of the closet is better for most, it is almost always harder, much, much harder, so that when the futility reflected in the mirror and in the suspicious eyes of others shatters the delicately fashioned crystal illusion, God only knows how many obituaries fail to reveal the true cause of death.

Likewise, coming out takes place in stages with the first visible manifestations frequently seen on National Transsexual Coming Out Day – otherwise known as Halloween, the one day of the year when transfolk can strut their stuff with virtual impunity. Even wives are willing to be part of the fun on Halloween. Of course, it's a little hard to explain the panties, since they're not really a visible part of the outfit, but, heh! you just want to be authentic.

The Halloween season is also a good time to do some shopping that might otherwise raise eyebrows. For instance, when else can you shop for a woman's wig and convince yourself that the clerk actually believes you when you claim to be plunking down several hundred bucks on a

Halloween costume? Ditto for the clerk at the thrift store as you paw through the women's second-hand finery.

With the delicious taste of Halloween stuck in your mind like a milk dud in your teeth, you decide to proclaim yourself a crossdresser, an otherwise straight man who just enjoys wearing women's clothes. If you're lucky, you can find safe places to go out crossdressed, and if you're *very* lucky, your poor, anxious, befuddled wife will half-heartedly participate in your "fun."

Now I have a good friend who knows a lot more transwomen than I do who insists that cross dressers are not just transgirl scared-ta-be's; that there really are men who like to dress up in women's clothing for…well, just for the hell of it I suppose. I hope she's right. I think an epidemic of cross-dressing would be fantastically liberating for men – and fun to boot. What's more, done well, I think a lot of girls would get off on it, because mixing gender metaphors is sexy. I mean, what's sexier than a pretty girl in an old pick-up? A good-looking guy in a ruffled tux shirt with dark curls spilling over his collar? A muddied female combatant on a girl's soccer team? Blurring the lines is hot; it's suggestive of novel and naughty possibilities. As it stands now, guys and girls are just way too predictable. It's a wonder there hasn't been an epidemic of bi or trans-curiosity if for no other reason than sheer hetero boredom.

Some of my first tentative steps out into the big, bad world were on short excursions with Jan, my best friend and life-partner. I met Jan soon after moving to California when I enrolled adorable little Lia in the toddler program at the preschool where Jan taught. We were both in bad marriages at the time, though mine would end considerably sooner and less traumatically than hers. Our relationship as teacher of the other's child continued when her son, Dustin, came into my classroom in the 3rd grade. (This was still years prior to my coming out.)

By the time he was a sixth grader, Dustin had become one of those children I relied on for the sanity any reasonably healthy adult will lose when too long in the company of children. He possessed the jaded humor of an adult, and he was one of the few students with whom I could share an exasperated eye roll when a particularly immature student said something particularly dumb. He likewise could say things that professionalism forbade me. For instance, the day he called an exceedingly obnoxious little princess a bitch right in the group meeting, I could have kissed him. It was everything I could do to resist pumping my fist in the air and exclaiming, "Yes!" And with Dustin, I never had to fear he would use this against me or another student later.

Jan moved from the preschool to the elementary campus where I taught just as her marriage came apart like a car run too hard, too fast and too long over a washboard road. For months, she had all the symptoms of posttraumatic stress disorder, though her teaching scarcely showed it. As I found out later, she had also survived a horribly abusive childhood at the hands of a sadistic, alcoholic mother. When the old beast died, I thought the three daughters would clasp hands, dance and sing with the munchkins of Oz "*Ding dong the witch is dead, the witch is dead, the witch is dead. Ding dong the wicked witch is dead!*" Characteristic of abused children, however, they grieved her parting and flew the family flag at half-staff despite her atrocities. Through knowing Jan and her sisters, I came to appreciate the incredible power abusers have over the abused, a power that can raise a bony hand from the grave to grip a heart with icy fear.

Jan was in many ways the classic blonde; you know, the kind they make the jokes about, plus she was way too co-dependent for me to ever fall in love with. The last thing I wanted was to have someone trying to take care of me – emphasis on "trying." Besides that, the woman could never finish a sentence. It made me crazy. I am a writer; I pay very close attention to words and how they are woven together into sentences – you know, complete thoughts that end before new ones begin?

I had similar reactions to Lia when she was in high school. I'd be in the kitchen fixing dinner when Lia would come in and commence to expound on the drama de jour.

"Ohmygod, you're not going to believe what happened today! Remember, I told you about Stephanie breaking up with Joey?"

I would have no recollection of her ever having shared such priceless information with me, not a clue as to which blonde-haired, blue-eyed, Barbie-impersonating girl Stephanie was and not quite certain if this was the Joey up the street or another, but then, none of that mattered; she wouldn't wait for an answer anyway.

"Well, like, you know…"

She wads these four words up like they are a worthless candy wrapper and throws them on the ground. I take a deep breath.

…they broke up like a month ago, but he's so not over her?…

Is she asking me or telling me? The way her voice slides up at the end of a sentence makes it hard to know for sure.

…so today at lunch she went out to her car, and like, you're fucking not going to believe this!"

She had a foul mouth by the time she was twelve. I let it slide. Profanity isn't worth a battle.

"She found, like, a dead fox on her car."

She is looking at me waiting for a reaction, but by the fifth "like" my grip on the kitchen knife had tightened, and I was listening to the voices inside my head reminding me, *Okay, now, just remember, your daughter is talking to you. She's telling you about her day. Remember when you actually wanted to know about her day? Well, now you have to at least pretend...Meredith! Remember! She is your daughter. You love her. Infanticide is bad!...Wait! What did she say? A dead what? Is she kidding?*

Anything more than a ten-minute conversation with her – two minutes if any of her friends were involved – and small insects with prickly legs would begin crawling all over my skin beneath my clothing. By about the tenth "like" I felt if I did not find some avenue of escape in...say, the next two seconds, I would start screaming like a banshee, rip off my clothes and use them to throttle every teenager in sight! Okay, so I'm never going to win *Mother Of The Year* – big deal.

Where was I? Oh yes. Even as friends, I wanted Jan to know the whole story; I had already deceived too many people. So on a beach near the Golden Gate Bridge, I told her that I was transgender, that I wanted to live my life as a woman. By this time, I had had enough experience to be reasonably sure she would not flee in horror, or worse, break into hysterical laughter. In fact, I had learned from a previous relationship that the worst possibility was that Jan would appear to be very accepting and then later, use her acceptance as a tool to cultivate a relationship with me as a man. Jan, however, on nothing more than blind and naïve faith (and certainly, she must think at times, sheer insanity) accompanied me – at great personal cost – into unknown waters deeper and rougher than either of us ever imagined, and when the going got tough, she stood resolutely by me. I could never have made this journey without her, and to her I owe a debt of eternal gratitude.

While there were plenty of differences between us, Jan and I were alike in several important ways. For one thing, we had both lost our childhoods. I lived mine as someone else, and Jan's mother stole hers. While we couldn't go back and change the past, we did as much as we could to reclaim and relive our childhoods, and the horses we bought and the adventures we took with them were our little girls' dreams come true.

Back when I was in transactional analysis group therapy, one of the techniques we used to help identify and expose the hidden stories we tell ourselves was to imagine our life as a fairy tale. So, if I was to imagine Jan's and my relationship as a fairy tale, it would be something on the order of Beauty and Beast except ours would be about the unique bond that forms between a Freak and a Cripple. In this tale, each finds with the other unexpected acceptance, companionship and love. The Freak relies on the Cripple for the tangible rewards – e.g. food, clothing, shelter – given those afforded social acceptability, while the Cripple depends on the Freak for practical help, an adventurous spirit and the ability to solve complicated problems that involve the effective manipulation of power tools. Consequently, over time they form an intricate web of intimacy, mutually beneficial, unusually harmonious and dangerously dependent.

On the every other Sunday mornings when my kids were with Marsha, we'd typically make love, fix breakfast, get all dolled up and head for the Castro. This sounds easier than it actually was, because we lived in a small cluster of apartments that presented some rather daunting logistical problems. Especially if he'd smoked a joint that morning (and most mornings he had) Tim, our upstairs neighbor, would show up at our door on some lame pretext whereupon he would hang out and chat and chat and chat and chat. If I had already gone through the painstaking process of putting on my makeup, this posed a significant problem. Jan could cover for a while, but, I mean, how long can you be in the bathroom?

Once we had managed to get rid of Tim and were finally ready to go, the configuration of the buildings required making a short, terrified dash through open country on Jan's signal from the front door to the waiting car, then speeding out the drive as fast as possible before Tim or one of the other neighbors could intercept us. It was utterly nerve wracking, but coming home could be even worse, since we could never know for sure just where anybody was until it was too late. Often we'd make a pass or two, before turning into the access road, after which, there was no turning back. I always had extra clothes, so if worse came to worse, I could just change in the car but removing all traces of the make-up without benefit of soap and water was virtually impossible. It was also terribly, terribly sad, and often threw me into a depression that lasted for days.

Our first outings beyond the Castro were usually camping or else staying in cheap motels in small towns. Jan was of invaluable assistance during those early forays. For instance, if we were camping, she would scout out the bathroom situation, signaling me when the coast was clear or else engage other occupants in light conversation (Jan's very good at that) while I would slip quickly and quietly into or out of a stall. When we'd go out to eat, she'd order for both of us, since my voice was almost always a dead giveaway. Then we'd stroll down the main street and do a little shopping. Back in those early, pre-surgery days, it's hard to imagine I passed at all, but shop owners in those small, backwater places were so desperate for cash, they wouldn't have cared if I'd been impersonating a golden retriever so long as I had a functioning Visa. And, in fairness, I think most of them were good, kind, sympathetic people. Contrary to what the daily news would have you believe, the world has a surprisingly large number of really decent people in it.

Often, after speaking to a group, someone will say how much they admire me for my courage; but I don't feel courageous. Forty years in the closet enjoying the privileges of a tall, handsome, straight, white man doesn't seem very courageous to me. Nor – and in LGBT circles, this is blasphemy – am I always glad I came out. When I look at the costs, what I had to give up, especially my work as a teacher; when I see what it has cost others, especially my children; when I realize all the things I couldn't and can't do as a transwoman that I could have as a man, then I'm not so sure. So many times I wished I could have pulled off being a man, wished I could have kept up the pretense and still found enough peace to live a somewhat good and happy life. And though I believe life is always better out of the closet, there are plenty of times when it doesn't feel better, when it just feels harder.

But that's the rub isn't it? We can never be sure. We choose this instead of that and later, wonder if we should have done the opposite. At a critical moment we take this path rather than the four or five others we might have, and when the choice spins itself out in time and space, and we approach the end of our days, we cannot help but wonder – and sometimes wish – we had chosen another. Of course it doesn't help that with the passage of years, the forces at play, the reasons, the motivations for the original decisions have dimmed or plain been forgotten.

In the end, to live is to live by faith, good faith, bad faith, strong faith, weak faith, hopeful faith and faith that it's all meaningless and random, but faith nonetheless. My faith, grounded in Christianity, is that the work of God is redemption. If it is anything, the message of the cross is that there is nothing we can do, God cannot redeem for love. Some things are easier to redeem than others, intention influences outcome, and all decisions, both good and bad, exact a cost, but nothing is beyond the power of God to redeem for good. On that I have staked my life; and even if I'm wrong, which I could be, I'm glad I made that choice.

Penises

While it is rare for a Male-to-Female to emerge from the closet pretty enough to have even the slimmest chance of landing a date on Saturday night, *nobody* comes out without sporting that ultimate symbol of manliness – the penis.

While my sexual maturation was timely and appropriate to my physiology, I was so confused by the fundamental contradiction between my sex and my gender that I lived for years in what might be described as a state of suspended oblivion. Still, even *I* couldn't ignore that unsightly thing between my legs that, in addition to being infuriatingly visible, was likewise embarrassingly unpredictable.

I have often heard women accuse men of thinking with their dicks. Well, as a woman who had the misfortune of being born with one, I have great sympathy for men, because penises *do* have a mind of their own. I could be having the most random thoughts imaginable, thoughts about as sexy as fried squirrel brains (an unsavory and definitely *un*sexy delicacy I ate once – and only once) when all of a sudden the damn thing would rise up like Moby Dick from the sea. Why? Had some relics of my olfactory past secretly detected pheromones in the air setting in motion a hormonal chain reaction totally outside my awareness or desire? Had Priapus suddenly demanded adulation? Was the moon in erection phase? It made no sense. The damn thing would regularly wake me up in the middle of the night from a sound sleep with throbbing, insistent urgings akin to being awakened and asked if I wanted to play. "Hell, no I don't want to play; I want to sleep!" It's impossible to appreciate just how powerful and persistent a penis can be until you've had to live with one 24x7.

But, truth-be-known, I did not hate my penis. Nor did I think of sex reassignment surgery (SRS) as the rite of passage whereby I would attain the status of true womanhood. (Oh God, that it could be that simple!) For me, the biggest problem with having a penis was the significance everyone else gave it.

A friend once told me that she could more easily refer to me in the feminine once I had "the surgery," which just goes to show that in a society dominated by the concrete/literal thinking appropriate for young children even the intelligent and well-educated have trouble thinking abstractly. Given that I am not prone to public nudity, why would a penis be more significant in defining me as a man than a prostate? Not to mention why a man-made vagina qualifies me for being a woman even though I have no uterus, no ovaries and have never suffered a menstrual period much less the agony of child-birth. The first person I ever heard make the cogent and catchy distinction that "sex is what's between your legs and gender's what's between your ears" was also the proudest of her new post-SRS vagina and clearly viewed it as her lifetime pass into womanhood.

If indeed sex is what's between your legs and gender's what's between your ears, what difference does it make if you have a penis or a vagina? Why spend up to twenty grand turning your penis inside out if gender is what's between your ears, not what's between your legs?

I'll tell you why: because I, like everyone else, desperately, utterly, and with all my heart want to look into a mirror and see – me. And I'm not talking about a thinner rendition of me or a younger, taller, stronger, shorter, darker, lighter likeness. No, I want to look into the mirror and see *me* looking back at me, not some man. As the classic feminist tome maintains, our bodies and our selves are hopelessly, infuriatingly, inextricably bound.

Like it or not, for the bulk of the world, a penis is THE identifying mark of manhood; it is to manliness what chlorophyll is to plants, what gills are to fish, what feathers are to birds. Consequently, it is no wonder that men – gay and straight – transsexuals and even women (though they are less apt to admit it) are obsessed with The Penis. It defines who we are and who we are not. It imposes all sorts of unwritten, unconscious, irrational rules, restrictions and constraints on our thinking, our language, our behavior, our wardrobes, our architecture, our relationships and our laws. It is the one thing about which we must never be mistaken. I can misread your race, your accent, your political affiliations, your religion, even your sexual orientation, but to misread your sex is the ultimate *faux pas*. To complain that men think with their dicks ignores the fact that dicks loom unaccountably large in the collective imagination of more than just men.

Given its significance, it is no wonder that male-to-female transsexuals beg, borrow, lie, scrimp, steal and sacrifice virtually everything, including love, to have our penises converted into what most closely approximates the equipment we should have been born with in the first place even though most of us never intend to use it for intercourse with a man, and we sure as hell are not going to birth any babies through it much as we might insanely wish we could. Not counting its role in reproduction, lesbians and hetero-women over forty seem to be the only ones who appreciate a penis for what it is: a sex toy.

For me the real culprit was not the penis but the testicles. They were responsible for the accursed hormones that sculpted and shaped my body into the likeness of a man's. While it's true that in my vain attempts to be normal, I encouraged their dastardly work by "picking up the heavy things and putting them back down" as I once heard a femme gay man derisively characterize weight lifting, well beyond that and to my continuous dismay was the shape they gave my face, my neck with that horribly disgusting Adam's apple, my huge hands, my oversized feet and, above all, my height in excess of six feet. It was these factors that conspired against my ever living comfortably and confidently as a woman. These were the permanent, irrefutable evidence of a birth defect no amount of surgery could fully erase. My penis was simply annoying – in large part because of the importance everyone else gave it. The hormones did the real damage. Because of them, I could never be pretty.

Hunting, Football and Boy Things

From the beginning of remembered time and in countless ways, great and small, spoken and unspoken, conscious and unconscious, I observed that others thought of me as, treated me like and expected me to behave in the manner of a boy. My clothes were simple, drab and ugly; my hair was buzzed in the summer and if not buzzed, plastered down with Brylcream or Vitalis or, on really windy days, both. My dolls were rubber soldiers that we shot with BB guns, blew up with firecrackers, buried or – on really bad days – burned alive. Virtually all my toys involved some sort of weaponry, and with them, I engaged in many a rousing game of Army wherein – dressed in camos complete with authentic helmet liners purchased from the local Army surplus store – we killed hundreds, even thousands of Krauts with our realistic bolt-action M-1's onto which were fixed equally realistic-looking rubber bayonets. (This was back in the days before the mavens of political correctness sought to ban toy guns and knives and authentic steel dummy hand grenades heavy enough to shatter car windshields in favor of winner-take-all team sports wherein little boys get to ape the behaviors and adopt the values of egomaniacal, drug abusing professional athletes or else seek stimulation in front of television screens with large bags of fatty food-like substances to sublimate their violent tendencies through countless hours of blowing off people's heads or ripping out their hearts complete with spurting blood – virtually, of course – and without the worrisome inconvenience of having to go outside where they might damage the valuable landscaping and actually get sweaty, soiled and dirty.)

Of course, being male, I early on participated in the true religion of the South – football. It was one of the most redeeming things about being raised a boy. Hurling my skinny body into boys larger and stronger than me, grabbing them around the waist and dragging them to the ground and having them do the same to me was nothing short of ecstasy. The only thing better than a rousing game of tackle football was football in the mud - heaven!

Many years later as a Montessori teacher for 9-12 year-olds, I staunchly defended the right of the boys to play tackle football over the objections of my mostly female colleagues who considered it too rough. What they didn't understand – having been raised girls – is that football is one of the few forms of intimacy allowed boys. While girls can play with each other's hair, hold hands and touch each other affectionately, such tender intimacy is forbidden boys. Two boys skipping playfully across the playground holding hands will elicit more than just jeers from their male classmates, plus it's likely to raise a few staff eyebrows in one of those simple, small, telling gestures that exposes homophobia as surely as a taunt. Football was one of the few ways we boys got to touch each other without fear of being humiliated, hurt, or enrolled in aversion therapy.

This surreptitious and serendipitous goal of football was not entirely lost on the girls, either. In what would turn out to be my rather ironic role as guardian of male intimacy, because of my support of tackle football, I was awarded the unenviable prize of recess supervision.

On the sidelines one particularly cold winter day, I was watching the boys play football, when one of the sixth grade girls joined me. For a few moments, she just stood there watching the game before she asked, a distinct edge of disgust in her voice, "You know what they're doing out there, don't you?"

I looked at her puzzled, since it seemed quite obvious what they were doing out there. "Well, yes, Elizabeth. They're playing football."

"No they're not," she replied caustically. "They're humping each other."

"Elizabeth!" I remonstrated. But when I turned my attention back to the boys, several more minutes of careful observation, now informed by Elizabeth's provocative suggestion, forced me to concede, "You know, Elizabeth, I think you may be right."

I never played school-sponsored football where you put on all that sexy gear that makes even skinny guys look like the Incredible Hulk, then gallop around a well-manicured field in front of cheering fans and prancing cheerleaders with their bouncy pony tails and adorable short skirts. That was way too scary. Not the game. Football in pads was actually a lot less painful than the inglorious way we played it in jeans and T-shirts on rock-strewn lots with neither adoring crowds nor pretty girls. It was the locker rooms that terrified me – all those naked boy bodies strutting around, maligning each other with degrading, misogynistic, homophobic taunts and threats.

I'm convinced that in the South, making the varsity football team, more than physical ability, required having a sufficiently pathological character disorder. I suspect a reunion of the team would find half of them in the penitentiary and the other half in the legislature. It wasn't until much later that I realized I probably felt like most girls would feel in a locker room full of boys - terrified. Still, I loved the game and played it with reckless abandon and for the sheer brutal intimacy of it.

If it is true, as I have sometimes postulated, that I am a good example of a girl having been raised like a boy, I think all girls would profit the way I did from playing football. Based on my experiences as an elementary school teacher and the parent of both a boy and a girl child, when two boys get into a fight, it usually involves some pushing, shoving, swearing, maybe even some kicking and hitting with an occasional bit of real blood; which is to say, it is a rather brutish affair, easily observed and readily adjudicated. Unless a two-by-four or similarly hard object is also employed, the consequences usually require nothing more than, "Okay, Ross, you sit here and Dustin, you sit over there, and when you've both cooled down, we'll talk about how we settle our problems without resorting to violence" a sermonette that, by sixth grade, they could virtually recite by heart.

With girls, however, it was rarely so clear-cut – or clean. For one thing, the fight itself was seldom visible to the naked eye – especially one untrained in the ways of girls. It usually started out with something said or someone snubbed – intentionally or unintentionally, it didn't really matter – which resulted in an exchange of cuttingly cruel words usually spoken in undertones always accompanied by hateful looks and expressive body postures the inevitable consequences of which were a profusion of tears and a lot of emotional bleeding. Nor did it stop there. Whereas, in a matter of minutes, Ross and Dustin would be back playing together like a couple of adorable and rather doltish puppies, battles between girls could rage for days, weeks, months, years – maybe even lifetimes. And whenever I dared accuse one of them of wrongdoing, they would invariably look up at me in innocent, moist-eyed incredulity shocked that I could question for even a moment that they were anything other than poor, helpless victims of the other's unjustified cruelty. At such times, I halfway expected them to hold out their dainty, little hands as further proof that no traces of blood were visible – though, wait a minute! Was that the glint of a rapier I saw tucked deftly inside a sleeve?

I think football might help girls learn, as I did, how to deal with conflict and channel their violent tendencies, if not creatively, then at least with a lot of good physical exercise. It would teach them how to get knocked down and then get back up without taking it personally, as well as how to knock someone else down without malice or intent to inflict lifelong harm to their fundamental sense of worth.

As it is, after years of teaching and observing the insidious cruelty girls are capable of inflicting on each other, I sometimes think we should thank the gods of patriarchy that the world is run primarily by men.

Like real southern boys, I fished, camped, played games that involved throwing knives at each other's feet, swung from wild grapevines like a skinny Tarzan and built rafts out of trees downed with my slain Uncle Howard's WWII K-bar knife. Once lashed together with bits of twine, we floated down the Sunflower River where snakes, turtles and floating human turds served as targets for our rocks, sling shots and BB guns. I even killed small animals with large weapons; I mean, how much more manly can you get than that?

While I loved hunting, I did not actually enjoy killing. That probably explains why I could blast clay pigeons out of the sky like a pro but spent untold boxes of number 9's with nary a dove to show for it. By the time meat finally managed to make it to my table, its dollar value would have rivaled that of albino elephant steaks.

Nor do I oppose hunting. In fact, I think everyone who eats meat should at least once in their lifetime experience the entire process: the predatory stealth of the hunt, the thrill of the kill, the agony of watching the light in a wounded animal's eye fade into the opaque mystery of death, the feel of fresh blood, the pungent stench of bloody entrails, the savory tang of wild meat. It gives a whole new meaning to the word "food." Plus I believe animals understand hunting, and, given voice, probably would make little complaint even against the modern technology that puts them at such a disadvantage. (Still, you have to wonder where the sportsmanship is in possessing a weapon that can drop an animal dead at 500 yards.) Rather, it is the routine, thoughtless, systematic destruction of their habitat and homes that must seem so maddeningly insane to them and constitutes not only a greater threat to their existence on the planet but – in fact – is a cruelty and barbarity far greater than any hunter's gun.

Still, to this day, I remember the last animal I killed.

It is early winter in Northern California when I slip my canoe into the Russian River for a couple of days of solitary squirrel hunting. There are two frames through which I have most enjoyed watching Nature pass. One is over the bow of a canoe, and the other is between the ears of a horse. (My old friend, Zephyr's, were the finest – rich brown edged in a velvety border of dark chocolate. If there is an afterlife, the first face I hope to see on the other side is Zephyr's.)

Overnight, a rain moves in so heavy at times I worry my tent is set too near the river's edge. By morning it has turned into a steady drizzle, what I am told some Native Americans call a feminine rain, the kind that enlivens the senses like a spice. Well dressed for the weather, I break camp and slide my canoe into the river's embrace.

Being alone in a canoe on a gently moving river in a soft rain shortly after dawn fills the senses so entirely as to invoke a peculiar kind of euphoria, so much so that hunting became less a way of getting food than as a tether holding me to body and earth lest in such bliss I sail like Elijah straight to the bosom of God.

From a canoe, a squirrel hunter gains a distinct advantage, since squirrels do not expect a predator to approach from the water. Consequently, the bushy-tailed little creatures noisily feasting on the bay nuts are particularly unwary when I beach my canoe a short distance upstream. Nor is it hard to get within shotgun range, since a wet, drippy forest is much easier to creep through silently than a dry, crunchy one. Still, they are definitely on the move industriously gathering the fruits of the bay, which, unlike the naked hardwoods of the East, still offers concealment within a protective covering of dense, winter foliage. Thus obscured, my shot rips through the small animal's hind quarters rather than her head as I had intended, so that when she hits the ground, she is by no means dead.

Immediately she begins pulling herself toward a protective pile of brush, dragging her mangled hindquarters behind her. When I rush from my hiding place to intercept her, she begins a long, pitiful, aching cry, a cry less of pain than a heart-wrenching plea for her life. As a young female, she is probably coming into her first year as an adult, soon to be impregnated and bearing young of her own. I have caught her in a moment of youthful exuberance gathering the bounty of bay nuts to set aside for a life she was just beginning to live, a life, because of me, she will never have. As she desperately claws the ground while her life oozes slowly, inexorably out onto the earth, red and wet, her piteous cries rip through my heart like the pellets of the shotgun have ripped through her flesh; yet it is clear she is mortally wounded. No tears of grief, no expressions of regret, no amount of heart-felt, gut wrenching, God-why-did-I-do-this repentance can restore her, mend her, send her back to her happy chore high in the leafy branches of the fragrant bay. Death is inevitable, and having brought her down, I have but one moral choice: to end her life as quickly as possible. I don't remember in what brutal manner I did it, nor do I distinctly remember cleaning her small, mangled body. I do remember unloading my shotgun, stowing it away in the canoe and vowing to eat her flesh with reverence and never again to kill an animal for sport.

Several months later I am back in Maryland visiting my dear friend Robert who has recently started exploring the possibility of past lives with an equally esoteric friend. About such things I have no strong opinion, since I consider myself scarcely qualified to judge well the things that more easily lend themselves to knowing. Still, I am open and curious, so with Robert's help I enter into a semi-hypnotic trance to search for any real or imagined former lives I might have had. There are actually quite a few, but in the most memorable, I am a pretty, dark-haired girl, probably sixteen, living in colonial times. Something terrible has happened; either I am wounded or ill, I'm not sure which, but I am dying. I can feel my young life draining away and there is absolutely nothing I or any other can do to stop it. Still, I try. I fight desperately to hang on to this life I so passionately want to live. Instantly, the memory of the little female squirrel flashes before my eyes, and I see her again as I can see her still, crying out so pitifully as she pulls herself forward, trying with all her might to escape the doom that has already befallen her at my hand, fighting against death as if by sheer force of will she might push it back to the time when she was still young and whole and happily gathering bay nuts. But it was not to be for she nor me, though God knows how much I wish I could make it so, if not for me, at least for her.

44

Therapy

In my Mississippi hometown, the ultimate degradation for a girl was getting pregnant before she was married. (For the boy who impregnated her, however, it was considered little more than bad taste. After all, boys will be boys. Furthermore, even as he overtly upbraided his son for stupidly "knocking some girl up," covertly the father might feel relieved, even proud, since this would constitute irrefutable proof in his mind and, more importantly, the minds of others that he no longer had to worry about the ultimate paternal horror of horrors – that his son might be gay.) On the other hand, if it was discovered that a boy was seeing a therapist – always in a city some distance away – a full-page ad might just as well be run in the local paper, complete with a full frontal photo in drag, announcing his homosexuality. Therapy was the sort of thing discussed in furtive whispers like a crime. It is no wonder, then, that rather than seek it, I had to be driven to it.

While I had cross-dressed on and off my entire life, after my father's sudden death midway through my senior year in college, I became obsessed with it. The church where I was serving as youth minister collected second-hand clothes for the needy, and bereaved and bereft as I was, I was definitely needy. Late at night by the dim glow of streetlights leaking through the first floor windows, I would pilfer through bags of clothing, searching for garments that might scratch the itch, relieve the near constant ache, comfort the unspeakable sadness that arose from wellsprings of sorrow deep within me tapped by the death of my father. Once I found a suitable outfit, I would put it on and prowl the darkened halls silent as a cat, terrified and exhilarated, drunk on toxically fermented hope. In places where the light cast my shadow on a wall, I would stand for what seems like hours admiring my feminine silhouette with unspeakable, aching, desperate longing.

Compulsively, night after night I would do this, until one night a good friend spied my car in the parking lot. Supposing me to be devoutly tending to my ecclesiastical duties, Mike somehow managed to get inside the locked building and, thinking to have some fun, decided to sneak up on me. When he burst into the room where I was decked out in forbidden finery, he might as well have come in spraying the place with bullets, for I could scarcely have been more mortified. It was an unforgettable moment of brutally horrifying shame. No one had ever seen me like this. I had kept it hidden my entire life, guarding against even the suspicion. With him standing in the doorway wide-eyed in disbelief, I felt completely and utterly exposed, though nakedness would have been a mercy.

What happened next could have gone a variety of ways other than the way it did; for in addition to being a good friend, Mike was a kind and sympathetic gay man. When he realized what I was up to and saw the complete and utter horror on my face, he backed out of the room without a word and beat a mercifully hasty retreat, leaving me to soak in a cesspool of shame. For a moment I was so stunned, I couldn't move. My mind fought against belief. It couldn't be. It just couldn't be. I had hidden it all my life. Now someone had seen me. I had been caught. I ripped off the clothes and with a firm resolve to never, ever do this again, frantically put mine back on.

I know now that being discovered was probably my unconscious intention all along. I was too embarrassed and too ashamed to tell anyone; yet with the death of my father and the stress of school and graduation, the pressure inside me was building dangerously. It was a terribly risky strategy on the part of my unconscious. Had it been anyone other than Mike, who knows what might have happened. Perhaps it was just dumb luck that Mike, of all people, found me; for I knew, even as mortified as I was, that he would not betray me; nor would he judge me. He, of all people, might even understand. That it was Mike who found me – and in church, no less – I now believe was pure Divine grace, and to this day, I stand amazed.

Looking back, I regret he didn't stay. As I said, he was a person who might have understood. He knew that I knew he was gay, and he knew that I didn't care. He was my friend; in a couple of years, we would be roommates in seminary. I could have talked to Mike. Had we both been willing to stand in that place, that terrible place of humiliation and shame where all our instincts told us to run, who knows what might have happened? Maybe if I had allowed him to see me at my worst, and he had been willing to look upon me as I was with eyes of understanding, compassion and sympathy, the nut of shame might have been cracked. As it was, his attempt to spare me further embarrassment and my desire to be so spared, left it harder than ever. How many opportunities do we miss, and what damage do we unwittingly do by simply bowing to the familiar injustice, averting our eyes, making a polite retreat and in so doing, allow it to stand unseen, unnamed, unchallenged, unhealed? Shortly thereafter I made what might be called my only real suicide attempt.

The horror of what had happened almost immediately turned into a deep sense of dread. If Mike had discovered me, I could be discovered. And if I kept this up, it was only a matter of time before it happened again. It had to stop. It had to stop now!

So again, late one night, I drove back to the church determined that God was either going to heal me or take me. A storm, big by even southern standards, was roiling in the sky. I stripped down to a pair of cutoffs, and as the wind whipped the tops of the pines into a mad frenzy and huge raindrops splattered against my nearly naked body, I ran round and round the empty field behind the church.

Great bolts of lightning tore through the night sky, exploding like heaven-hurled bombs around me, but on I ran, determined to either be normal or be dead, and God could witness just how serious I was.

Looking back, I don't think I actually believed God would miraculously cure me. What I think I wanted was to die, and I wanted God to be responsible – as He clearly was – and to bear the blame – as He certainly did. I had not chosen to be this way, nor could I live with it; yet, it would not go away.

I don't know how long I ran, hours it seems, but obviously, I did not die, but then again, neither was I healed.

Finally, confronted with the very real prospect that I was either going to cause myself an early demise or – worse still – be exposed to the world for the perverted freak I was, I sought help.

I went in order to be cured of my deviancy. I was living proof of what Eric Berne, the father of transactional analysis used to say, that people don't get into therapy to become winners; they get into therapy to become braver losers. I was determined to be a normal man – a truly losing proposition, because no matter how hard I tried, I was simply not a man, normal or otherwise.

My initiation into the world of psychotherapy took place in the psychology department of the university where I was enrolled in graduate school. They were always on the lookout for willing guinea pigs on which the graduate students could practice their dark craft, so they gladly took me in like a coven of hungry witches and graciously agreed to support me in my quest to become a braver loser.

I am convinced that late one night while stoked on coke (and I am not referring here to the soft drink) a group of these psychology doctoral candidates came up with a technique to cure my deviancy by what amounted to self-torture. First, they had me record one of my favorite fantasies into a tape recorder. As if this humiliation in and of itself wasn't enough to cure me, I was then to lie down on an examination table in a darkened room, the tape recorder was turned on and whenever I felt the least bit aroused, I was to scream NO loud enough to be heard three buildings over. This brilliant Pavlovian procedure was supposed to rid me of all desires for the despised perversity. Of course, it didn't, though, over time, it did result in some pretty hot sadomasochistic fantasies.

While I was by no means cured, the therapy door was at least open, and the next time I went through it, I was out of seminary, married and into my first job as an assistant minister at a medium-sized Baptist church in a small town in southern Mississippi near where I'd gone to college. This was the beginning of what ended up being a mercifully short four-year period in my life when I attempted to drive a round peg – me – into a square hole – the Southern Baptist Church.

Transactional analysis, or TA as it was called back in the day, was the rage in therapy circles. For one thing, it was a hell of a lot cheaper and considerably more effective than individual psychotherapy. I figure TA fell out of grace because it was way too easy for ordinary people to understand, too effective at helping people deal with their real issues (which, remember, is the last thing most people in therapy want), demanded skills for which conventional psychotherapists had little training, talent or interest, plus required too much work and took way too much money out of the pockets of all those MDs and PhDs who could otherwise charge obscene amounts treating individuals interminably.

One particular event emblematic of the power of group therapy stands out in my mind.

About two-dozen of my therapist's clients had gathered for a weekend marathon, two intensive days of weeping, wailing and gnashing of teeth. I can't remember how it came up, but Nancy, the woman therapist in the husband-wife team and clearly the better of the two, told me to imagine the worst thing I could; I wouldn't have to reveal it, just imagine it. Well, that was easy. I imagined all those times I secretly dressed in women's clothing. When I indicated that I had the image, she instructed me to look around the room directly at each person. As ridiculous as it sounds, even consciously knowing they couldn't see what was safely locked inside my head, this was still hard to do. To consciously imagine myself a woman in the knowing presence of others, gave it a reality it was hard to believe they could not see.

After I painfully met each pair of eyes, she asked what I saw. After a moment's thought, I replied that some people looked curious, some seemed to disapprove, others showed interest, support, even love, while some people looked bored, others sleepy, one person was looking out the window and a couple seemed totally uninterested in the whole damn thing. She cocked her head, bounced her eyebrows and smiled. I just looked at her. Could it be that easy? I don't know what I imagined would happen if people ever found out, if they ever even suspected – surely terrible, awful, dreadful things. Never had I imagined that people's actual responses might include a random mixture of curiosity, disapproval, support, love, boredom, distraction, sleepiness and disinterest. I burst out laughing. Suddenly *The Big Secret* didn't seem nearly as big as I had always imagined. Instead of an angry elephant threatening to crush me beneath its massive foot or rip me apart with its trunk and tusks, it was just a stuffed animal whose oversized shadow cast on my bedroom wall I mistook for the real thing. It was an epiphany. Heavenly bells pealed, angels cheered and shook their starry pompoms. It was The Truth, and, sure enough, Jesus was right; The Truth did set me free, or, at least, it offered to. As it turned out, I did not yet possess the requisite courage to embrace this Truth that might have set me free. It is one thing to know the Truth and quite another to embrace it.

Still, especially when I'm feeling depressed and sorry for myself, I ponder how my life might have looked had I come out as a young adult rather than at the onset of old age. Given the time and circumstances in which I lived, it is hard to imagine it being anything other than an unmitigated disaster; but, then again, it's hard to imagine even now, even in Northern California how a young adult male, particularly one like me with all the feminine charm of a bulldog bitch, could live a successful, satisfying, moderately happy life as a transwoman. As an older woman, I am afforded the luxury of anonymity, even indifference by virtue of nothing more than my gray hair. Younger women – especially femmes, even not particularly attractive femmes like me – are objects of interest to precisely those whose attention is most potentially lethal. Looking at it from this perspective, maybe I was right after all. Maybe it really was an elephant – only now it's old and tuskless and blind; a mostly harmless shadow of its former self.

By the time I moved to California and TA had gone the way of the rotary phone, I was forced to accept the fact that I was never going to enjoy the luxury of being a normal man, even by the most outlandish definitions of "normal." Turning to what my therapist called "bibliotherapy," I read everything the psychologist Robert Johnson wrote about the importance of men incorporating their feminine and took it more to heart than I imagine he ever intended and in ways he almost certainly never envisioned. Based on Johnson, Jung and what I managed to glean from a variety of other sources, I set about to consciously create visible and viable ways to overtly embrace and express my feminine. In so doing, I hoped I might sufficiently satisfy her so that she would, in turn, allow me to live with some degree of contentment as a man. I grew my hair long – very long – and wore it in ways no man would dream of, dressed in flowing pants and shirts in colors and styles usually forbidden to men.

Additionally, I began attending a weekly improvisational movement class based on the teachings of Gabriel Roth. After years of imprisonment, my body was finally set loose, and to my amazement, I took to dance like a bird to flight. It was just one more thing I had been denied as a boy. But as much as I loved movement, as important and liberating as it was, my inner feminine was still not satisfied. Repeatedly, she drove me into depths of despair and depression, whereupon I threw her even more outrageous offerings. I started dancing in a leotard and skirt. While it must have seemed strange to others, by this time, the power and grace with which I moved and my increasingly well-developed male musculature left no doubt as to my sex even had I taken to wearing a tutu. Oddly enough, the more I allowed my feminine visible expression, the more attracted women were to me, which was not at all what I had anticipated, was certainly not what I had intended, and was not what I wanted.

Movement was a profoundly effective and immensely satisfying expression of my inner feminine, plus it equally energized and expanded my experience of the masculine. I heartily recommend it for everyone, especially men. But as much as I loved movement, as healing as it was, in the end, it proved no more successful in removing the need to live my life as a woman than all the traditional male things had.

There is a story in the Bible where Jesus becomes the hit of a wedding party when he changes ordinary water into uncommonly fine wine. Well, no matter what I did, no matter how much I begged, prayed, danced and read, regardless of all the time, energy and money I spent trying to be normal, I was, in the end, utterly unsuccessful at changing his perfectly good wine back into ordinary water.

Religion

My earliest memories of religion are as a five year old sitting in the spacious sanctuary of a colonial style Southern Baptist church, Mom decked out in her Sunday best with me sitting beside her ridiculously handsome in my suit and tie with my hair all slicked down. Often I passed the time waiting for the service to begin carefully examining Mom's hand with strange, intense curiosity, or else, I colored in my coloring book until – announced by majestic organ fanfare – a scowling Dr. Horton strode regally onto the rostrum as the congregation rose in unison singing "Holy, holy, holy! Merciful and Mighty! God in three Persons, blessed Trinity."

The stirring words of that stormy prelude were indelibly imprinted on my impressionable brain. But it was when he occupied the massive mahogany pulpit for the sermon that the real torture began, because in short order, he would be ranting and raving like a pudgy, baldheaded lunatic. I could never figure out what in God's name he was so mad about. What provoked him to yell and scream and pound his fist on the pulpit until his face turned red, while, conversely, the congregation sat passively before his verbal abuse like a convocation of spiritual masochists?

Prior to the hell of worship, I spent an interminable hour in purgatory, sitting on a cold metal folding chair in a sterile, prison-like cinder block room, listening to some befuddled adult read boring, moralistic platitudes from Sunday School manuals written by spiritual zombies. While the adult droned on, I would have been studying the girls, imagining how it felt to wear a dress, to feel the cold metal chair touching the bare skin behind my knees, to look down and see my feet enclosed in a pair of shiny, black Mary Janes with short, white socks edged in lace. It's the sort of thing I did when forced to sit still and ponder the impossible, imagine what could neither be acknowledged nor understood and never shared.

After my two-hour decent into the religious netherworld, I invariably returned home with a splitting headache, which abated only after an hour's nap. After a few hours of playful reprieve and just as *The Wonderful World of Disney* was coming on TV, we loaded back into the station wagon for BTU (Baptist Training Union) followed by yet another hour of hell, fire and brimstone boredom.

Following the evening services and with almost an entire day of our precious week-end wasted, I vividly recall the unholy specter of a group of us crazed children running amok in the luminescent blue glow of the church's garish neon moniker manically stomping the guts out of June bugs and roaches the size and heft of half dollar coins. For this act of senseless violence I am doubly contrite, since, not only were the bugs innocent of any wrongdoing – other than their ontological bugginess – I realize now that they were likely the only creatures that actually found light in that godforsaken place, and there we were murdering them like crazed disciples of a mad dog – god, that is.

So, being an overly compliant child desperately in need of approval, at about age eight – or maybe I was all of nine – I, in the parlance of Southern Baptists, "walked the aisle to take Jesus as my personal Lord and Savior" thereby becoming a full-fledged member of the church. (Don't ask me how a nine-year-old casts an intelligent vote on the church budget; divine inspiration I suppose.)

At the age of about twelve in what can only be described as a pathetically desperate attempt to earn the approval I knew I didn't deserve, I preached my first sermon. I dimly recall it as an intensely disintegrating out-of-body experience. Others, however, took it as a sign that I was destined to become the next Billy Graham – an internationally recognized evangelist of unparalleled respect and admiration in Southern Baptist circles. This lofty expectation was encouraged when, after successfully managing to survive high school through a concerted effort at anonymity (Are there any places – with the possible exception of maximum security prisons – so full of latent male violence as American high schools?) I accepted the mantle of leadership laid on me by the church's suspiciously squirrelly youth minister to lead a great youth revival. From a carefully cultivated non-descript nobody, I overnight became a charismatic crusader for Christ, bringing into the ranks of the redeemed many a sin-sick teenager guilty of such weighty immoralities as dancing, listening to rock and roll, drinking and – gasp! – "petting."

It's hard now to imagine what possessed me and brought me to such depths of spiritual degradation, but I think it was mostly about sex. Sex, of course, at least, sex outside of marriage was wrong; and, for me, it was not only wrong, it was terribly, terribly confusing. I could never quite figure out with whom and as whom I wanted it. Sex involved a complicated mixture of lusting after Vicki, the pretty blonde tease in the Wednesday evening prayer group, even as I desperately envied her the curvaceously female body that evoked the deliciously forbidden sensations I felt throbbing in my loins for her as her. Try untangling that one. So, instead of screwing them, I converted them, which, come to think of it, probably screwed them anyway – except without the fun.

Because I lived in determined denial about my desperate desire to be a girl, my naive, unquestioned and unquestioning belief in the puerile god of my childhood religion was never seriously tested until I went off to college. Now a small Baptist college in South Mississippi would seem a pretty safe place to cultivate ignorant devotion to a lily-white god, but as it turns out, there was this war thing going on in some faraway place called

Vietnam. Politicians had only recently discovered that drafting the children of white, affluent, educated voters to serve in the military in a time of war would eventually undermine their mercenary aspirations, which they had hitherto successfully hidden behind the veil of patriotism. As a concession to these powerful constituents, eligible young men of means were allowed to postpone their patriotic duty through college deferments.

Not so far away in the heathen land of Louisiana State University, a fairly large number of young, affluent, eligible, white men were quite literally in danger of partying themselves into a premature South East Asian death. Rather than flunk out of LSU and be drafted into the U.S. Army, they transferred to our little Baptist college, which was always on the lookout for tuition-paying students – heathen or otherwise.

Away from their dens of iniquity, they dried out their alcohol-saturated brains enough to resurrect their GPAs so that they could return to their frat houses and once again anoint themselves with the spirit of Mr. Jack Daniels. It was, you might say, a match made in heaven. That God, what a kidder.

These LSU flunkouts brought into our citadel of righteousness the religious sensibilities of Attila the Hun. Somehow between bouts of lewdness, debauchery and drunkenness, they had managed to take real philosophy courses, which, unlike ours, had not been filtered through the extremely fine sieve of religious fundamentalism. Against this mob of beer-bellied barbarians, we, God's stalwart Christian Soldiers "marching as to war with the cross of Jesus going on before," were mowed down like so many rag dolls. They beat the holy shit out of us.

For example, when informed that they needed to accept Jesus as their Lord and Savior, these heathens countered, not with blasphemous curses against the precious name of our Lord and Savior, not with philosophical arguments questioning the existence of God. No, they were far too cunning for that. Instead, they responded with a genuinely perplexed, "Why?"

Years of Sunday school, Training Union, church camps, revivals, not to mention a nauseating number of sermons had left me utterly unprepared for this simple, seemingly innocuous query. Suddenly I found myself struck dumb by nothing more than a three-letter question – why? I had never thought about *why* someone might want to follow Jesus. Wasn't it obvious? Well, come to think of it, not really.

Of course, I could have replied in classic Southern Baptist fashion, "So that you will not burn for all eternity in Hell," but this required being more of a religious Nazi than I could stomach. I could, however, have promised, "eternal life with God in heaven," but even dense as I was, I realized that this presented some rather significant problems, problems I had never before bothered to ponder. For one thing, it required dying, and I didn't know anyone, no matter how deserving of a heavenly afterlife, who was anxious to cash in on their godliness and go six feet under. It likewise omitted the time between the here and now and the eternal hereafter, which, when you really stopped to think about it, seemed like a pretty significant oversight. So, appealing to the joys of the afterlife, which were, after all, impossible to demonstrate, wasn't very satisfying, and on top of that, there was the nagging recognition, undeniable, really, if you had even a smidgen of honesty, that their hedonistic lifestyles and devil-may-care attitudes were a lot more interesting and way more fun than mine, racked as it was with sin and guilt and shame. So there I was laid low by a three-letter question. It was embarrassing.

Worse still, with nothing else to do, since possessing alcohol – a thing of the devil – was one of the quickest ways to get gone from this shitty little Baptist school in the middle of nowhere to getting your ass shot off in some rice paddy in Vietnam, they entertained themselves by going on the offensive. One of their favorite topics was the issue of evolution versus creationism, which, unbelievably, still rages to this day. "So how many days did it take God to create the world?" they asked ever so innocently, though I could imagine pointy little teeth beneath their self-satisfied smiles, smiles that sent a shiver up my spine much like a deer must feel when it spies the yellow eyes of a lion peering from the underbrush. "Seven," I replied knowing damn well I was stepping into a trap but unable to see any way around it. "So how do you define a day?" Well, now that was an interesting question, one I hadn't anticipated. "Twenty four hours. Sunrise to sunrise, I suppose." "So then how do you explain that God made the earth in seven days when the sun wasn't created until the fourth day?" Damnit! You would have thought those idiots at the Sunday School Department in Nashville would have at least prepared us for that one! It was so damn obvious.

While it was brutal, to my credit, rather than banish them to the fires of hell – well deserving though they might be – I began to awaken to the possibility that the mawkish platitudes and simplistic slogans of my childhood religion might be nothing more than self-delusions of the ill-informed. For the first time ever, I had to face the terrifying possibility that what I had been told all my life might be – gulp! – wrong. If only I could have known then what I know now: that the opposite of faith is not doubt. The opposite of faith is certainty, and what a wonderful irony that when forced into doubt by these draft-dodging, beer-swilling, Christian-bashing flunkouts, I actually awoke to faith for the first time. That God, what a kidder indeed.

But the crucible in which my faith was tested and transformed came during my senior year in college when the dean of students unexpectedly appeared at my dorm door in early December saying the president of the college needed to see me. It was unusual, but after all, I was president of the student body, so a meeting with the president of the college might have involved a variety of things other than the sudden death of my father.

Except for a brief period when my younger brother Greg lived with me during his college internship, I never felt particularly close to my family. They always felt a bit like strangers to me, though, as it turns out, I was the stranger. Of course, it didn't help that each of the four children was born seven years apart. (Don't ask me what was going on in the interim, and, in typical Southern fashion, Mom wouldn't tell.) Still, as a child, I fondly remember my father coming into our bedroom on Sunday mornings to awaken us for breakfast with tickles and roughhousing. Richard, with whom I probably shared a bed until he left for college, would complain bitterly at this interruption of his precious sleep, but I loved it, longed for it, ate it up like candy. I never got enough of it, but I was, after all a boy, and only so much and only certain types of affection were allowed between boys and fathers. Eventually, denied the relationship for which I longed, I just withdrew and even more so after he died.

Secretly, I think I worshiped Dad. For one thing, he was strikingly handsome, with sharply etched features and piercing blue eyes. A look from those eyes could either make my heart soar like a swallow or else, make me want to crawl like a worm into the nearest hole. But it was his laugh that I remember best, how it carved deep creases into his permanently tanned face. Whenever something I said or did evoked it, I would try – invariably in vain – to make it happen again, because that laugh was like a fire in the darkness of self-doubt and kindled hope, if only for a moment, that he actually loved me a fraction as much as I loved him.

His honesty and honor, traits characteristic of the finest southern gentlemen, became something of a family legend when we got an unexpected phone call one evening after a powerful hurricane smashed into the Mississippi gulf coast. The caller told us that he and his family lived in one of the houses Dad built, and according to him, the hurricane had destroyed all the houses in that neighborhood except for the ones built by my father.

Dad was also wise, though in the tragic manner of someone upon whom too much is laid too early, one who struggles to carry a load he is unable to bear, yet bears it all the same. Much of the time he was around – which wasn't a lot – he was irritable. Mom attributed this to his ulcer, which, of course, was due to his smoking, which she steadfastly maintained was the root of all his problems. But he was a kind and gentle father, never physically violent like so many other men of his generation. Only once do I recall him spanking me. Compared to Mom's beatings, his was almost embarrassing. I cried just to get him to stop, mostly for his sake, since he clearly had no heart for the unpleasantry.

At his funeral, I viewed his finely chiseled profile from across the room. They say it's important for closure to see someone you love dead, but I'm glad I kept my distance. I did not need to see him dead. In a way, we had never really been alive to one another. Dead, and safely at home in the other realm – or so I imagined – he finally knew who I was, though, at the time, that was terribly bitter comfort.

After several hours at the funeral home pretending to be the dutifully brave son, I borrowed Richard's car, an overpowered Ford Torino, and drove out into the north Mississippi countryside. They call this part of Mississippi the delta, though actually, it's the flood plain of the Mississippi River. Before levees contained it, the river would flood vast tracks of land, laying down multiple layers of dark, rich soil, which now bear abundant crops of cotton, soy beans and rice.

If the land was once covered, as I imagine, with dense hardwood forests of oak, maple, sweet gum, pecan, walnut, hickory, ash, locust and cypress, you could never guess it. It was as flat as a proverbial pancake for endless miles. Skinny ribbons of forest one tree deep followed muddy, moccasin-infested watercourses; all else was cleared, plowed, disked and sprayed with an arsenal of pesticides for cultivation. It was a raped land into which I fled for solace. I found it down the second or third dirt road just past one of those ubiquitous wooden shacks in which an impoverished Black farm family lived. ("They may be poor, but they're happy," Mom once said in defense of such wretched living conditions.)

When I got out of the car, the emotions I had been so carefully containing at the funeral home exploded like a severe case of emotional projectile vomiting. Through a slurry of screams, wails, tears and snot, my fury, my rage and grief spewed forth at the only Power I could imagine responsible for this outrage, this injustice, this unspeakable tragedy. "How could you? How could you take Dad from me, so suddenly, without warning, before I ever got a chance to know him? Don't you know how much I loved him?"

It was so wrong, so terribly, terribly wrong and so hopelessly irreversible. What I had known of God prior to this moment was little more than hints and rumors. I had never looked into the face of God, much less shaken my fist in it. Surely anyone brazen enough to do so would be struck dead, but what did I care? He had taken my father from me, and I was calling Him out. I was ready to do battle with the Almighty even if it cost me my life – *especially* if it cost me my life.

And God came out. He stepped out of the shadows, from behind the veil, down from his lofty throne on high, and he wrapped me in his arms like I was his only precious child. My anger, so pure, so real, so fierce, rather than drive God away or provoke his wrath, evoked a love I never imagined possible, a love so real, so tender, so sweet, so pure it could indeed have killed me with its sheer intensity.

As a child, I used to puzzle at the biblical expression "the bosom of God." It made no sense. How could God have a bosom if he was male? But that is where I fell, headlong into the ample bosom of God where I wept until there were no more tears, until all that remained was a heart full of clear, clean, crystalline sorrow.

Eventually, I drove back to the funeral home – but I never returned to what had been. Before that, I knew about God as one knows about fire from a candle. With Dad's death, the temple of what I deemed holy went up in flames, and I knew fire as never before. In that crucible, the pious platitudes and simplistic clichés were consumed like so much straw. In the heat and light of that fire, something so much bigger, so much more powerful, so much greater and grander than I had ever imagined was revealed. It was the last and greatest gift my father gave me.

It would be easy to remember religion as a singularly bad experience, but that would not be the whole of it. Somewhere along the way, I heard the stories: the story of David and Goliath, Abraham's near sacrifice of Isaac, Samson, Daniel in the Lion's Den, the birth of Jesus, the Sermon on the Mount, his passion, the empty tomb, the prodigal son. What is it about stories that live on in us like imperishable food? To this day at unexpected moments, I find myself stumbling upon a feast laid out long ago but somehow newly fresh.

There was another period of evangelical fervor in my life, though it was decidedly different. I was in graduate school at the University of Southern Mississippi on the pretense of studying philosophy, which, when reading Emmanuel Kant, I felt about as much aptitude for as your average barnyard animal.

Inspired by the philosophers, I decided to become a *tabula rasa*, a blank slate. I would no longer pretend to know anything. Instead, I would completely open myself to whatever life sent and experience it without preconception or prejudice. This would be my new attitude.

That very week someone invited me to one of those ad hoc prayer groups that spring up from time to time like exotic weeds in the carefully manicured gardens of the mainstream church. Ordinarily, I would have rejected this as just another group of religious nuts the likes of which I had seen before – been there, done that – but now, I reminded myself, I was a blank slate. I would go see.

The group met at night in the dingy shell of an abandoned gas station. An attractive woman, probably in her early forties, who had about her an angelic, mythic air, like maybe she surreptitiously slipped away from heaven or, at least, Camelot, led the group with her guitar. Her voice was indeed angelic, and sitting at her feet on the floor shoulder to shoulder with the other devotees, we sang songs of praise that transformed the old gas station into a grand and glorious cathedral. If she spoke, I don't recall it; mostly, I think it was just her presence, her radiance that imbued the place with power and rendered it magical. Perhaps for the first time in a religious setting, I felt happy.

A feature of this little, unauthorized community of Jesus worshipers was a phenomenon called speaking in tongues. It is a kind of ecstatic language spoken of in the Christian Scriptures, particularly in the writings of the Apostle Paul, in which a believer's voice is taken over by the Holy Spirit and he or she begins to prophesy or praise God in a language that sound a lot like gibberish. In this particular group, a time was given when those who wished to receive the gift of tongues could go into another room and with the assistance of those to whom the gift had already been given, pray. Well, that seemed a bit far-fetched to me or, at least, very undignified, but, hey, I was a blank slate, remember? So I went into the back room, got down on my knees, some people I didn't know put their hands on me, and I began to pray.

It started out sane enough. I said something about how I wanted to be open, how I wanted to be healed. Stuff in therapy began to run through my mind, and then, it got all jumbled up with other stuff and suddenly, something snapped inside me like brittle metal and out of my mouth gushed a profusion of speech, incomprehensible and wondrous. Like pus from a long-festering boil, the confusion, grief, pain, shame and fear poured out of me in a way that could never have been contained or expressed in ordinary language. When it left me in a rush of sound, it was like being exorcised of a legion of demons. I literally slumped face-forward onto the floor completely spent and utterly blissful.

From this little group, I went forth onto the university campus to preach the Gospel; for what had happened to me was the very meaning of the term Gospel: good news, good news indeed. I no longer condemned people for their sins. I didn't want to save them from hell. I didn't even care if they joined a church. I wanted them to know that what had happened to me could happen to them; they, too, could be saved. I was in love with God, and I wanted to share God's love with others.

It was very simple and dear and sweet, and it didn't last very long. Shortly afterward, some young, handsome, charismatic man full of godly delusions of grandeur took over leadership of the makeshift church, since, according to the pseudonymous letters attributed to Paul, men, not women, were supposed to be the church's leaders. When he started trying to cast demons out of sick children, I left in disgust. "Why," I complained to God, "does our side always end up with the idiots?"

Had it not been for ministers like Graham Hales and Craig Ratliff, the cruelty, barbarity and ignorance of the Southern Baptist Church would surely have driven me to permanently reject my faith like even the hungry reject rancid meat. But they were men of thought who did not fear the hard questions nor wield the sword of faith like a weapon. They were the great corruptors about whom the revival preachers had warned us; the despoilers of virgin faith, the whores of Truth and in their troth, I met and fell madly in love with a God of infinite compassion and boundless mercy. It was this God, so marvelously, wondrously revealed in the person of Jesus, who I wed myself to and steadfastly set out to follow.

Following a feeble attempt to write a master's thesis to complete my MA in philosophy from USM, I spent three years getting a Master of Divinity degree from the Southern Baptist Theological Seminary in Louisville, Kentucky. After graduating, I married the woman I dated when I was a graduate student and she a high school senior. A psychologist of mere mediocrity could offer a variety of reasonable explanations as to why I took up with someone so much younger than me. At the end of the day, however, they would leave wanting what such explanations so often leave wanting. I am convinced that in the theater of human passions, forces are at work of which we have little knowledge and over which we have even less control. As the playwrights have imagined, in this realm, we who take such great pride in knowing the inner workings of the atom are destined to play out the eternal loves and epic hatreds of the gods and thereby, suffer in our tender flesh and infantile psyches the devastating consequences of maintaining blissful ignorance of the inner workings of our own souls and the invisible forces which act upon them.

After I finished seminary, we were wed, and soon thereafter, I commenced my blessedly short career as a Southern Baptist minister. Like so many young ministers newly minted from seminary, I started out in a medium size, rural church as the associate minister in charge of education and youth.

The pastor was a man some ten years my senior who, like so many ministers serving small, rural churches, was looking to move up. He had his sights set on one of those huge Baptist churches in the state capitol. Those positions, however, with their prestige, power and lavish salaries were highly prized, so Pastor Jim, whose preaching was about as inspiring as instructions for a toilet installation, found himself stuck where he was. He was at least as frustrated as me, though for entirely different reasons.

While a small town might have a medical doctor, it almost never has a mental health professional, so mental and emotional health issues fall to a variety of people, including ministers. Like all towns, we had a few bona fide nuts, our share of alcoholics – closeted and otherwise – plenty of annoying, though harmless neurotics, lots of marital discord, and from time to time, a real, god-awful tragedy.

Most of these were the purview of the senior minister. I got the angst-ridden teenage girls from troubled homes who developed crushes on the handsome, young youth minister – me. These would show up at my office at the most inauspicious times to pour out their troubles with ripe, doe-eyed seduction. Sometimes it was all I could do not to take them in my arms, caress their fevered brows and whisper soothing words of God's passionate love in their delicate ears just before our lips met in delicious, forbidden desire.

Thankfully, I never did. I wasn't that stupid – or that desperate. Besides, I wanted to *be* them, not have sex with them; though when one's not possible – or allowable – the other can become that much more attractive. Ask a Catholic priest.

I think it's fair to say that small, rural church going people are often characterized either as superstitious simpletons or fundamentalist, neo-Nazi rednecks. Based on my experience, both stereotypes are as far from the truth as are the stereotypes of gays as child molesters or atheists as hedonistic, immoral, blasphemers…well, okay, maybe atheists are blasphemous, but so am I. While there is plenty to criticize about religion, what I observed of the people in the pews was that religion, for all its faults and frailties, usually had a salutary effect on its practitioners, especially those who gave it a practical priority in their lives. Nor are ministers of small, rural churches rubes and charlatans as they are so often depicted. Usually they are men (and yes, they're almost always men, unfortunately) of genuine caring who must not only bear the impossible burden of trying to be the standard by which all men are measured; they must also be the ones who single handedly hold out hope when all is hopeless, who are expected to find meaning in the ashes of despair, or who try with little more than baling wire to repair relationships that have been tearing themselves apart for years. Maybe they don't always do such a good job, but who can throw stones when it comes to that? And do we really think we will be better off when religion has been replaced by rationalism, secularism and science? The last time I checked, it was not the followers of God, even the most misguided ones, who were in danger of destroying the planet. For that dubious distinction, credit must go to the rational, secular scientists.

In one of his excellent novels, my favorite author, Wendell Berry, speaks sympathetically of the requirement laid on small town ministers to try and speak words of comfort and hope in situations that can only be endured. What do you say to the parents of a teenage boy who kills himself with a drug overdose – intentionally or unintentionally will never be known? What comfort can you give? In what can they place their hope in the face of the senseless death of their child? God? Heaven? Anyone who thinks so has never really been there. And yet, as a minister, I was expected to say something, if not by the bereaved, then by the others standing around not knowing what to say. And so I did, knowing that whatever I said would likely be swallowed up like a whisper in the cataract of hopeless grief.

Fortunately I was never one of those ministers who offered pietistic platitudes like: it was just her time, or, they're at home with God now, or God just wanted your precious child back with Him in heaven. I was myself too acquainted with grief for that. Mostly I tried to just be there, which in the end, is all anyone can do – including God.

Sometimes in their role as spiritual first responders, ministers are called on to try and staunch what – metaphorically speaking – turns out to be a lacerated artery.

Joe was the son of one of the finest families in our church, what we called "salt of the earth" people, plain, down to earth people who embodied the highest ideals of what it means to be a decent, honest, caring human being. Glen was a farmer and Virginia a high school teacher. They had four children – Joe, his brother Bill and his sisters, Laura and Beth. Joe was about my age, around 27 or 28, Laura was married to a postal worker and living in town, Bill worked on the place with his dad and Beth would have been about four or five years younger than me still living at home on the farm.

Beth was knock down gorgeous and sweet as honey to boot, one of those girls who was so far beyond me, so out of my class, so perfect that I didn't even desire to be her. All I could do was ogle her in rapt awe.

Joe was as handsome as his sister was beautiful, funny and brilliant. At the time he was living somewhere in south Louisiana with his girlfriend who I met once at some family function to which I was invited. My only clear recollection of her was of her laughing. She had a beautiful laugh and was herself a lovely young woman. Unbeknownst to us – and perhaps unbeknownst to them at the time – she was pregnant with their child, a child she would never bear.

One day Joe unexpectedly showed up at home highly agitated. He was talking apocalyptic, end of the world nonsense, so his parents, not sure what else to do, sent him to talk to the minister. Since I was newly out of seminary and had studied philosophy, he came to me with his wild visions. Listening to him, I got the notion in my head that, while the words themselves made little sense, they might contain some sort of hidden meaning, just like in biblical apocalyptic literature. Maybe he was trying to tell us something, and if I kept asking him questions, kept probing, kept listening, I might be able to discern what was going on beneath the surface; I might be able to break the code. Finally, I was told to stop; it just made Joe more agitated. Even though I felt like I was onto something, I complied like a good boy.

Joe returned to Louisiana in the same state of mind with which he had come. A few days later he took a knife and with it, murdered his girlfriend and cut from her womb their unborn child.

Clearly, I did not have enough training to deal with whatever was going on with Joe. I did not have the requisite skills to understand it. I had no way of predicting or even imagining such a horrendous possibility. And I can tell myself over and over again what others so readily told me, that there was nothing I could have done that might have prevented this tragedy, this horrible, unspeakable, unimaginable tragedy.

And yet, I was there. He was talking to me. What if I hadn't given up? What if I'd kept on asking? What if there *was* a message that with more time I might have discerned? What if I had listened better? Maybe, when there was still time, I might have done something, said something, realized something that would have saved the life of that beautiful woman, the child and Joe. Probably not, and yet, I will never know, and I can never forget. It haunts me at times still, because every day of their lives afterward, Joe's family suffered and wondered, and those who loved that young woman thought of her, remembered her, missed her; yet for all time, she remains dead.

I testified in Joe's behalf at his trial. He was found not-guilty by reason of insanity, and sentenced to a prison for the criminally insane in rural Louisiana. Marsha and I would go visit him every month or so until we moved away. While in prison, he wrote a humongous novel that to my knowledge was never published. His writing was incredible. After many years with no more psychotic breaks and no evidence of insanity, he was finally released. By then, we had completely lost touch. Joe died in his 40s of cancer.

One day during the long, agonizing ordeal of the trial I was over at the home place, paying a pastoral call. The feeling inside the house was comparable to what must hang over a battlefield during a lull in the fighting. There was fear. Everyone was afraid, some more than others and not all of the same things. There was bone-aching fatigue, the kind you know it will take years to recover from, if ever. There was drama and even excitement as the battle of wits between the prosecutor and Joe's bright, young defense attorney played out in the courtroom. In equal measure to the fear and the excitement was dread, gray and heavy as lead; for there were no good outcomes. The only hope was that maybe it wasn't entirely hopeless, that some good, some hidden, some unimaginable shred of good might emerge from somewhere like a banner in the midst of devastation. And behind and beneath and around it all was the dark specter of death, as if the cold, gray, dead woman cradling her lifeless fetus moved about the house like a wraith.

"You wanna talk?" I asked Beth as she stood alone like a stranger in her own home.

"Yeah," she agreed.

"Let's go outside," I suggested.

She didn't hesitate.

We walked across the expanse of lawn toward a nearby field of corn, eight feet tall and tousled out.

"How are you doing?" I asked as we walked. It was the standard, textbook question a minister asks troubled souls, but I really wanted to know.

She looked down and shrugged. How could she wrap in words what was going on inside her? Her parents had mortgaged everything they owned and gone to everyone they knew and even people they didn't know to borrow the money to get Joe out on bail. They had hired an up and coming lawyer to defend him. God knows what sacrifices this had required of everyone, including Beth. Now, after more than a year, the trial was upon them and everyone was as tense and tight as a bow string.

We walked into the shade of some towering pecan trees. I didn't know what to say to Beth. Clearly she was suffering, as were they all. Everything I could think of seemed trite, even stupid given the gravity of the situation. I wasn't inclined to touch her; she was, after all, Beth. Plus, it didn't seem like the gesture that was called for at the moment, and given what I sensed coming off of her, it might have gotten me decked.

Beneath the trees, the ground was littered with fallen branches. Suddenly, as if dropped into my head like a nut from heaven, I had a moment of inspiration. Had I taken even an instant to think about it, to give it proper consideration, to critique or analyze it rationally, I would have almost certainly rejected it as crazy. Instead, I reached down, picked up a tree branch about as big around as a baseball bat and three times as long and held it out to Beth. "Here," I said, "take this and hit that tree."

I half way expected her to look at me like maybe I had lost my mind, or at least, ask why. Instead, she took the branch without a word, lifted her gaze to the sturdy trunk of the towering pecan, hauled back and swung. When it hit the tree, the limb exploded. Without encouragement, as if this is what she'd walked out into the yard to do, Beth hauled back and swung again, this time, giving voice to her rage. The rest of the limb exploded. Tears streamed down her face and snot bubbled out her beautiful nose.

It was such an incredible thing to witness. The fury bottled up inside this beautiful young woman, the fury she could not even acknowledge much less express exploded with the force of a bomb. She didn't have to say how much she hated him, hated him for what he had done, hated him for his betrayal, hated him for what he was putting everyone who loved him through, hated him for the fear she would have to live with the remainder of her days of what a man might do. She just let it go without hurting anyone or anything, save the poor tree.

In this moment I saw for the first time the power of ritual. Whereas words could only encircle the emotions roiling inside Beth like an angry sea, the ritual allowed her to momentarily circumvent the long, circuitous paths of reason and language. It gave her immediate, unimpeded access to the thoughts and feelings she couldn't express and which were growing inside her like a malignancy. Afterward, she seemed relieved and better able to allow in psychic resources and reinforcements for what still lay ahead. I never forgot what I learned that day with Beth, and I've used it many times since with others and with myself.

After the full fruiting of the Civil Rights movement had led the country to recognize the injustice and rank stupidity of segregation and outlaw it, I was caught completely off guard when the grim specter of the KKK appeared at my door.

On weekdays a kindergarten not affiliated with the church, rented space in the church building. When the people running the kindergarten – some of whom *were* church members – accepted a Black child, suddenly we had an issue on our hands. I was flabbergasted. Surely not. How in God's name (precisely) could anyone be upset about kindergartners? We're talking four and five-year-olds here, cute, adorable, innocent little kids. "Are you fucking kidding me?" I wanted to scream. Yet they weren't – and they weren't a bunch of old farts either. The leader was a young, mean, college educated accountant.

I was outspoken; I didn't hold back; I was up in arms. The senior minister – you know the one with aspirations to move up the ecclesiastical ladder to one of those big, fancy churches in the capital – he was...how shall I put it?...discretely silent. He judiciously withheld his opinion on the matter. On Sunday mornings he could rant and rave about sin in the abstract, but when sin marched right through the front door dressed in one of its most hideous guises, he seemed to have nothing to say about it.

The Wednesday night business meeting when the issue would be discussed by the membership was packed to the gills. In truth, I don't think the opponents had a chance, but if there was any doubt, it was obliterated when Archie stood up to speak.

Archie was a farmer and a rancher who lived out near Joe's family. He was a mountain of a man; I mean huge and not huge as in fat, huge as in strong as an ox. His close cropped blonde hair, his clear blue eyes, his strong masculine features made him look like the very image of Nietzsche's superman. Hitler would have put his picture on

Nazi recruitment posters – except he was about as much a Nazi as Gandhi.

After the discussion had been going on for some time, Archie lifted his huge frame out of the folding metal chair and ambled slowly to the lectern. He grasped the sides with his two massive hands, stood looking down for a moment as if to collect his thoughts, looked up and began to speak. His voice was soft, almost small, without a hint of anger or accusation. He was sad, he said, deeply sad, because he couldn't understand how anyone could be upset about a small child, regardless of their color, wanting to attend our kindergarten. Who were we? he wanted to know. How could we, he asked, his voice cracking with emotion, refuse a small child and still claim to be followers of Christ? Tears flooded his eyes and began rolling down his cheeks as he stood and stared out over the crowd, waiting for someone to answer his simple question. A few people coughed and shifted uneasily in their chairs at the sight of this huge man standing before them openly weeping, but no one answered.

The vote was taken. The child was welcome to stay in the kindergarten that met in our building, and some of the members withdrew.

These, however, were exceptions to my time as a minister. Beyond the tedium of Sunday morning and evening worship services, planning and carrying out youth activities, visiting the aged and the sick, I recall spending an inordinate amount of time praying over the corpses of old people whose waxy faces I had never before laid eyes on and about whom I knew only one thing: their lives, for good or ill, were over.

By this time there was a fairly compelling body of evidence raising serious questions about the efficacy of my attempts to manipulate God through good – no, *excellent* – behavior into making me normal. Not only were my noblest efforts to earn normality being constantly trampled by my obsession with being a woman, on the two great social issues of my time, the Civil Rights Movement and the Vietnam war, the Southern Baptist Church was, at best, deafeningly silent in contrast to the Bible, which was unequivocally clear. (Does it seem like such a stretch to believe that when Jesus said "love your enemies," he probably meant not to bomb them?) As a result, I became increasingly aware that the church in which I had grown up, the church which I had dedicated my life to serve, and the church in which I was employed at a rather handsome salary had the practical value and spiritual legitimacy of professional wrestling. That's when I discovered Church of the Savior through the writings of Elizabeth O'Connor whose books my famished faith scarffed-up like so much red meat.

An ecumenical Christian Church headquartered in Washington DC, Church of the Savior was in the best tradition of that thoughtful, intelligent, compassionate strain of Christianity that runs through the otherwise dull rock of religion like a shimmering band of crystal. I began regularly attending retreats at Dayspring, Church of the Savior's retreat farm in rural Maryland. I made the pilgrimage from Mississippi to Maryland in hopes of finding some way to reinvigorate the church of my childhood, in which, by this time, I had spent considerable time, energy and money preparing to work. At a deeper level, however, I was desperately searching for something real, some concrete, identifiable incarnation of faith that had intellectual validity and that offered comfort where I hurt and hope where I increasingly despaired.

Every year I would go, and for a goodly part of four or five days, I would cry. I didn't know why I was crying or what I was crying about. Inside me lived a pool of grief, deep and invisible, from which flowed a seemingly endless stream of tears. Someone once said that the beginning of wisdom is a firm grasp of the obvious. In my youthful, exhausting, desperate race to escape being grasped by the obvious – that I was not a man – Dayspring became a crucial resting place, a refuge, a sanctuary. God knows what I would have done without it.

After two and a half years at the rural Mississippi church, I started my expected climb up the career ladder by accepting a good-paying associate minister position with a renowned pastor of a prestigious church in the state capitol.

Northminster Baptist Church had distinguished itself by being one of the few Southern Baptist churches that had taken the side of justice during the Civil Rights Movement. Based on this radical act – and this act alone – it was considered a bastion of liberalism. I went knowing that I would either make it there or I would make it nowhere as a Southern Baptist minister.

I had been there less than a year when, in the senior minister's absence, I preached a sermon based on the story of the Hebrews' exodus from Egypt. In it, I postulated that if the story was reenacted today, the U.S. would be in the role of Egypt, the oppressor. The priests of the pharaoh who pronounced divine sanction on his acts of exploitation and cruelty would be the modern church, while the world's poor and oppressed would be the Hebrews, God's chosen people. Even though I made a compelling Biblical case, this largely white, wealthy, Republican congregation welcomed my words of wisdom with the same enthusiasm they would have welcomed a tax audit.

While the sermon ruffled some feathers, the vigilantes really mounted up when, in a moment of prophetic zeal a few weeks later, I published an article in the church newsletter proposing that the Iran hostage crisis presented us with a perfect biblical metaphor. In this metaphor, we, the U.S., were just like the Iranians who were holding our innocent citizens hostage; except we were holding the entire world hostage to serving and satisfying our selfish interests and insatiable greed through the threat of nuclear annihilation.

As further evidence that I was not the sharpest tool in the shed (as if more evidence was needed), I thought my article was nothing short of brilliant drawn as it was from the finest of the biblical prophetic tradition – and Southern Baptists were, after all, great believers in the Bible, weren't we? What in my youthful naiveté I failed to foresee was that, also acting in the finest of the biblical prophetic tradition, the Powers-That-Be decided to bestow upon me the special reward reserved for prophets.

When the newsletter article hit the streets, the deacons along with the senior minister were on retreat. Someone must have called them, because when my incendiary suggestion that we, God-fearing, white, Christian Americans were no better than those evil, dark-skinned Iranian Muslims reached them, they actually broke off the retreat. Instead of saying something like, "This newsletter article is disturbing, but since we're here on retreat to do the work of the Church and discern God's will, maybe we should discuss it, pray about it even." What a fucking concept! No, they break off the retreat and by the end of the day, I am without a job. "We think you'll be happier elsewhere," the senior minister crooned soothingly in that professionally manicured voice of his. And even though he was right – I *was* happier elsewhere, *much* happier – it still didn't justify what they did.

Unlike Jesus and a lot like Judas, rather than make a stink, I accepted a handful of silver and resigned like a good boy. Mr. Bigshot senior minister eventually left, too, though he joined the Episcopalians, which, according to Southern Baptist thinking, means he turned out to be a bigger sissy than me.

After being fired from Northminster and working for a year at a private Montessori school in Jackson,

Marsha and I moved into one of the houses on Dayspring farm in order to become part of Church of the Savior.

One of the chief tenants of Church of the Savior then, as now, was the belief that God called every person – not just ecclesiastical professionals – to some particular work. This work, no matter how seemingly small and insignificant, was an integral part of God's intention to redeem the entire created order and restore it to the purposes of Love. As such, this calling brought healing to the world as well as to the one called. Faithfulness to this call was exercised principally and practically through a mission group, a small group of similarly called believers who were likewise committed to serving the world through a stated mission.

Shortly after moving to Dayspring, I joined *Emaneos*, the mission group that managed Dayspring's 50 acre fruit and vegetable farm. *Emaneos* met each week, usually somewhere on or near the farm. Our little group of six was about as screwed up as any, though I think we functioned together better than most. Each meeting started with about ten minutes of silence after which we did a quick check-in, part of which was a report on how well we had kept the daily disciplines of 30 minutes to an hour of silence, prayer, Bible study, reflection and journaling. (Alice was the worst at keeping the disciplines, but at 83 and crotchety as hell, we figured she deserved some special considerations. Plus, I figure the Almighty didn't mind either, since, given the hardships of Alice's life, he no doubt got a well-deserved earful whenever Alice got around to addressing him.) Then we'd talk about the mission.

We talked about the faith implications of pesticide use. They were almost certainly a sin – some more so than others – but, given the circumstances, particularly the financial circumstances, not to mention God's obvious love affair with weeds and bugs, we kept on using them, though at as low a rate as possible.

We spent a lot of time talking about labor, who to hire and how much to pay them. We talked about which crops to grow. At one point, Robert, the farm manager and my dearest friend, and I semi-seriously debated growing a small crop of marijuana in the middle of the apiary to try and solve the constant threat of financial collapse. Though we had no moral objections to marijuana, we were forced to concede that growing an illegal crop that would do nothing to help feed the hungry didn't exactly fit our mission.

We took great pride in marketing our produce, the gifts of God's good earth, in underserved areas of DC. We never tried to convert people; we just tried to feed them good, fresh, wholesome food grown with love and sold at a fair price. That was our mission.

It sounds rather ordinary, certainly not dramatic. It's not like we did anything exotic or esoteric. Oh, sometimes we celebrated communion with one of Judith's delicious scones, but that was about it. No sacrificial lambs, unblemished calves or suckling pigs, no dancing around fires, no psychedelic drugs, not even wine.

Yet there was something about those weekly gatherings, something about having a common call and being committed to one another in ways that required significant sacrifices of time, energy, and money that transformed the ordinary and otherwise mundane tasks of farming into something else, something more, a sacrament in the truest sense, an offering we gave and a blessing we received. Had the risen Christ visibly appeared in one of our meetings, I would scarcely have been surprised; such was the tangible presence of the Divine Numinous when we gathered.

After the meetings, I would walk back to my house in the dead of night, inwardly aglow, following trails through the dense forests of Dayspring that on moonless nights were navigable solely by the feel and sound of my footfalls.

    I loved working on the farm. Tractor time was some of my favorite. Tractors are incredibly powerful machines, and watching a two-bottom plow tear open the earth like a ship parting the surface of the sea was awesome. Once the job of plowing a field had begun, there was nothing to do but ride the lurching beast of a machine and allow the roar of the engine to fill my ears until it became its own kind of silence, then sink into a euphoric trance for long, slow hours as the earth rolled neatly off the plow into dark, rich rows.

    No one had to tell me that a straight line is a geometric mandate intrinsic to plowing, and I quickly discovered that the best way to achieve this was to fix my eyes on some point at the far end of the field and focus solely on it for the entire run, then lift the plow, turn the tractor around, find another object on the other end of the field in line with the next row, drop the plow and keep my eyes fixed on the new focal point. This was not always easy. For instance, indigo buntings, birds so startlingly blue a tree full of them could easily pass as Christmas ornaments, nested in the raspberries, and even the hint of one would distract me. Suddenly the row I was plowing would bulge outward leaving a section of unplowed ground that would cause problems in later stages of cultivation.

    Fall, however, was the worst. Growing up in Mississippi, I had never witnessed the glory of a sugar maple in its full fall splendor. They are unspeakably beautiful, so much so they cause themselves to blush. The trees festoon themselves in a riotous orgy of golds, scarlets, limes, maroons, each seemingly in competition with the others for attention like a horny group of girls at a military parade. Were they not so elegantly earthy in their beauty, they would be shamelessly gaudy. There was this one tree in particular. She stood alone at the end of the uppermost field where in the summer we grew a small crop of lilies for the cut-flower market. In fall, she was breathtaking, a princess of some ancient arboreal lineage descended directly from the One True Sugar Maple that dwells in the metaphysical realm of Plato's perfect forms. When I plowed the upper field, all rows led to her. She became the apex of a triangle, for whenever I turned the tractor in her direction, she alone became the object of my attention, yea, my devotion. Every fall since moving to California, I remember her like a long-lost lover, gone but never forgotten.

The most promising crop from both a mission and a financial perspective was strawberries, which we marketed primarily as pick-your-own. After Caleb was born, the financial demands of a family (not to mention the obligations of fatherhood) forced me to quit working on the farm as a paid hand and accept a teaching position at a Montessori school. I remained a mission group member, however, and on weekends during strawberry season, I would take Caleb with me to help at the strawberry field checkout stand. While I was weighing produce, taking money and chatting with customers, Caleb would crawl into the field and proceed to pick and eat every red, pesticide-covered berry he could lay his chubby little hands on. In a matter of minutes his face, hair and round Buddha belly would be sticky with sweet red juice and speckled with tiny strawberry seeds. He never seemed to suffer any ill effects of his gluttony, nor, given that he is now a gorgeous, intelligent, healthy triathlete, is there any indication of long-term damage. I am glad to report, however, that his manners when eating strawberries have improved significantly.

The intellectual framework within which faith and action were understood within the Dayspring Church were significantly influenced by Jungian depth psychology with a particular focus on Jung's feminine and masculine principles and energies. This way of thinking about faith resonated with my own struggle like the sound of a well-tuned drum, and to be told that the struggle between the masculine and feminine was also the battleground of contemporary faith was compelling to say the least. I latched onto it like one falling grasps a rope. Unfortunately, however, I didn't reveal how in me these two forces were locked in mortal combat. I just hoped that as we worked with them, I might find some way to reconcile their opposition in me even as we struggled to find ways to reconcile them in the larger society. It was a terrible disservice, as well as a gross breach of faith that I did not reveal the trans stuff to these wise and good people. I deeply regret that now and ask their forgiveness.

Among other things, our work with Jungian depth psychology at Dayspring helped me finally cleanse myself of my fundamentalist past. In keeping with good Jungian depth psychology, it started with a dream.

In the dream, a bearded man dressed in priestly black vestments with an air of malevolent hostility is threatening me. The exact nature of the threat is unclear, but I awaken terrified. Years earlier in group therapy, I had learned a technique for working with dreams like this that originated with the Senoi tribe of the Malaya Peninsula. The first thing I do before working with the dream to discern its meaning is find a protector to accompany me back into it. On this occasion, it is a black panther who possesses the power, upon my command, to rip the black-robed figure to pieces. Protected by the panther, I ask the figure what he is doing in my dream and what he wants. As usual with this sort of malevolent figure, he wants me destroyed. I inform him that my destruction is not an option, whereupon my protector growls a threatening assent. I ask what else he might want? I can't actually remember the entire conversation, but eventually, I realize that this figure in my dream represents the oppressive power fundamentalism still has in my life. In order to honor the dream, I decide to do a ritual to rid myself of fundamentalism's lingering influence.

It takes weeks to finally come up with the ritual, but when it comes to me, I instantly know it is right. On a beautiful, clear day in early spring, I take a shovel and the leather-bound King James Bible with the words of Jesus written in red, the Bible I used throughout my childhood, out into the woods that surround the house in which I live on Dayspring. Without a clear destination in mind, I follow that mysterious, inexplicable leading I have come to expect when in the mystical realm of ritual. It takes me to the outdoor pavilion where the Dayspring Church worships in summer. Near one corner of the pavilion I find a concrete tile about the size of a large stepping-stone on which a mosaic of what looks like a medieval saint is inlaid in smaller colored tiles. In all the times I have gone by this spot, I have never noticed this tile, though it has obviously been there for a long time. I roll it over, dig a hole, bury the Bible, and replace the tile. When I walk away that struggle, at least, is over.

Eventually, the farming operation failed financially. The Dayspring Church, which had always had something of a love/hate relationship with our mission, generously assumed the debt for which each of the mission group members was otherwise legally responsible, and the mission group dissolved.

I remember vividly the day we gathered for a last farewell.

I am standing on a small rise overlooking the strawberry fields, feeling confused to the point of vertigo.

Something is not right, but I can't figure out what. This intimately familiar landscape has mysteriously taken on a strange, surreal quality. It is like seeing someone you love dead for the first time. You know it's them, but in the exact same moment, you know it's not them at all. When Robert approaches and stands beside me, it suddenly snaps into horrifying focus; he has plowed the strawberries under. The fields in which we worked to bleary-eyed exhaustion, the fields over which we rejoiced in successful years and wept in failure, the fields from which hundreds of people had picked sweet, red fruit, the fields in which my child had feasted like a glutton, the fields in which we had placed our hope and that were the very incarnation of our mission are gone. It is over, finished – dead. Spontaneously I cry out, turn, and fall into Robert's arms, wailing like a mother when she first views the body of her dead child.

In the churches of my childhood and in the churches where I worked, faith was something we talked about, an idea, a concept, a doctrine, a principle, a tenant. In the daily struggles of life, however, faith had the practical value of small change. But at Dayspring, faith lived on the point of a plow, and it had a way of ripping open more than just the fertile earth.

Leaving Dayspring was the most excruciating experience of my life. In many ways it was similar to the death of my father, except the pain of losing my father was the pain of losing a relationship that might have been, whereas, my relationships at Dayspring were as real and rich as the foods we had so lovingly grown. When I drove off in the U-Haul bound for California, it felt like my skin being torn from my flesh.

The Bible says that the Hebrews' journey from the Promised Land into exile was made with much "weeping, wailing and gnashing of teeth." That pretty much describes what I did the lonely three thousand mile journey across the country. Recalling the trip is like reliving a nightmare, a murder – a rape. Save for Caleb and Lia, I left everything and everyone I loved. We moved to California on the pretext of saving the marriage, which was akin to trying to save someone's life by giving mouth-to-mouth resuscitation to their decapitated head.

My eight years at Dayspring were the richest period in my life. No high has ever surpassed the way I felt plowing a field, no touch so sensuous as being soaked to the skin with early morning dew picking sweet corn, no thoughts so worthy, no work so meaningful, no struggles so urgent, no silence so pregnant, no relationships so rich. It was the emotional, spiritual and intellectual watershed of my life, and everything since feels like commentary.

Children Introduction

As I moved more and more deeply into the life of Dayspring Church and the farming mission group, Marsha's involvement in the church waned. The demands of membership in a CofS faith community like Dayspring were costly in time, energy and money, and Marsha would not have been the first person to find them excessive when piled on top of being the family's major bread winner, holding down a full time, demanding job with an hour's commute. Plus, I think it was probably more religion than she was looking for, and, again, she would not have been the first to find it so.

For me, moving to Dayspring was like crossing the Jordan River into the Promised Land. In time my loyalty, my love, my affection came to rest on the farm, on the land itself, on its fields and forests, streams and ponds, and on those with whom I shared it. The demands of membership were not a burden to me. What became a burden to me was Marsha.

In exchange for my ministerial services, the Dayspring Church gave us a large house surrounded by beautiful hardwood forests. Attached to the house was a small apartment in which a single woman lived alone. I knew her name, and I knew that she was a lesbian. About the only other thing I knew about her was that I envied her something fierce. Sometimes I would stand for long minutes just staring at the door that joined our domiciles, imagining myself living alone in that little apartment, fixing dinner, reading, coming and going as I wished without the need to negotiate it with someone who was often resentful and jealous. Living alone in that little place I could do what I wanted and wear what I wanted and be with whoever I wanted *as* whoever I wanted to be without interference or disapproval.

By our fifth year at Dayspring, I was making plans to leave Marsha. Not permanently, or so I said. I just wanted to get away, out West where I could hike the Pacific Crest Trail and try to get my head straight, especially about this relationship that was becoming increasingly unsatisfying, about the Church and my relationship to it, and about the trans stuff, which threatened to overwhelm and destroy everything. Two months before I was to leave, Marsha announced that she was pregnant.

The only thing more damning than being born with a penis is using the accursed thing for Nature's intended purpose. Had I been smarter and in anything other than total denial, I would have run screaming in the opposite direction at the suggestion I make a spermatozoic contribution to the conception of children. Nonetheless, because the rules of manhood to which my phallus tethered me like a chain demanded it, I did my part. Besides, I was playing with a full testosterone charged deck, and Marsha was a great lover. But more than sex and more than obligation, I was motivated by guilt. I felt guilty for wanting to be a woman, guilty that I couldn't be normal and couldn't give her a normal life. I felt guilty for not telling her about it before we got married. I felt guilty about losing the church job and the life that went with it. I felt guilty for taking her away from her family to a place where she obviously wasn't happy. I felt guilty for not making more money than she did. I felt guilty for not wanting children. I felt guilty for loving what I was doing and the people I was doing it with more than I loved her. About the only thing I didn't feel guilty about was having sex with a person I loved and to whom I was married.

I tried to comfort myself with a narrative that once Marsha had a baby she would be happy; she would have what she wanted and in return, I could have what I wanted – without guilt. What an idiot. Did I really think I could make a contribution of sperm and then be done with it? I was the wrong species for that. And did I really think I could have a child, even as its father, and not fall in love with it? I was not that person – thank God.

What I never asked myself and consequently, never asked Marsha was why she didn't leave? By the time we moved to Dayspring it was abundantly clear that the trans stuff was not going away. She couldn't cure me, I couldn't cure me, God couldn't cure me, nothing could or would cure me; I was transgender. I wanted to live my life as a woman, and all the evidence suggested I would never be happy until I did. We both knew that was never going to change. The best we could hope for was that I would be able to continue repressing it and somehow bear the depressing consequences of so doing.

There were plenty of opportunities for her to leave, and, lord knows, there was plenty of reason. In addition to the trans stuff, being a farmer's wife was not what Marsha had signed on for. She had married a handsome, young minister with a promising future who could have supported her in a manner to which she was looking forward to becoming accustomed. It was clear I was never going to do that, plus she was terribly homesick.

And no one would have blamed her for leaving. Once she told them about the trans stuff, she would have had nothing but understanding and sympathy. Was it love that kept her? I have no doubt that there was love, but just as love didn't stop me from doing what I knew hurt her and hurt our relationship, love didn't keep her in it. There was perhaps some irrational shame on her part, but that's not enough. Down deep there was something else. People don't freely stay in uncomfortable, hopeless circumstances for no reason. The reasons may be unconscious – they usually are, giving them all the more power – but something else was at work that I suspect had little to do with me.

Maybe she thought that becoming a father would cure me. That's what I thought when I married her, and we both knew how that had turned out. I was so quick to take the blame for everything that I never stopped to consider that in choosing me to be the father of her children, knowing who and what I was, Marsha took upon herself a portion of guilt equal to mine, if not greater. At least the person I deceived was an adult who could have in less than a day had her stuff packed up and gone. Children, on the other hand, are pretty much stuck with the parents they get, and for their father, Marsha consciously and knowingly chose me.

Both of the children were born at home on Dayspring Farm. At the time, hospitals were suspected of causing more problems than they solved, nor had they yet come up with the idea of birthing rooms, so home births were making a comeback.

At the time I didn't appreciate the courage it took to give birth at home with only a midwife, me, and our good friend Deborah who, though primarily there as the photographer, was also a nurse practitioner. Giving birth at home removed the prospect or promise of pain killing drugs, and we were at least a half an hour from the nearest hospital. I'm sure Marsha considered all these things, and surely she knew from the stories of other women what she was in for. Still, she chose to give birth at home, a feat for which I shall always be grateful and utterly in awe.

Having a child at home required considerable preparation on our parts. There was a list of supplies as long as my arm. We never did figure out what the hell Witch Hazel was and why we were suppose to have it – but we had it. Of course, there were emergency plans, especially with Caleb who was born in the dead of winter. We faithfully attended all the birthing classes. Marsha attended breast feeding classes. We did everything they recommended and everything we could to be prepared.

When the contractions with Caleb came about two weeks past his due date, they came faster and harder than we expected. We had been coached to stay relaxed when labor began. "Most likely it will be hours before the midwife even leaves her house once contractions begin," they had assured us. It would depend on the duration and frequency of the contractions, which I dutifully timed and recorded.

After only about an hour into labor, the contractions were already approaching the magic threshold. It was hard to know what to believe, what I'd been told – don't worry, relax, it'll take time – or what I was seeing on the hands of the stop watch. Two hours into labor, the timing was irrefutable, and Marsha was clearly into hard labor. I called the nurse midwife. She sounded very casual on the phone; we were, after all, first time parents, and she knew how hysterical first timers could be. "How long are the contractions?" she asked casually. I told her. She seemed more interested. "How long between them?" I told her. "Okay," she said, "I'm on my way." I didn't know whether to be relieved or scared shitless. I was prepared to be Marsha's birth coach; I was not prepared to deliver our child.

Fortunately, the midwife made it in plenty of time, and Marsha's labor went on its un-merry way. One thing they had warned the coaches about was a phase of labor called "transition." I remember the instructor trying to describe how we would know it. Finally, she just said, "You'll know."

Throughout labor Marsha and I had been doing great together. I remembered what to do, how to coach her to breathe in the contractions, when to touch her and when not to, what to say between the contractions, how to encourage and comfort her, how to leaven the horror of it all with judicious doses of humor. After several hours of labor, as another contraction began, I leaned in to begin coaching when, without warning, an expression came into Marsha's face that could, without exaggeration, be called demonic. Even if I hadn't been forewarned, the look in her eyes would have pushed me back as surely as a hand to the throat. "If you touch me, if you so much as lay a hand on me or say one more word, I will fucking come off this bed and rip your goddamn head off and spit down your throat," her visage said without so much as a word. I sat back, became silent and tried my best to become invisible. "Transition," I thought, "That's transition. Wow."

Unlike Caleb, who seemed to be training at birth for the triathlons he would do as an adult, Lia's birth was downright leisurely. Of course, by then we were old hands at the birthing thing; still, it seemed to take Lia forever to get serious about getting born. My fantasy is she was taking her sweet time, because she wanted to very carefully examine each new stage of the process and reflect on it, evaluate it and see how it made her feel. Finally Marsha got in the shower to see if she could speed things up, while I took a nap. I don't even remember a transition. Whereas Caleb had been a hefty 9 pounds, ten ounces, Lia was a healthy 8/2. My only regret through the whole incredible process was that when the midwife asked if I wanted to "catch" Lia, I declined. I didn't trust myself; and besides, I didn't want to get that far and then, screw something up. I could have done it, though, and afterward, I wished I had.

Because they were home births and because Marsha and I had an Rh incompatibility, we had to be particularly vigilant about jaundice, which manifests as a yellowing of the skin. Anyone who thinks Caucasian babies are born pink has never had to worry about jaundice. To the eyes of a parent anxious about jaundice in their newborn, it wasn't a question of whether or not the child looked yellow; it was a question of how yellow is too yellow. "Just bring him in," they said when I called, so we bundled up our five day old, and I drove him to the hospital to have his billirubin checked.

I was filling out the admission form when I came to the question "Relationship to the patient," and for the first time in my life, I saw myself write the word that would change my life forever: "Father." Up until that moment, I had been doing what needed to be done. I had been on deck, on duty, on guard – as a good father should be. I had not stopped to consider, to reflect on and appreciate the significance of what had just happened. For good or for ill, whether I liked it or not, wanted it or not, who I was had fundamentally changed forever, and what I might do and who I might be were no longer entirely mine to choose. When they pricked his finger and he cried out in pain, I knew then what I would know many times thereafter, that I would never be safe again. I could be hermetically sealed inside a container able to withstand a nuclear blast, and if one of my children was somewhere out in the world, I would not, could not be safe; for whatever happened to them, happened to me, whatever pain they suffered, I too would suffer.

When they're small, parents, at least, parents in the developed world, can with some degree of confidence enjoy the illusion of control and protection. Of course, stuff can – and does – happen. When the weather warmed sufficiently, we would leave the sliding glass doors open to the backyard so Caleb could crawl outside whenever he wanted. Of course, we were always nearby, but one day when I went to check on him, Caleb was sitting on the flagstone patio picking tiny mushrooms that had sprouted in the cracks and aiming them toward his mouth. I scooped him up, called for Marsha, and whisked him to the kitchen sink where I pried open his mouth with my finger and looked for evidence of mushrooms. By this time, Marsha had the phone and was dialing poison control. They instructed us to give him syrup of Ipacac to make him vomit, (which, of course, we had), and then to bring him in. On the way to the emergency room, he finally threw up with no evidence of mushrooms, so we turned around and went home.

By the time they're too big to scoop up without risking the need for chiropractic care afterward, the illusion of protection begins to crumble like fortress walls of old clay. I remember vividly the day I first truly realized this. By that time we had moved to California, and I was living in what amounted to a small neighborhood of odd, little apartment houses where the neighborhood gang of six or eight kids was never out of sight or earshot of at least one adult. One family had a boy a little older than Caleb, about 8 at the time, who was rarely there but with whom Caleb played when his best friend Nick wasn't around. He was a mean little kid who I didn't trust, so whenever they played together, I kept a particularly close eye on them. Still, one day I looked up from the kitchen window to see Caleb running back toward the house holding his mouth. I dropped what I was doing and rushed out the door to meet him. His lip was bleeding, so we came inside where a closer inspection revealed that one of his newly grown permanent front teeth was chipped. Shithead had thrown a rock that – quite accidentally, he insisted – had hit Caleb in the mouth.

I did all the things a parent does. I stopped the bleeding, cleaned the wound, iced it, and packed him off to the dentist. When all was done that could be done and Caleb was upstairs with Nick, I sat down on the couch and wept – sobbed, actually. It was a permanent tooth, and as such, it was a wound he would carry with him for the rest of his life – as would I it turned out; for after all these years, I cannot write these words or read them without crying. In that moment, I saw with terrible clarity that I could not protect him from the evil in the world, from the bad things that could and would happen, from injuries that would leave scars regardless of how much I might try to love them out of existence.

When they got old enough to know better, some of that changed. I did not, for instance, suffer their hangovers. In fact, I was only too glad to let them suffer their hangovers when they drank too much. Yet even now that they're adults, I am still not, nor will I ever be safe; for, if anything, my love for them has grown with the freedom to be myself. Now, sometimes I can see through the aging eyes of experience futures in which I grieve for them losses yet to be lost, sorrows they have not yet felt, pains that await their awareness. Daily I make my prayer for them and hardly a week goes by that I am not moved to grateful tears that they are in my life.

Sometimes I grieve just because I miss them, and because I can see that time will have its way with me and the opportunities to suffer their losses, to celebrate their joys, to weep when they weep, to laugh when they laugh, to tend their wounds and kiss away their tears will pass into memory. Just as I cannot imagine my life without them, I also cannot imagine theirs without me, even as I pray with all my heart what every parent prays, that my good and proper end will come long before theirs, and that when I am gone, they will carry me in their hearts as I have carried them.

Children – Part 1

By most accounts and measures, I was a good father. I provided for their needs; I roughhoused, played and cuddled with them; I taught them the rudiments of popular sports; we camped, canoed, and worked together; I taught them how to use tools, even the dangerously powered kind; I took Caleb hunting. I tried to take Lia. I insisted that if she was going to eat meat, she should engage in the whole bloody process, but Lia adamantly refused, and by that time, I had lost most of my predatory interests, never very strong in the first place.

Regrettably, I could also be mean in ways often associated with fathers. I was too often irritable and impatient, like my own father, and on one occasion, I was violent, though that was more like my mother.

When he was about ten, I took Caleb on a long weekend hunting/camping/canoeing expedition on the river. We returned Sunday afternoon tired and dirty with a truck full of camping equipment to unload, unpack and clean, supper to fix and the demands of Monday morning in the classroom waiting for me like the stone of Sisyphus. I told Caleb to start unloading the gear. He pulled a bag out of the truck, dropped it on the ground and started playing with a friend who had discovered we were home. I told him to take it in the house. He took it in the house, dropped it on the floor, came back out and began playing again. I told him to keep unloading the gear, but every time I came out, he was back playing with his friend. Exhausted and exasperated, at the end of my physical and emotional rope, I snapped, and the next thing I knew I had slapped him hard across the face.

It was one of the worst moments of my life. Instantly, I felt sick with guilt; yet, rather than admit it, I screamed "If I'm going to do all this work for you, you've got to help out!" This, of course, was a reasonable expectation, which I had every right to demand it of him, but it in no way justified what I had done. For hitting your child in the face, there is no justification.

Yet, is this not the gift of children? They call forth from us a love we never thought possible, and yet, by their very natures, children have a way of ferreting out the unhealed places inside us like a mole finding a worm. In this sense, every child is the Christ child, a gift from God given for our salvation in direct conflict with the empires of our egos.

The incident still lives in my memory like a crime. It is one of those terrible moments in time I would give my right arm to take back, and yet, time moved on as time does, leaving it there indelible and undeniable, etched permanently in my mind like an obscenity carved in stone. Later that evening, I apologized, and from time to time in the ensuing years I brought it back up – as I do now – if only to repent anew and say again how much I regret it. I think Caleb has forgiven me. I hope so.

I remember with both joy and sadness a few times when I cared alone for them as babies. If Marsha was to be away long enough, I would paint my nails, don a skirt, apply a little make-up, and with the aid of these small symbols, feelings of love and tenderness would emerge that were otherwise inaccessible to me. The impatience, frustration and anger would leave, and like a stone rolled away from a tomb, a version of me would emerge that felt otherwise inaccessible; a version denied me as a man and disallowed me as a father.

These moments were rare and fleeting. Stuck in the roles of husband and father, I was frequently angry, and in the shadows, lurked rage. Realizing that I had dangerously little patience for the demands of young children, I mostly assisted, supported and facilitated Marsha, who did the bulk of the parenting during the first few years of their lives. She was an excellent parent of young children and more than made up for my shortcomings. She held an almost perfect balance between strictness and permission, discipline and nurture. Unlike me, she had a seemingly endless supply of patience, and while she had no qualms about giving either one of them a pop on their diapered behinds if they needed some kinesthetic reinforcement, mostly she was able to redirect them with a kind of creativity that I found mystifying and marvelous.

If I had any of Marsha's genius for parenting, I think it was in the role of teacher. The curriculum was anything I could imagine they might one day need to know, and my pedagogical techniques were unconstrained by ed code or sterile professionalism.

When Caleb started crawling, we lived on the bottom floor of a two-story house. Since both floors were completely self contained living units, there wasn't a lot of traffic between floors, but the stairs definitely posed a hazard for a baby as yet unfamiliar with the impartiality of gravity. To make matters worse, there was also an outside set of stairs leading to the upper deck which the upstairs tenants used frequently. We blocked off both sets of stairs with gates, but the gates were a nuisance. Nor did I trust them to hold against the persistent tugging of a child drawn to stairs as a moth is drawn to the flame or the adults to remember to replace them. (I was the worst.)

One Sunday morning I took Caleb with me to worship in order to give Marsha some much needed extra sleep. At the time, the Dayspring Church was worshiping in the living room of the original, old farmhouse. I took a seat between the wooden staircase and the front door, a position from which I could make a quick, unobtrusive exit should Caleb get fussy.

Most of the time he was a good-natured little guy, pudgy and ugly and cute as a puppy. I put him on the floor to crawl around and explore this new territory, and it didn't take him long to discover the stairs. He put his hands on the bottom step and craned his oversized head back to gaze up the long staircase. I watched but made no move to interfere. He began to climb. He succeeded in getting himself up on the first step and began to work on the second. I calculated the relative heights from which a fall might either teach Caleb a valuable lesson about the dangers of stairs or actually cause injury. He mounted the second stair, the nadir of his journey and what I had determined would be the limit of my allowance. When he leaned back to assess his progress, gravity had its way with him, and though he was barely out of arm's reach, I made no move to catch him. He did a complete backwards roll – a quite nice one, actually – before crashing onto the hardwood floor flat on his back, his head hitting with a loud "THWACK!"

There was that long second of silence when a baby seems to be struck dumb by the sheer incomprehensibility of it all, with the horrifying realization that the Universe has betrayed him into the hands of what are clearly incompetent adults. Then came the scream, a scream of fury, of pain, of accusation. "YOU CALL YOURSELF A PARENT!?" he seemed to wail in complete and utter despair. I scooped him up and hurried outside with him. From then on, his attraction for stairs was tempered with a healthy dose of respect and caution, and shortly thereafter, he became quite the expert at navigating them safely.

I give credit to the secret workings of my inner feminine that I did not abandon Caleb and Lia at the first opportunity. When Marsha fell in love with Thom within months of our moving to California, I had the perfect out. Though I longed to return to Dayspring like one dying of thirst longs for water, I could not, would not, did not leave my children. I marvel still that I stayed, for they were the only reasons to do so.

When Caleb was four and Lia two, I finally got my chance at mothering when Marsha and I established separate houses. I cooked meals, cleaned house, washed their clothes, made their beds, got them up and ready for school in the morning. At night, I would don my long, flannel gown, the kind I had dreamed of having as a child, tuck them in, read a bedtime story and sing *Kumbaya* as they fell asleep. As sweet as it was, trying to imagine myself a mother was like trying to conjure a difficult spell.

While I often dressed in skirts in front of them, rather than liberating, it was often fraught with frustration, since I could never know when one of their friends might show up at the door, or some neighbor drop by. I couldn't even go outside to call them in from play without having to change. Still, I did it often enough that when Caleb was in sixth grade he very innocently outted me.

As a Montessori teacher of 4-6th graders, I taught both of my children, Caleb for three years and Lia for two. It was the custom of the sixth graders to give the teachers (Susan and me) a special gift on the spring campout. Knowing that I enjoyed wearing skirts and utterly ignorant that such a thing was forbidden to men, Caleb somehow managed to convince his fellow sixth graders that the best gift they could give me was a skirt. How he convinced them that this would be a suitable gift, I have no idea. I guess they just went along with it. Who better to know what I wanted than Caleb?

They went to Jan, who was teacher in the lower elementary at the time and not yet my partner and enlisted her help finding such an item. To hear Jan tell it, this put her in an extremely awkward position. To refuse would have been to confirm that there was indeed something wrong with a man wearing a skirt and by extension, something wrong with Caleb's father and their teacher – a message she did not want to promote. Additionally, how do you tell a child their gift is wrong? Yet, at the same time, she knew that the presentation of this gift would be a very public affair, and that word of it was sure to spread. So, not without trepidation, she helped them find me a skirt.

For my part, I can't imagine what Jan was thinking. Surely she could have found some way to redirect them. How about a good canoe paddle, a new pair of binoculars, hell, even a piece of jewelry? Anything but a skirt! Then, once it was decided, why she didn't give me the heads up is something I will never understand. Surely she knew how terribly awkward this would be for me.

And what was going on with me that I never confronted her about it? It was unconscionable for her to just allow me to be exposed in front of everyone. Why I ever trusted her again, much less married her, I will never understand. Yet, I never held it against her, never even got mad. Looking back, I find my lack of response mystifying – and vaguely disturbing. Was I secretly glad? I didn't *feel* glad. Did I want people to know? If so, it wouldn't have been *these* people and certainly not in this way. I think I found the whole incident so painful, so traumatizing, I simply shut it out of my mind and tried never to think about it again.

So, on the sixth grade campout, in front of the entire class and all the parent helpers (mostly men) they gave Susan a manly shirt with a bear embroidered on the pocket and me a long, green skirt. I was stunned almost beyond comprehension. "Oh wow!," I managed to say, trying to sound politely surprised rather than completely mortified. It felt like one of those dreams where I'm on a busy street naked – except this time, it wasn't a dream, and, though fully clothed, I felt very much exposed.

I started folding it up and was about to say something that would take everyone's attention in another direction when they cried, "Try it on! Try it on!"

I left my body, just left it then and there and went away…somewhere else, somewhere above and beyond it all. Only a remnant of me remained, enough to try on a long green skirt over my boots and jeans and notice the men standing in the back laughing.

I must have turned more shades of red than a sunset over the desert before a storm; that is, until all the blood drained from my head into my leaden feet, leaving me sweaty, faint and disoriented. To the parents, I must have looked like a worm squirming in a frying pan of hot grease, burning with shame and embarrassment.

Now, looking back, I feel embarrassed at how embarrassed I felt. The shame about the trans stuff was just so overpowering I couldn't see the moment for what it was: absolutely hilarious. I wish I had worn the thing the rest of the evening just to prove that there's *not* anything wrong with a man wearing a skirt. I wish I could have celebrated it, if not for the liberation it offered, at least for the irony.

Not long thereafter, I sat both Caleb and Lia down and informed them that most fathers did not wear skirts and dresses around the house or gowns to bed, and that my doing so needed to be our little family secret.

This forced deception intensified the inner conflict I felt about my relationship to them. I loved them; about that there was no doubt. As my students for several of their grade school years, I spent uncommonly large amounts of time with them. Still, it now seems to me that I rarely enjoyed them, reveled in them, delighted in them the way they deserved and the way I might have had the impersonation not been required.

Then again, what parent doesn't feel this way? One day you look up and discover that adorable child you cuddled, kissed and read bedtime stories to has transformed into a full-fledged, long-limbed, independent-minded semi-adult, and you find yourself wishing you could recapture, if only for a moment, the beauty, the innocence, the magic of their childhood. Too often I simply endured the week they were with me, waiting impatiently for when they would again be with their mother, and I could more fully and freely try to conjure the spell without them innocently jinxing me.

There were, however, notable and memorable exceptions to the ambivalence I often felt. One particularly rich time was the summer we went on a five-day canoe camping trip on the Russian river when Lia was about six and Caleb eight. Away from the demands and distractions of work, free from the roles and expectations automatically imposed by others, we spent long, slow hours simply enjoying the outdoors in one another's company. While we had canoed and camped many times before, it had rarely been just the three of us, and I made special preparations for the trip.

Drawing from memories of my own childhood, I brought along rubber soldiers, the kind I had played with, and we made up an elaborate war game using stones, slingshots and even the pellet gun. It took us a couple of hours to mostly annihilate the other's army, and I think we were eventually forced to come up with some natural disaster to finally end the game.

I also borrowed a friend's 22 pistol, which we target practiced with against a high bluff. I can still remember little Lia, the gun clutched tightly in both hands, blasting away at a hardboiled egg. I thought the hillside would give way under the weight of lead before she gleefully blew it to smithereens. (My children, I am glad to report, seem not the slightest bit inclined toward violence, military service, or membership in the NRA as a result of these martial experiences.)

Two nights we camped on a gravel bar where a small tree jutted out over the river, providing a perfect four-foot high diving platform. We'd throw these foot-long colored rods weighted on one end into the water, then dive off the tree and try to find them all before surfacing. Given the current, it was no small task, even for me. We cooked over an open fire. We even made a sweat lodge in which I led them in a simple ritual that I regrettably can no longer remember.

Diving with masks and snorkels, Caleb and I discovered a submerged canoe, which we managed to free from its captivity and, with Caleb solo in the stern, bring home as a prize. With an extra craft, Lia was forced to paddle the little kayak (more like an oversized piece of Tupperware than a real kayak) rather than ride like the River Princess in the bow of my canoe. I still smile remembering her slouched down inside it, sulking, a large straw hat protecting her face from the sun, paddling down the river all the while whining and complaining that her arms hurt, which I'm sure they did.

Our last night we camped on a sand bar where a huge boulder sat on the water's edge some ten feet above a deep swimming hole. For hours, as darkness slowly descended, they repeatedly climbed up its backside, then hurled their small bodies into the water far below screaming in terror and delight.

There were other memorable times on the river, like the time Lia started running a fever during the night, so that the next day I had to build a tent in the middle of the canoe to protect her from a steady rain as Caleb and I paddled back to the pick-up point where Marsha was waiting. Or the time Lia, Jan and I built a shelter from another unexpected rainstorm and passed the time smoking wild grapevines the way my mother had shown me. These times in particular capture the essence of how I wanted life to be with them, free from both the oppression of fatherhood and the obsession to be female, each of which in its own way threatened to upset the delicate balance, contaminate the rich medium every child needs to grow into healthy adulthood.

Sometimes I wish I had come out when they were much younger, since, living as a woman, I think I would have enjoyed them more. But little good it would have done me if, as a result, I had lost them both forever.

Children Part 2

When I could no longer perpetuate the lie of
manhood, and, by extension, fatherhood, Caleb was poised
to begin his sophomore year in high school, while Lia was
entering ninth grade. At the time, Marsha and Thom were
living in Sonoma, a town some thirty minutes away where
the children also attended school. I had all but been fired
from teaching (more on that later) and, no longer with a job
to lose, had decided to make a break for it and come fully
out of the closet. It was then that Caleb decided he wanted
to switch schools and attend Petaluma High, the town
where I lived.

By that time I could not have crammed myself back
into that closet had I wanted to, and I told him so in no
uncertain terms. As I recall, my exact words were: "I'm
coming out of the closet, Caleb, and I won't go back in for
you." I reminded him that he had a perfectly normal
mother, and that he might seriously want to reconsider
staying in the high school where she lived, since going to
school in the same town where I lived could prove tricky,
to say the least.

Still, he insisted, so I pressed him. "For instance," I
said, trying to paint the picture for him in horrifyingly
graphic terms, "One day you're going to be standing
around with your buddies when someone walks up and
says, 'Hey Caleb, I saw your dad downtown in a dress.'
What are you going to say then?" He looked annoyed at the
question and answered, "So," in one of those semi-
intelligible grunts common to high school boys.

"So?" I almost shouted. "Is that all you can come up
with? How about, 'Oh, my God! She wasn't wearing the
mini-skirt was she? I hate it when she wears the miniskirt!'
or 'So, was she hot?' and wiggle your eyebrows like this,
see? Or better still, 'And you thought *your* parents were
weird.'" He was not amused. Still, I forced this sort of

conversation on him more than once, and yet, he enrolled in Petaluma High.

While there were moments of discomfort for everyone, it went much more smoothly than I think anyone expected. While it was odd that I was their father and dressed and lived my life as a woman, once their friends got to know me, *I* was not particularly odd. While I was a little funny looking, I was likewise, just plain funny and friendly and more interested in them than I thought they should be in me. And while being their father and dressing like a woman was strange, I did not dress strangely for a woman. (Truth be known, I dressed a good bit more like the traditional image of a mother than most mothers did.) And how can you feel too bad about an adult who, on the sole condition that you surrender your car keys, provides a safe place where you can hang out with your friends, drink beer and smoke pot and then, the next morning medicates you with liberal quantities of water, ibuprofen and homemade buttermilk biscuits? Okay, maybe she's weird – but she's cool.

Don't get me wrong; I did not *try* to be cool. While I definitely appreciated their acceptance, I did not approve of their drug use. I particularly didn't like that drugs and alcohol seemed to be prerequisites for fun, and I said so. If I'd had my way, they would have sat around drinking sodas, eating popcorn and playing Twister. But given that both Marsha and I had always promoted the values of curiosity and exploration, I knew that regardless of how either of us felt about it, they would eventually use their freedom to explore the world of intoxicating substances. I simply wanted to make sure that their first experiences took place in as safe an environment as possible and before they left home. That way we could talk about it, reflect on it, debrief it, critique it, and by relinquishing attempts to control, I hoped I might be allowed influence and thereby help them avoid abuse and addiction. So far it seems to have worked, though not perfectly, and I will be the first to admit it is a parenting strategy fraught with peril.

I encouraged my children to question values society tries to instill, especially the ones invoking blind and ignorant patriotism. I insisted they think critically, question assumptions – even those made by authorities – and value tolerance, respect and wisdom. I encouraged them to explore possibilities most parents pray their children never will. For instance, just before Caleb's fifteenth birthday, Lia and one of her friends discovered a *Playboy* hidden under his mattress. Of course, I was concerned – not that he had a *Playboy*, but that he felt a need to conceal it. So, for his fifteenth birthday, I went to The Sensuality Shop and bought him a tube of Men's Pleasure Cream along with an assortment of pornographic magazines that included the latest issue of *Playboy*, a gay magazine, a lesbian one and even a trans one (though, on second thought, maybe I bought the trans one for me.) Anyway, I got him a wide selection, which, on his birthday, I laid out on his bed before he got home from school. Later he came into the kitchen smiling sheepishly and thanked me for his gift. I told him I just wanted him to know that life offered lots of possibilities, and I hoped he would remain open to them all. About a month later, he gave me money for another issue of *Playboy*, which I got for him, and then, he quit asking. I suspect he discovered my Victoria's Secrets were just as good and free to boot.

Then, when Lia became sexually active, she complained that she rarely had an orgasm during sex with her boyfriend. Seizing this as one of those "teachable moments," I informed her that what few people realized was, that for giving a woman sexual satisfaction, a penis is a blunt instrument. If it was an orgasm she wanted, I suggested that Kelly or Katie or Amber would be a lot more likely to satisfy her than some boy. That both of my children have turned out straight is no fault of mine. I actively promoted homosexuality as an entrée on the menu of their sexual explorations, if for no other reason than to scandalize the relatives.

I know having a trans-parent has not been easy. I'm sure there were times when it embarrassed them, times when it made *them* feel queer, awkward and uncomfortable. Given our society's views and values, how could it not? I tried my best to minimize those times. I discretely kept my distance in public situations; I tried to read their body language to know when I was unwelcome, though those times were notably few; I never asked them to call me mother; that would have been too weird even for me. Soon after I came out, however, I insisted that they call me Meredith. This eventually evolved into Mer, which, ironically enough, if spelled Mere, is the French word for mother. Other than that, I made few demands. I didn't like that they still referred to me as their dad to their friends, but I made little fuss about it and never tried to forbid it. I didn't get bent out of shape when they or their friends used a wrong pronoun – a masculine one – though I was very clear that in a public place that mistake might elicit some very unwelcome attention. I often made jokes at my own expense, both to remind them of the reality in which they were stuck – lest they fall into the illusory comfort of denial – as well as to keep light what I knew at times felt heavy. Mostly, I just kept my distance and chose my battles carefully, which, when all is said and done, is probably the best thing any parent of a teenager can do.

For their parts, my children handled it remarkably well. Since boys are arguably more homophobic than girls, I expected it to be harder for Caleb, but Lia had her own times of difficult misgivings. In a classic case of insult added to injury, Lia reported that the most annoying thing she had to deal with was, once she revealed that her dad was transsexual, not only did she have to explain what that meant, but that then, she had to assure them that I did *not* dress like a hooker.

Truth be known, beyond the initial discomfort attenuating the formation of new friendships, they paid it little heed; their own lives were far more interesting to them than mine. They both talked to therapists about it, but I did not ask and I do not know what was said. Lia specifically requested to see a therapist, which I gladly arranged, but after the first session never expressed any interest in returning. And until Lia's senior year in high school when on Diversity Day, she bravely made a presentation about her transgendered father, neither of them were advocates for the cause of gay rights. This I did not begrudge them, since their choice to stay in relationship with me when they might easily have chosen otherwise made living what to others was a normal life for them a daily act of advocacy.

Later, as my experience of living as a woman deepened and matured, I became much more comfortable introducing myself to new friends and their parents as Lia's or Caleb's queer parent. It usually broke the ice and acknowledged with a touch of comic relief who I was and that there was no need to pretend otherwise. In fact, I'd like to promote it as a recognized title; rather than Dad or Mom, you can be someone's QP.

Even though I knew the kids wanted it, for many years, I resisted and avoided family gatherings. They always threw me back into roles I was trying to rid myself of. The kids knew how I felt, and either they told their mother, or she figured it out on her own, and with characteristic grace, she accepted it. In times of crisis, however, reticence was put aside and we all pitched in to do whatever was needed. One such time was when Marsha needed to return to Mississippi to help take care of her dying father.

There are two things you should avoid having – a heavy-duty pick-up truck and a watertight storage building, because an unending stream of people will be showing up at your door begging you to help them move and beseeching you with pleas of, "Can I please store a few things in your building for just a few weeks?" which, of course, turns into years if not decades. Most of these people will be related to you, and thus, especially hard to deny.

With only a small window of time to remove her things and prepare her house for rent, all members of the family were pressed into service, including me. By this time, "Hank" was some eight years in the past, and I was enduring my fifth year driving a school bus. Her house a chaotic mess and the relationship with Thom pretty much the same, Marsha spent the nights with Jan and me.

Unfortunately, that year the rats had made an unseasonable early assault on our house, which normally they try to take over only after the winter rains have driven them from their outdoor domiciles. Especially unfortunate for poor Marsha, who desperately needed some well-deserved rest, they had established a beachhead in the walls of Lia's bedroom where she was sleeping. I immediately set up a counteroffensive using the customary weaponry – the shotgun, pellet rifle, traps and poisons, but I had fought this battle often enough to know that it would take weeks to declare with the same illusory certainty as our benighted past president, George W. Bush – Mission Accomplished.

Since much of the stuff housed in plastic storage bins safely tucked away inside my outbuilding was family memorabilia, Marsha, Caleb and Lia spent considerable time sorting through old photos? There are no photos of Meredith gracing our walls; the mirror is hard enough to deal with. And there are absolutely no photos of Hank anywhere to be found on the premises save, perhaps, in a sealed box crammed way back in the dark recesses of the attic. During the week of the move, however, they were on full display. Even Jan was fascinated. And as the decades old photos emerged, the stories about them were told, and I had a wonderful realization: for the first time ever, I could talk about the past without feeling like I was getting sucked back into it. Even looking at the photos of Hank, I felt almost wistful; like he was a person I had known, not a person I had been.

Some of it was hard. At one point a teary eyed Lia lamented, "I miss my dad." Though I have grieved her lesser losses, I was so relieved to be free of that persona, I could not offer comfort, solace or even sympathy. So sitting around our little living room with a few good beers and mediocre wine, we all got to reminisce, the kids got to hear the old family stories, and I got to appreciate just how far I had come.

When this backbreaking process was finally over, about two weeks remained of our precious summer. Jan and I had originally hoped to spend another week camping with the horses in the Sierras, but when Caleb asked if he and I could take a backpacking trip together, I quickly agreed, and Jan gave her whole-hearted blessing. Only after plans were firmly established did it occur to me that even as a fit 57 year-old, to hoist a backpack – something I hadn't done in years – and undertake a trek at altitudes reaching over 10,000 feet with a 22 year-old triathlete was…well, stupid. One thing was certain: I'd have to stick him with all the heavy stuff, something to which he willingly and graciously agreed.

After brief deliberations, Caleb and I decided on a 25-mile loop trail through the Jenny Lakes Wilderness area in Sequoia National Park.

Standing in the check-out line of Trader Joe's preparing to purchase our camping fare, an attractive, middle-aged woman with weary eyes turns to me and asks, "Do you remember when they were still little and cute?"

I am accused to questioning glances, blatant stares and sympathetic smiles, but I am caught utterly off guard by such relaxed and easy friendliness.

I laugh and agree, "Yes, yes, I do."

She continues wistfully, "They were just so adorable and easy then, but not anymore." She is joined by two teenage girls, one of whom she reaches out and touches affectionately. "Now they're just trouble," she adds. The girl eyes her coolly before saying something and leaving the store.

"How old are they?" I ask.

"Fifteen and thirteen," she replies wearily.

"Oh, those are hard ages. It gets easier," I assure her, tall, handsome Caleb at my side, living proof.

She turns away as the checker begins processing her items.

For me, it doesn't get any better than this. This brief exchange with another mother has made my day over and over again; for she graced me with a rare moment of normality.

When it's just my kids and me, our relationships work extremely well. In public, however, my discomfort increases exponentially, so going into the Sequoia National Park Visitor's Center with Caleb to get our backcountry permit was particularly unnerving. (God, if I could just be shorter!)

The young man at the front desk with the open-mouthed Oh-my-God-what-are-you? look on his face finally manages to reply to my query that the person responsible for the permits is out to lunch and will not be back for half an hour. With time to kill, I wander over to the permits desk to look at a map. Caleb has disappeared, off looking at books I suppose, or else, he also caught the look and decided to create a little space of his own – something I do not begrudge him.

As I am looking at the maps, a young ranger comes up, says he overheard the conversation and asks if I have any questions he might answer. Times like this make me believe that there are angels in the world. No, really, there are.

As we look for our intended destination on the topo map, I comment on his Mickey Mouse watch. "Yes, I worked at Disneyland for five years," he informs me. "That must have been fun," I reply. "Oh yes, every day I got to be a new character. It was like dress-up every day of the year." What I know and what he knows and what most of these heterocentric breeders don't is that more than just a few of those dancing Disney characters, clowns, pirates, singers and performers are gay in more than just the happy, happy Disney way. While my gaydar does not read him as gay, working for five years at Disneyland, he has been around enough queers to read me as easily as if I had danced through the door in a Dolly Parton wig singing at the top of my lungs "I love being a girl!" and he kindly has taken it upon himself to come to my rescue. Bless you, adorable young ranger wherever you are. Bless you.

We get the permit, I successfully and safely navigate the women's bathroom without incident, and we go to the store for the required bear canister. If Caleb had run for the hills earlier, he certainly shows no inclination to do so in the store, and I think it safe to assume that the young girl renting us the bear canister acts so stupid because: 1. she just *is* stupid or 2. she is so taken with the tall, handsome young man next to me she has gone a bit brain-dead. It is one of those wonderful moments when *I* am not the center of attention.

The problem with outdoor activities like backpacking, horseback riding or canoeing is that skirts, dresses, Mary Janes, and make-up are about as out of place as a fur coat at a PETA party. However, I depend heavily on these things to queue others as to my true gender, and without them, I feel as exposed as a plowed-up earthworm in a flock full of robins. So, again, when it's just Caleb and me hiking along, everything is great. Whenever, we meet someone on the trail, however, I stop breathing, which, at an elevation of 10,000 feet carrying a backpack, I am having considerable trouble doing in the first place.

Backpacking parties passing each other on the trail almost always stop and exchange friendly information about the condition of the trail ahead, distances, weather, camping spots and the like. Deprived of my irrefutable symbols of femininity, the discomfort I feel during these encounters reminds me of a recurring dream in which I am in a vehicle speeding backwards along a road that grows steadily narrower. On one side, the bank rises steeply while on the other it falls away into an inky abyss. Unable to slow down or stop, the tires eventually slip over the edge, and I awaken in a panic as the truck plunges downward into the abyss. The dream mirrors my fear of what disastrous consequences might follow if I am mistaken for a man, though not so much to me personally as to those with me, whose company I cherish and enjoy, who might themselves be embarrassed or even humiliated.

On the third day after we have crossed the 10,000 foot pass and are headed down, we stop to rest at a large alpine lake. By this time the sweaty grime and dirty hair have become intolerable, so I decide to take a bath. Now that sounds simple enough, but baths are usually taken…you know, naked. Being naked had never been a problem before. One summer on a canoe trip to a really remote place when Caleb and Lia were still small, Jan, the kids and I had spent the better part of several days naked. But now…now things are different. Now, thanks to the wonders of science, I have breasts, and I don't know whether to be casual about my altered anatomy or shy. I opt for shy. I find a private spot, change into the swimsuit I have brought along, and wade out into the lake. Once in deep enough water, I remove the swimsuit and begin scrubbing away the grime.

While these isolated moments were difficult, the majority of our trip was nothing short of wonderful. Best of all, I *felt* like a woman. At times, I felt positively girl-like, more like Caleb's female friend than his parent – certainly not his dad. Not even a tiny part of me ever wanted to be a man, and walking through the grandeur of Nature as a woman feels so right and good and true. Several times I thought how much more fun I am to be with than Hank, though I don't know if that was true just for me or if Caleb felt the same. Except for those moments when I felt like I was about to plunge into the abyss, I enjoyed our time together immensely and all the more so as Meredith.

Children Part 3

Our trip also gave me a chance to see Caleb's new digs, a tiny house he shared with Greg, another member of the Cal Poly Triathlon team. Let's just say the place has character. For one thing, both boys have three bicycles, each of which is specially designed for some very specific function other than the simple locomotion afforded me by my childhood Schwinn. If you've ever tried to store a bicycle, you know how difficult it is with those handlebars and pedals, and in this house, six of them lined up in a row would take up well over twice the available floor space. Of course, it doesn't help that the living room has three full-length couches, a coffee table and a refrigerator devoted exclusively to the cooling of beer.

To address this vexation, the boys have come up with a rather novel solution: they hang the bikes from the ceiling, which fortunately, is high enough to allow passage underneath. Caleb's fancy yellow road bike actually looked quite decorative hanging above the state-of-the-art sound system. The mud covered dirt bike hanging over the kitchen table, however, is another matter. It is not hard to imagine sitting down to breakfast only to have a dirt clod plop into your fried egg; except that the table is so covered with tools, bicycle parts and all manner of non-culinary paraphernalia, sitting down to eat a meal at it is out of the question.

Now I imagine if I were a real dad, after a quick inspection of this bachelor's pad, I would open the fridge devoted to beer, pop the top on a cold one, plop down on the couch, prop my feet up on the coffee table and say something like, "Boy, I remember when I had a place like this..." That is not what I do. That does not occur to me. What I do is start cleaning the kitchen.

But it's putting away things that proves to be the real challenge. After washing and drying a large plastic pitcher, I discover that there are about eight large plastic pitchers. "Caleb, what in heaven's name are you doing with all these pitchers?" I ask. He looks annoyed. I realize I am starting to nag, which, while a motherly trait, is an annoying one nonetheless. I soften. "I mean, really, Honey, how many large plastic pitchers do you really need?" Whereupon, he proceeds to explain that the pitchers along with the 50 pounds of flatware, five spatulas (Lia swears that at one point she counted eight), ten different pieces of coffee making apparatus, multiple lidless pots, enough plates to feed five times what the house could even remotely accommodate, countless coffee mugs, beer mugs (okay, those I can understand), more spices than on display at the local Safeway, including half a dozen boxes of baking soda, all open, twenty boxes of herbal teas, eight ugly plastic mixing bowls, three large colanders – in other words, enough kitchenware to open a small restaurant chain – all of these represent strata left behind by previous occupants. Oh, so it's not clutter; it's archeology!

Finally, I persuade him that, given the very real limitations imposed by space, just this once he should violate the unwritten protocols of college apartment living and simply trash all but a couple of the best pitchers. Reluctantly, he does so, and I can almost hear the place breathe a sigh of relief.

In Caleb's room, I get a glimpse of his life that I no longer get to see on a daily basis. While there is a section of wall devoted to the identification numbers he has worn in various races, there is otherwise little evidence that the room is occupied by a serious athlete. In fact, the largest piece of decoration is a huge poster of a laughing Jimmy Hendricks given to him as a present by Lia. How wonderful, I think, that the most square footage of wall space in his bedroom is dedicated to a Black musician; we definitely did something right.

He also has an altar on which is the sword I gave him for his eighteenth birthday. On the blade I had engraved a passage from the Hebrew prophet Micah which, in response to the question, "What does the Lord require of us?" reads, "To do justice, to love mercy, to walk humbly with your God." You may need it someday to cut an umbilical cord, I prophesied at its giving. (I gave Lia one, too, on her 18th birthday with the same engraving. We all need a sword we know when and how to use.) But there are other things I do not recognize on his altar, artifacts and talismans of which I know nothing. Admiring them, I realize that there are things about my son that I do not know, that, in fact, he has become a person I do not know, his own person, a man, and as his parent, I find this strange – and disturbing.

On my last night there, Lia, also a student at Cal Poly, treats me to a local performance of *The Chorus Line* in which her friend Cassie has a part. We have just taken our seats near the front when a man about my age and his teenage daughter enter and sit beside me. I like men, particularly men my age, and being with them as a woman is especially interesting. Unless they know me or read me as trans or find me too unattractive to merit interest, a whole new range of possibilities exists, possibilities I find fascinating.

He looks my way, smiles and strikes up a conversation. He's pretty cute, too. I, of course, ask him questions. Maybe it's true that men like to talk about themselves more than women, but my experience is that most people like to talk about themselves. I think that's why I get along with people so well; I'm interested in them. Of course, some of this has to do with keeping the attention off of me and to curry their favor in the event they suddenly have an epiphany. From years of practice, I've gotten good at asking people questions that sometimes yield information that surprises even them. For instance, in a matter of minutes, I know this guy has two daughters, that they don't get along very well and the one sitting beside him is probably gay.

I can also tell he likes me and, more importantly, hasn't yet read me – or else, he's hiding it really well. I think he might even be considering asking me out, except I make a point of revealing I live some five hours away and will be leaving early the next morning. Besides, he has only seen me sitting. Once we stand up, and he realizes I am at least four inches taller than him, he won't be interested anymore. Still, in so far as I am able to squelch the fear that at any minute he is going to read me, I love this. It is titillating, a little scary and fun, like the rollercoaster.

So much of what it means to be a woman – *too* much of what it means to be a woman – is found in a man's desire. It's not hard to understand how some transwoman, especially young, pretty ones, get themselves hurt – and sometimes, killed – messing around with men. And how would it be to live with a man as a woman? So many things would be easier. For one thing, I would fit. I would be normal. God, what must that feel like? And who doesn't want to feel like they fit, like they belong? But in my case, it's all flirtation, flirtation not just with this guy, but with normality itself, a dream, an illusion, a fantasy. Still...

The summer following Caleb's and my 25 mile jaunt through Sequoia National Park, Lia ask if she and a couple of her friends can use the camping equipment to go out for a few days. "Oh, I want to come!" I reply without thinking. Such a response is totally out of character for me, since I have made it a point never to foist myself into my children's relationships uninvited.

Lo and behold, however, Lia and her friends think this is a great idea. Perhaps their enthusiasm has something to do with the fact that none of them knows how to assemble and operate the camp stove, much less how to cook a three course meal on it. The bears also pose a problem, and they still believe that my presence affords them a degree of protection. It must be one of the last illusions of childhood to fall.

We buy our food, no simple task since Michelle is a vegan while Kelly and Lia are hard-core carnivores for whom bacon is one of the essential food groups when it comes to camping. It is a long, long journey to the park, especially when Lia and Kelly decide they have sussed out a short cut on the map. Before long we are lost.

We stop at a Forest Service fire station for directions. I send the girls in, knowing that three lovely damsels in distress will summon forth considerably more assistance than I could ever hope to garner. We find our way back and, in the process, I suggest in true parental fashion that they might learn a valuable lesson from our misadventure. I quote the mountain climbing proverb: "Plan your climb and climb your plan;" last minute changes can sometimes lead to disastrous results. They nod in humble assent.

The last torturous hour of the drive is along an insanely narrow, winding road, but when we finally arrive, it is worth every agonizing minute. I have never camped in such a beautiful spot alongside a rushing mountain stream with exquisite snow-capped mountains rising in the near distance – and the weather is perfect.

For three days, we cook and eat and hike and afterward, take quick dips in the freezing stream and gather firewood and build a nightly campfire and sit around talking and drinking, and smoking a little pot and giggling like girls at a slumber party. Better late than never.

I know that many of my ideas of what it would have been like to grow up a girl are myths and illusions that any woman could easily disavow. I know from being a parent and a teacher that girls can be snippy and bitchy and mean to one another in ways uniquely female and that they face trials and hardships about which I know little. Still, from what I can see during our four days together, what I had so often fantasized it would have been like to be a girl is just as wonderful as I had always imagined.

Being with Lia and Kelley and Michelle, watching them interact with one another, greeting their sleepy-eyed, messy-haired faces each morning, following their strong, lithe female bodies along the trail is the very essence of what I always wanted to be and to do. They are playful and affectionate with one another in ways that are sometimes shocking. For instance, Kelly will be standing alongside Lia, when suddenly, out of the blue, her hand will dart over and clamp itself onto Lia's boob. And the poor ranger must have wondered what he stumbled into when he entered our campsite unannounced to place some sort of bear warning on the food box and found the girls cuddling affectionately on the cot. Their acceptance and willingness to allow me into their lives was stunning and amazing and moving.

Still, like so many other times, our time in the mountains together has a bitter/sweet quality; for it reminds me that I have spent most of my life standing in the cold and the dark looking into a room full of girls in their beautiful gowns with their hair all fixed, laughing and talking and living their lives. This time, however, the door suddenly swings open, and there are Kelly and Lia and Michelle calling, "Come on in, Mer. Join the party." At first, I can't believe it; it's disorienting and even a little intimidating. I have stood outside so long looking in I have grown comfortable in my tattered suit of hopeless longing. But once inside, I am immediately aware that over the years the girls I've watched so wistfully through the window of my imagining have all stayed young and pretty, like Lia, Kelly and Michelle, while, conversely, I have grown old. And much as I want to don a lovely satin gown and fix my hair and join the party, it is too late. Oh God, it is too late. I must content myself with the dubious rewards wrung from a life well lived, while the hopes and dreams and desires that I have clung to over lo, these many years are like faded photographs of what might have been but never was. All I can do now is transform my longings into blessings and bestow them upon those for whom it is not too late. And so I do. With gratitude to Lia and Kelly and Michelle, so I do. Blessings! Life's richest blessings be upon you, my dear ones.

Nowhere has being transsexual felt so heavy as in the realm of my children. Few terms are as determinative as 'Dad.' Its gender appellation is as hard and pure as crystal forged in the fiery bowels of earth. It is a title from which there is no escape; it is ubiquitous, omniscient and omnipotent. Even God cannot escape it. And as I have struggled to find some other interpretation of our relationships that might bind us differently, nothing seems powerful enough to supplant fatherhood. I might as well try moving a mountain.

Yet, looking back over the years and the distance Caleb, Lia and I have come, I am reminded of the words of Jesus: "If you have faith the size of a mustard seed, you can move mountains." As I survey the landscape of our relationships now, I am aware, gratefully aware, humbly aware that, amazingly enough, that mountain is gone. But it was not faith that moved it. It was love.

Outlaw

I was a divinity student in Louisville, Kentucky, when I first came to appreciate that facts do not equal truth. Ironically enough, I learned this from the Bible, which, in service of the Truth, often plays fast and loose with the facts. As a young theology student from a fundamentalist background, I initially found this disturbing. After all, didn't God write the Bible, and who better qualified to get the facts right than The Almighty? Over the years I have come to appreciate that an identifying characteristic of the God of the Hebrew and Christian Scriptures is a unique brand of humor that can be appreciated and enjoyed only by those who – to paraphrase Jesus – "have eyes to see and ears to hear."

Examples abound, especially the parts of Holy Writ composed by the capable quills of nothing short of divinely inspired drama queens whose shameless embellishments, historical fabrications and downright factual errors, reveal God with such complete and utter opacity that some are drawn into lifetimes of grateful devotion while others are driven to ridiculous convolutions of logic in defense of lame-brained ideas sucked from a smattering of isolated, disconnected, irrelevant passages of Scripture that have been bent, warped and distorted in order to fashion a humorless god created in the image of their fear and after the likeness of their folly.

After many, many years, I have finally come to realize that the facts about *what* I am do not equal the truth about *who* I am.

According to Jesus, it is the Truth that sets us free, not the facts.

But the facts were nonetheless compelling, too compelling, disproportionately compelling, so much so that I spent the majority of my life staring wide-eyed and terrified into them like a deer caught in the headlights of an oncoming car. But just as the lights of the car – for all their brightness – do not enlighten the deer to its peril, the fact of being a male-to-female transsexual did not enlightened me as to my true identity; but rather, concealed it, obscured it, confused it and left me to be repeatedly run down, torn open, broken, bruised and bloodied by the emotional Mack trucks of shame, guilt and fear.

"The facts, ma'am. Just the facts" were all our favorite detective, Joe Friday, star of *Dragnet* in the era of black and white TV, needed to find the bad guy. So it is that the culture's preoccupation with the facts rather than the truth makes me what I am: an outlaw.

Given that there are no outstanding warrants for my arrest and the only probation officer I know happens to be my little brother, my claim to fame as an outlaw is based on proclivities rather than legalities. You won't find my picture posted on the bulletin board at your local police station, but if you did, it would have to be my baby picture, since I was born an outlaw. Which is not to say I was a rebellious child, one of those spunky, impetuous, little hell-raisers from the get-go. Quite the contrary. I grew up with such a neurotic need to please, I spent thousands of dollars in therapy before I could even recognize and admit that I *had* needs and then thousands more learning that I could actually have them met without necessarily depriving others of life, liberty and the pursuit of happiness. It was money well-spent.

Even though my friends scoff at the idea of my being an outlaw, my friend the high school teacher, much as she might like to, can't invite me to speak to her class – not without alerting the administration and sending notifications home warning parents of the impending visit from a TRANSSEXUAL, as if – in addition to being an outlaw – I had some sort of contagious disease.

I am quite certain that were a real outlaw to visit a high school classroom (you know, one of those ex-cons who exhorts young people to avoid a life of crime) similar precautions would not be required. Of course, those most threatened by me would argue that I – unlike the ex-con – would be promoting a life of abomination and debauchery. Truth is, I'd promote transsexuality with the same enthusiasm I'd promote limb amputations; I wouldn't wish it on my worst enemy.

In his brilliant little book *Ishmael*, Daniel Quinn makes the astute observation that every culture has a Story, a Story which plays continuously in the background of our lives like music in the mall, haunts our collective consciousness like a ghost, guides our thinking, informs our judgments, insinuates itself like fog into the fissures of unconsciousness, and surrounds us like a wall protecting and preserving the familiar. Rarely do we actually notice this Story, and even more rarely do we question it, since questioning it threatens to disrupt the social homeostasis upon which the status quo, and we as parts of it, depend. The Story can be changed but only at great cost.

I had a first-hand experience with the dramatic power of the Story when I was a student at William Carey College, a small Baptist college in South Mississippi. At the time I also attended University Baptist Church, a small, rather liberal Baptist church, which, given that this was Mississippi and these were Baptists, after all, explains why it was small. From my earliest memories of going to church, I had heard about intrepid missionaries working in the remotest parts of Africa, spreading the Gospel to the dark-skinned heathens. We had prayed for them, collected money for them, heard stories about them, saw homely photos of them with nauseating regularity.

One place where Southern Baptist missionaries were most active was in Nigeria, so it should have come as no surprise when a young Nigerian man applied to attend our little Baptist college. It was, after all, run by the denomination responsible for his eternal salvation. I say *should* have come as no surprise, because judging from what happened next, it seems as though no one had ever imagined such a thing. Since he, like most of us, could not afford the costs of a private college education, he applied for a scholarship. In order to get a scholarship to a Southern Baptist college, he had to be a member of a local Southern Baptist church, and he was…well, you know, black! There were no black members of Southern Baptist churches, at least, not in Mississippi in the early '70s. The very idea was as unthinkable as…well, gay marriage.

Given that our small congregation was considered liberal, the Powers That Be, you know, the ones in charge of protecting, preserving and passing on "The Story," suggested he try us. It was a good idea, actually, and might have worked out fine, but, as luck would have it, his first appearance at worship was in the company of a lovely, blonde-haired, blue-eyed southern belle. You could hear sabers rattling in Confederate graveyards as far away as South Carolina.

When he presented himself for membership, the vote of the congregation, which, up to this point, had always been a meaningless formality, had to be delayed. A meeting of the congregation was called for the following Wednesday night. Members who had not shown their faces in years, members who had long since moved away, as well as a few whose appearance was downright scary – Hey, wait a minute! Didn't we bury her last month? – showed up to vote on the young Nigerian convert's request for membership.

It was a heated affair. Passions were strong on both sides of the issue. I remember one man, a local contractor who I had never seen in the years I had attended, stood up and announced, "I just want ya'll ta' know, I don't have anything against niggers. Some o' my best workers are niggers and I'm good to 'em. You can ask 'em. I just don't know why they cain't stay with their own kind."

If those weren't his exact words, they are more than a fair representation of the sort of thing I heard more than once. And truth be known, that old racist son-of-a-bitch probably was good to his workers and likely contributed more to their economic well being than most of those liberals ever did or ever would.

Eventually, the young Nigerian was granted membership, got his scholarship and never bothered showing up again. Some convert he turned out to be.

Not only is The Story hard to change, but, according to Quinn, defying it results in a very persuasive punishment: we are not fed. Most male-to-female transsexuals are living sad, frustrated, tormented lives inside their closets for primarily one reason: they're afraid of losing their jobs. No job, no food.

Even those who wisely choose fields where it's practically impossible to get fired, still risk losing patients or clients or finding themselves ostracized by peers and the social groupings on which they depend. Those few who successfully transition on the job often find themselves in untenable situations where they are confronted daily with overt and covert expressions of ridicule and rejection such as being addressed by their old, male name, referred to in masculine pronouns or being required to use either a special bathroom or the men's.

Relationships with colleagues are queered, those above you are either resentful or patronizing while those under you lose trust or respect. Over time and with the invaluable help of nondiscrimination laws, some of these things can be worked through, but it's frequently brutal, and often the transsexual is driven to look for another environment where she can just start over, where no one ever knew her as John or Bob or Bill. But make no mistake; starting over is terribly costly and not just in money.

Nor does it help that in an attempt to eradicate any doubt in the eyes of others regarding his manliness as well as in service to his own determined attempts to be "normal," many transsexuals prior to coming out chose stereotypically male occupations. Oh sure, some women do carpentry, drive big rigs, operate heavy equipment, fly fighter jets but in her new life, the up-and-coming transsexual wants to wear skirts and pretty blouses, pantyhose and heels (go figure), makeup and French tips, all of which don't really work so well on a Caterpillar D-3. Plus those hard-hats are so rough on your do! Pretty soon, you can find yourself getting very hungry.

After my teaching career came to an ignominious end, I found a job as a *barista* at a gay owned coffee shop in San Francisco. Working at a small coffee shop with a three-hour commute did not exactly pay the bills, so I started doing a little journalism on the side for a bi-weekly queer rag called *The San Francisco Bay Times*. Unlike most other reporters, I was not bound by the conventional rules of journalism that account for the soporific quality of most news articles. The guiding principles at the *Bay Times* were "anything goes" and "nothing is sacred" and while I loved it, I wasn't willing to do it for free, and they paid whenever they felt like it, which wasn't very often. Still, it was a great place to come out – fertile soil in which a budding trannie could blossom in all her glory.

When Jan's dad died and she inherited a sizable chunk of change, I quit the coffee shop to focus fulltime on writing. Writing is like manna to me, the food given to the Hebrews by God during their sojourn in the wilderness, but while I had hopes of becoming a successful writer, I never allowed myself to nurse illusions of fame and fortune. I could see our financial peril should I not someday generate income from my writing, so to forestall the day of reckoning, I invested heavily in the stock market during the internet boom of the late '90s. I take solace in knowing that people much more financially savvy than me were as equally stupid. (In addition to appealing to the basest qualities of the human character, I think rich people dreamed up the stock market because they got tired of having to think up new ways to rip off poor slobs like me, so they created a mechanism whereby we could just hand our money over to them – and pay for the privilege to boot!)

At first, we made money hand over fist, some of which I withdrew to pay the bills. I wrote like mad; I wrote a novel; then I wrote a children's book; I started an impressive collection of rejection letters; and then the bubble burst. Virtually overnight, we lost thousands upon thousands of dollars. I bailed out, banked what little was left and started looking for work – this time, in the real world.

Fortunately, we had used some of the money for facial surgery performed by an outstanding surgeon in San Francisco, Dr. Douglas Osterhout, who worked nothing short of a miracle in making me mostly passable as a genetic female.

I knew that finding a job would be no small task, given that all my training and experience were in: 1) the ministry and 2) teaching children – jobs in which a queer like me had about as much chance of success as a paraplegic ice skater with Olympic aspirations.

When my old job at the private school opened up, Jan suggested to the director that he hire me back to the position I had created and served with distinction for twelve years. But by then I had gone through my transformation, a metamorphosis, given the response of many who had known and loved Hank, was considered nothing short of a butterfly turning itself into a dung beetle.

According to Jan, he wouldn't even consider it. "I don't want to be known as the school where the transsexual works," he told her.

In other words, he was prepared to let the program die rather than let it be taught by an outlaw, and this from a man who had been raised in the segregated south. Forty years earlier this would have been equivalent to saying, "I don't want to be known as the school where the nigger works." Why can't people make that connection?

Still, had I been in his place, who's to say I wouldn't have done the same? Private schools depend for life on the willingness of people to pay outrageous sums of money for their children's education, and it was an open question as to how many would have wanted their child taught by an obvious transsexual – for all intents and purposes, an outlaw.

To make matters worse, society's Story portrays people like me as somehow a threat to children. Supposedly, we want to do hideously obscene things to them and convert them to the "gay lifestyle." What most people don't realize in their homophobic ignorance is that there are no straight, gay, lesbian or transgender child molesters. There are male pedophiles who molest little boys, but they are no more gay than male pedophiles who molest little girls are straight. They are both pedophiles, and I think constitutional prohibitions should be amended to allow for mandatory castration; it is, after all, a logical consequence – and probably a mercy.

How the myth that LGBT people are more likely to molest children ever got started is a mystery to me – probably the Catholic Church.

Fortunately, the Staff Work of Omnipotence went to work again, because for some inexplicable reason, I was actually reading Lia's monthly high school newsletter (an act which for a writer might be considered literary self-flagellation) wherein I found an announcement that they were hiring school bus drivers. I responded, and either because they were desperate or because they were good or, perhaps, desperately good, they hired me.

That the transportation department, the red-headed step child of the educational system, rather than the professional educators with their lofty talk of diversity and tolerance were willing to take me in without qualm or question seems further evidence that God does indeed have a wonderful sense of humor as well as a justifiably low regard for the qualifications of the chosen. (I'll believe schools are serious about teaching tolerance when they start recruiting people like me.)

While I was grateful for a job that, in addition to helping pay the bills, allowed me a little time to write, bus driving was excruciatingly boring, that is, when it wasn't like being a counselor at Camp Lord of the Flies. While I had the academic credentials to teach at the local junior college, those jobs were hard to come by, plus the status given new hires rarely provided health benefits. I have always been good with people, but initially my appearance often throws them off – I'm a bit freakish in a handsome sort of way. The technology sector could be promising, but my love of computers rivals my love of nose hairs. Faced with the possibility of a lifetime of near poverty working at dead-end, boring jobs with only Nature's retirement plan – Death – to look forward to, I have sometimes rued the day I came out of the closet. In almost all ways my life as Meredith is better, but it is likewise harder, much harder.

Little did I know that when I opened that closet door, a thousand others would slam shut.

Teaching

I never set out to be a teacher. I set out to be a minister. "Teacher" was nowhere on my radar, not on the menu, not part of *GOD'S PLAN FOR MY LIFE.* No one in the family had, to my knowledge, ever been a teacher. No one ever suggested I be one. I didn't even like school, plus I was way too ADHD to be a good student.

I got into teaching because Marsha gave birth to Caleb in January. Since there was little paying work on the farm at that time of year, I subbed in Marsha's class while she stayed home with our newborn. When Marsha returned to her classroom in the spring, a woman in the adjoining classroom left on maternity leave. Since I made more money subbing than I did working on the farm, I moved next door.

It turned out that putting me in a classroom was like throwing a duck in water; I just knew what to do. What's more, I liked it. Recognizing a gem in the rough when he saw one, the director of the school offered to pay for my Montessori training if I would teach for him the following year. Now a family man with obligations and responsibilities, it was an offer I couldn't refuse.

It has always been hard to know what to think about that decision. I loved the farm, and I loved the work of farming. I loved the land. Oh, God, I loved that beautiful piece of land, and I loved working it with my dear friend Robert. Leaving it was like leaving the Garden of Eden to take over the family insurance business, or worse, like Judas selling out his beloved for a handful of silver.

Of course, leaving was the only sensible thing to do and for a host of reasons. Like all small farms, we had to compete with agribusinesses that, using cheap immigrant labor and taxpayer subsidized water, fuel and roads, could grow and ship produce all the way across the country cheaper than we could grow, harvest and market it locally.

Plus, the corporately controlled supermarkets weren't interested in buying our fresh, locally produced food. The Dayspring Church, the farm's patron and landlord, was ambivalent about our mission at best, downright hostile at worst. (It seems we were too noisy, too messy, too…too…farmie.) I was also just a farm hand, low man on an already short totem pole, making just above minimum wage with no benefits other than the sheer love of what I was doing. Staying on the farm after the children came would have required sacrifices I'm sure Marsha would never have been willing to make, and honestly, I don't think I could have countenanced either. Like most women, Marsha did not aspire to be a farmer's wife. *I* might have made a good farmer's wife, but for that honored position, *I* was not qualified.

In the end, it's impossible to know. When redemption is the work of the Universe – and redemption *is* the work of the Universe – even our mistakes, our betrayals, our follies and foibles get folded into the loaf of Life, until it is all but impossible to know if they were ever anything other than ingredients vital to the recipe.

Despite what I was told in the training, it didn't take long to realize that being a good teacher had little to do with the curriculum. The curriculum was the easy part. I could learn the curriculum just by reading and studying, and I liked reading and studying. What I quickly learned was that the most important thing for being a successful teacher was the ability to manage a classroom full of children. Too lenient, and I'd spend all of my time trying to wrest order out of chaos. Too strict, and the students felt oppressed. Very little education happens in either chaos or repression.

It helped that I was brought up by no nonsense parents in a culture that did not worship children and in the days before discipline became a four-letter word. While the old ways of parenting could be harsh – a good thrashing was always one of the possibilities – we never had to bear the oppressive burden of wondering who was in charge. The adults were in charge, and about that, both they and we were clear. It was a comfort.

Consequently, when I walked into a classroom of children, there was never any doubt about who was in charge – I was in charge. They could test me and try me – and they did – but at the end of the day, I won the battles and in so doing, I kept one of the most important promises I never made to them.

This structure of power took some getting used to by children whose parents had abdicated the hard work of parenting from an imagined fear they might damage their children's precious self-esteems. Children raised by these parents thought they could run my classroom like they ran their homes; that every limitation was an invitation to a negotiation. My first task was to disavow them of this notion, which I did without hesitation, equivocation, or mercy. In truth, children don't want to be in charge despite their protestations and tantrums to the contrary. Tantrums are like jumping up and down on an untested bridge; you want to make sure it'll hold before you bet your life on it. For a child, being in charge is scary. They're children, for god's sake. They're not ready to be in charge. Once it was established that in the classroom, I was in charge and that there was no negotiating this fundamental fact, we could all relax and enjoy ourselves, which mostly we did.

The second most important skill for a teacher was the ability to teach. At this I excelled, primarily because I valued learning over knowing. For example, one of the best lessons I ever taught began: "I don't know how to find the area of a triangle." The students were some of my mathematically brightest. "I know there's a formula," I went on, "just like there's a formula for determining the area of a rectangle, but I can't remember what that formula is. Of course, I could just look it up and teach it to you, but that would take all the fun out of it, so *our* assignment this week – yours and mine – is to see if we can, using these Montessori materials that are designed to teach area, find the formula for determining the area of a triangle." During the course of the week, I would sit down with the materials, sometimes alone and sometimes with another or other students, and we would play with the pieces trying to come up with a formula that applied to all triangles. It was such fun I almost felt disappointed when we came up with it, because after that, I could never unlearn it for future groups.

When the farm eventually failed, I found teaching jobs for Marsha and me in Northern California. I was hired by a small, private Montessori school to begin their upper elementary program, grades 4-6. After only a year, the director of the school, a lovely man who had little interest in running a school and even less aptitude for it, gladly turned over the day-to-day running of the elementary campus to me, giving me almost complete authority to do as I liked. Marsha was hired by a different Montessori school in a nearby town.

Having come from Church of the Savior where I practiced daily disciplines, I decided I wanted to build a daily nonreligious spiritual component into the curriculum. This had already been started by Helena, the woman who, several years before, had started the lower elementary program, grades 1-3. From her, I inherited the peacemaker meeting. In this meeting, everyone – teachers included – got to air their grievances in a structured, safe environment where the only allowable response to a complaint was "I hear you." It's amazing how many problems have a way of working themselves out when the aggrieved can simply be heard. It was also during the Cold War, and in keeping with the Montessori commitment to peace, Helena's class was constantly writing letters to then President Reagan, begging for an end to the nuclear arms race. For significant success in this area, I give partial credit to Helena and her little class of 1st – 3rd grade gadflies.

In addition to the peacemaker meetings, I started doing daily meditation exercises. First thing in the morning, I'd have them find a comfortable place to sit or lie down. Once they were relaxed, I'd take them on a guided fantasy into a mysterious land where, over the course of several weeks, they would encounter all sorts of animals from the greatest to the smallest. Then, one night on the fall camping trip, around a campfire, under a canopy of towering bay trees, I'd have them lie down on tarps. After the customary relaxation instructions, I'd take them back into the fantasy land where, this time, they were to meet their own, unique spirit animal. The things they shared afterward regularly blew my mind.

After I began doing morning meditations with the class, I realized that I needed some way to close them. Early one morning on a fall backpacking trip in the Sierras, I climbed alone to the top of a large boulder where I composed, or, to my way of thinking, *received* these words, which I began reciting to them before they set to the day's tasks:

You have been given the gift of another day.
Receive it.
Use it in a lifelong quest for knowledge and understanding,
That you may be likewise a gift to the earth and all
her inhabitants.

To my surprise, before long, they spontaneously began saying it with me, so that each morning it became a choral recitation, a unison chant, a prayer.

Sometimes, rather than a guided fantasy, we'd just sit quietly on the back deck. There we looked out over a long, grassy hill on the distant top of which, silhouetted against the sky, grew two trees, bent and twisted by weather and time into almost mirror images of one another. In autumn, when the leaves would fall, and again in spring when they returned, it would be revealed that, though they were so alike in appearance, they were entirely different in kind. We'd witness the passing of the seasons in those trees, along with the greening and browning of the grasses, the passing of deer, an occasional coyote, the flight and cry of hawks, the lazy circling of turkey vultures, the cock-a-doodle-doing of quail. Sometimes a mouse or vole would venture out surprisingly close to us, which would always cause a stir. We didn't go out when the cows were there. The fence was flimsy and the cows, curious. Sometimes the bull would be there.

One hectic morning as I was doling out assignments from my daily planner, my attention was drawn up from my precious notes by a general disturbance arising from the class. Supposing one of the class clowns responsible for this annoying distraction, I looked up irritably, ready to read someone the riot act. What I saw, however, was everyone's heads turned away from me toward the back windows. Following their gaze, I immediately saw the source of the distraction. Not ten feet from the back deck, the bull was in full mount behind one of the heifers.

Having never been around unneutered livestock, I had never before considered the lengths a bull's penis would need to go to carry out its procreative function. It was as long as my arm and a ghastly blood red! The boys were in awe; the girls, mortified. The poor cow! She was not about to be mated; she was being impaled! It was horrifying – and fascinating! I felt like I should grab their heads and turn them away, but there were too many of them, and besides, we were all mesmerized. Unfolding before our very eyes, was a dramatic, uncensored, real-time depiction of bovine copulation. Sex ed, which, prior to this, had not been part of the year's curriculum, suddenly was.

As a personal commitment and in keeping with the spirit of Montessori, I tried my best to have a hands-on component for every new concept I taught. When we were studying one of the endless wars, I realized that growing up in affluent suburbia, these children had no idea of what a gun could do, much less the experience of killing something. Killing, as valuable as it might have been, was beyond the pale of what I could do with other people's children, but the school was located far enough out in the country that I could give them a small taste of what a gun could do. I set up straw bales on the playground and with me standing right beside them, they fired away with Caleb's pellet rifle at metal cans. I would have preferred shooting something wet and red, like a watermelon with a shotgun, but that would have risked a visit from the Sonoma County Sheriff's Swat Team. As a bonus, they got lessons on how to safely handle a firearm.

In chemistry they got to burn and blow up things. (Once I almost blew up my class. Who knew hydrogen and oxygen were so volatile?) We sacrificed a few yellow jackets to demonstrate the power of colorless, odorless, tasteless carbon dioxide. Sometimes I made up games, like the photosynthesis game, which was a complete flop. We dramatized parts of speech with a skit called The Little Lardy Lumpkin Show. In this exercise in pedagogical histrionics, Susan, my co-teacher and friend, would stand behind me, insert her arms under my armpits while my own arms would be hidden in a pair of cut-off jeans with my hands in boots simulating legs and feet. Susan's arms would be covered by the sleeves of a large shirt the back of which also covered and concealed her. Her arms and hands acted as mine, but without the ability to see, her movements were wildly unpredictable – and hilarious. I don't know if the kids learned parts of speech, but we had a great time.

In what might be described as a particularly telling, if not odd, example of the kind of teacher I was, I became something of a local celebrity when one morning I brought to class the skinned and dressed carcass of a yearling deer I had literally tripped over that morning while out jogging before dawn. It was a particularly propitious find, since, at the time, we just happened to be studying muscles and bones. For the entire morning, small groups of students took turns carefully studying the carcass, pulling apart the different groups of muscles, moving the legs to see how they worked, touching, observing, smelling real muscles, bones, ligaments and tendons. Since it had still been warm when I found it, after everyone had had a chance to examine it, I brought it into the classroom kitchen, cut up a back leg, and the next day, with additions brought in by some of the bolder class members, we cooked and ate a savory venison stew.

The poor parents. Upon hearing about this anatomical and culinary experience from their children (since I saw absolutely no reason to forewarn them or seek their permission) were riven with a mixture of horror and delight. On the one hand they wanted to brag about it to their friends, most of whose children were enjoying a safe and sterile public school education, but then again...did they really want people knowing their child had eaten road kill?

Another time on a camping trip, a group of students came running back to camp saying they had just seen a deer get hit by a car. I promptly loaded a few of them into my Nissan station wagon, affectionately known as the Wimpmobile, found the deer (a beautiful blacktail buck) brought him back to camp, strung him up by his hind legs and proceeded to go through the entire bloody process while they and the parents watched in horrified fascination. From then on, parents gave me every road kill cookbook, T-shirt, ball cap, bumper sticker ever made.

Even the playground was a novelty. While we had the traditional climbing structure, a wall ball court, basketball hoops and a sports field, we also had trees to climb – and occasionally fall out of – a sacred garden for quiet, intimate conversations, and – most popular of all – an area devoted to the building of forts. Materials for the forts – fallen tree limbs, 2x4s, and sheets of plywood that I sawed in half – were purchased by the student government from fundraising money. No nails were allowed but holes were drilled in the wood and rope supplied. As a result, the playground always looked a bit like a homeless encampment, but those forts taught more valuable life lessons than I can list or probably even know.

After about ten years, I left the idyllic, little private school where I was loved and honored, to help create a public Montessori charter school. I knew it was risky. Others warned me that public education and Montessori wouldn't mix, but I had always believed that a Montessori education should be available to children without regard to income, and the newly passed charter school legislation in California was designed to make that possible.

The Montessori mandate to customize the curriculum for each student as well as my commitment to a different kind of educational experience meant that I regularly worked 50-60 hour weeks. Six months into my work at the charter school as lead teacher of the upper elementary cluster, I had one of the young teachers under my supervision say candidly to me, "Why should I do all this work you're asking me to do when, for the same pay, I can teach in a regular school where I can be at work at 8 and home by 3 with evenings and weekends to myself?" What could I say? For the love of it? She left at the end of the year and did just what she said she would. The teacher who followed her left after one year and went to work for a sportswear company. And I had been doing this work for ten years in a private school for 25% less pay. So yes, for the love of it. Why else, given the choice, would you do anything?

As I feared and had been warned, the whole public school thing turned out to be an unmitigated disaster. Trying to teach in a public school – even an alternative public school – was, for me, like trying to run a race in leg irons. How do you teach children about the life of a stream without getting in it? Okay, they got wet. It was ninety degrees out; they dried. How can you learn about the organs of the body without opening up a freshly killed animal and looking at what's inside it? Yes, their little hands got bloody – all the better. Can you imagine what would have happened had I cooked them road kill stew? The departments of Health, Fish and Game, the Sonoma County Office of Education, along with about six other governmental agencies all would have been fighting for a piece of my hide. And why did the parents need to be informed if on a beautiful spring day, I wanted to take them on a walk off campus to admire and study the flowers? And what was with all this God-damned testing bullshit? Does anyone seriously believe a standardized test can accurately measure what students know, much less what they *need* to know? After what would turn out to be the worst two years of my life, the director, a wonderful woman, really, refused to renew my contract. "I'm tired of fighting with you," she said. It was a mercy.

I loved teaching. I know of few more satisfying experiences than watching the light come on in a child's eyes when he or she finally understands something that had hitherto been frustratingly obscure. And I loved my students. Not with a sentimental love. I wasn't a like doting, parent who thought the sun rose and set according to their desires; I wasn't a wise, avuncular sage bestowing words of wisdom upon them; I wasn't even a friend. I was their teacher, and I never lost sight of that. It was my job to prepare them for what was next, the next grade, the next level of education, and life beyond school. It was love with a kind of fierce clarity that could sometimes be harsh.

While teaching was, without question, the most unremittingly demanding work I ever did, full of its own peculiar frustrations (usually involving either parents or inept administrators) I honestly never tired of it. Imagining new ways to teach something, trying to find ways around the obstacles to learning, struggling to inspire and provoke curiosity in my students were challenges that constantly kept me on my toes and pushed me daily to the limits of my ability and beyond.

As a teacher, there were virtually no lengths I would not go to promote learning in my students. But when I came out of the closet, when I decided to be myself, when I dared defy The Story's rigid definition of what it means to be a man and what it means to be a woman, teaching, at least teaching children, for me, was over.

Years later, when my vocational life had degenerated to levels of unimaginable dreariness, memories of teaching would return, haunting me, filling me with regret and doubt about what I had done. In the loss of teaching I realized the full measure of what coming out had cost me. And while living a lie had been painful, unbearably so at times, had it really been worse than this? Worse than having no meaning, no purpose, no satisfaction in what I spent my days doing? While there were bad days teaching – every teacher has bad days – most days when I walked into that classroom, everything else fell away. In that classroom, I gave myself to my students and to teaching; nothing else mattered.

Dorothee Soelle says losing ourselves in something that is not us is the most wonderful way of disempowering the ego and becoming free. Was my longing to be a woman, my need to come out and live my life as a woman simply ego, or worse, obsession? Wasn't the fact that when I walked into that classroom it all but disappeared evidence that it was? Or even if not an expression of ego, might I have been able to successfully deny and repress the needs and desires through giving myself even more completely to teaching, becoming what I once heard someone describe as a Montessori monk? Wouldn't that have been better, maybe even more satisfying, than coming out and losing the work I loved and at which I excelled? Who are we if not what we do with our lives? And even if being trans shouldn't have mattered, which, of course, it shouldn't have, still I didn't want to be the poster girl for trans oppression and discrimination. I wanted to be a teacher.

144

Bus Driving

Toward the end of my tenth year driving a school bus, I drove a group of fourth graders to the De Young museum in San Francisco. I was out taking a walk when I ran into them outside the museum, gathering to come back to the bus for their lunches. The teacher, a delightful woman who seemed to truly love the kids, was surrounded by children as restless and inattentive as a swarm of bees.

"Would you like for me to take them?" I volunteered.

"Oh, that would be wonderful," she replied gratefully. "Children," she called, "go with Meredith back to the bus to get your lunches and then come back here."

"This way," I called.

They followed.

Walking the distance to the bus, I remembered the many times as a teacher I had been surrounded by such a swarm of children, some hugging close, others running ahead and still others straggling behind. Especially in places like the city, places with which I was unfamiliar, I'd be constantly on guard, circumnavigating the scene with the protective eyes of a lioness, accounting for all my cubs, alert to any danger. "Ya'll hold up there," I'd shout to the ones running ahead. To the stragglers, I'd turn, hold open my arm, and beckon, "Ya'll come on, catch up." Often in times like this, I would feel a small hand slip into mine, like a blessing, a benediction, and in that moment, I would know beyond the shadow of a doubt that I was where I most needed to be and most wanted to be. The pleasure of those times and that work come back to me as we made our disorderly way to the bus.

They got their lunches and, under my watchful eye, returned to their teacher.

Back on the bus, the pandemonium of sound and movement was replaced by a haunting silence, heavy and gray as lead. What had been a place of life and color filled with the music of children's voices was now a tomb. I was no longer a teacher; these children were not my students. I would never know them, and they would never know me, and I would not feel the touch of a small hand in mine, much as I ache for it.

Why? What had I done to deserve this? And where was my God now?

From Church of the Savior I had taken a theology that said that by virtue of being created in the image of God, I, like every person, had unique gifts. My primary spiritual task was to discover these gifts, cultivate them, and then, put them to work in behalf of that piece of creation that was uniquely suited to me. This work would be my "call," what Frederick Buechner defines as "that place where your deep gladness and the world's deep hunger meet."

The problem was: I had done that. I knew myself to be a gifted person, and I knew what it felt like to give those gifts in grateful service. That's what I'd done at Dayspring, and that's what I'd done teaching. That's even what I'd done working at the coffee shop in the Castro. Bus driving, by contrast, did not utilize my gifts. At the end of the day, I did not feel like I had helped make or do anything that served any purpose other than the creation of a meager paycheck. It brought me none of the inner joy and satisfaction that I had previously known when exercising my call. As a journal entry reads, "Bus driving sucks away my will to live, leaving me like an empty cicada shell, clinging to existence only because that's what I was doing when whatever was living inside me crawled out and took wing to parts unknown."

The theological problem for me was that God did not seem interested in my theology.

But if bus driving wasn't my call – and it definitely *wasn't* – why then, had it been given? And it *had* been given; about that I had no doubt.

As I said, I found the job reading through Lia's high school newsletter. We had lost almost all our money in the stock market crash of 2000. I wasn't making any money writing and the reserves I'd manage to salvage were dwindling, so I applied, was accepted and took the training. Originally, I intended to just be a substitute driver; that way I could continue to devote most of my time to writing.

One day as a substitute in training, I rode with Chris, a veteran driver, to learn her route. When we were back at the bus yard refueling, she told me that she had also intended to just be a sub, but something had happened that caused her to take a regular route that provided health benefits, and now she was glad she had.

I'm not really much of a mystic. I wish I was. Mystical experiences are kind of cool, but when Chris said what she did about being glad she'd taken a regular route, it was if an angel of the Lord appeared on her shoulder saying, "Meredith, listen to what she's saying. Go in there and tell them you want a route of your own."

Normally, I would check this sort of thing out before acting on it; let it sit for a while, bring it into my daily quiet time; talk to someone I trusted. Not this time. This time I walked into Janet's office, the Director of Transportation's, and told her I wanted a regular run, which she was all too glad to give me. In all the years I griped, complained, bitched, kvetched, and cursed bus driving, I never forgot that experience and how it felt, and because of it and because of the way bus driving just showed up right when I needed it and in such an unexpected way, I never doubted it had been given.

There is a cartoon in the September 24, 2012, *New Yorker* magazine in which a distraught king in his royal cape and crown is sitting outside an old camping trailer in the middle of nowhere. Beside him sits a plainly dressed woman to whom he is saying, "Even after all that's happened I feel no less regal."

It is almost impossible for the privileged to see their privilege – until they lose it. Because I never possessed great wealth or social standing, I never thought of myself as privileged. Like the cartoon king, even after all that had happened, even after abdicating my throne of tall, white, handsome, American, straight, male privilege, I didn't *feel* any different.

From a position of privilege, I could ask, What is it I want from life? To what am I called? What are my gifts and where might I give them? and with some assurance, believe that, with a little luck, a good education, perseverance and hard work, I might realize my dreams, aspirations, and ambitions. As a transsexual, however, it didn't matter what I expected or wanted from life. What mattered now was what life expected and wanted from me.

Stripped of all the external sources of meaning and purpose I had known before, I had to face the fact that when I stepped out of that closet "all dressed up with nowhere to go," my de facto call became to live my life as an out, open, and visible member of a stigmatized, outcast, and oppressed people. If, as I often complained, bus driving asked too little of me, this call asked too much.

With this, I was finally able to recognize and appreciate bus driving for what it was: an answer to one line of the Lord's Prayer, "Give us this day, our daily bread." On this long, difficult, painful journey I had to make, I needed a way to eat. Bus driving was daily bread, nothing less; and yet, as I would come to realize over time, quite a bit more.

One "more" of bus driving was revealed to me when I read Wendell Berry's novel *Jayber Crow*. One particularly tragic character in the book is described as a man who is obsessed with "making something of himself."

When I read that phrase, something clicked in my brain, and I found myself turning it over and over in my mind, often, ironically enough, while bus driving. Something about that haunting description, that tragic state of spiritual folly called out to me like one of the old prophets.

It didn't take a lot of digging around in the attic of my psyche to realize that one of the most important messages I got from my father was that, unlike him, I should "make something of myself," and to that end, he spent a small fortune on private college tuition.

Like so many of these early messages from parents, the need to "make something of myself" drove me mercilessly, and yet, I was completely unaware of it. It was like being beaten from behind. I could feel the stings of the lash, but I could never see the one who administered them. Or, to mix my metaphors, it was like a locomotive in the rear of a train that drives the cars in front of it heedless of what lies ahead. Journals from my twenties are full of angst and struggle and despair as I tried desperately to "make something of myself," something wonderful and special and important and worthy and, if possible, even heroic. They are painful to read. When I finally managed to "make something of myself," Dad would be proud and everyone would love, admire and respect me. (Dad's being dead for many years was, of course, no impediment to trying to please him.). Nor did anyone have to tell me that making myself into a woman was definitely not what Dad or anyone else had in mind.

But how could I ever make something of myself driving a school bus? It was impossible, and so, driven by this demand but deprived of the opportunity to succeed, I was constantly frustrated, angry and depressed. So desperate was I to find relief from this suffering, I was open to hearing what was revealed in Brother Berry's book. Finally I could see who was behind me wielding the whip and stay his hand. What a mercy it must be to let those beyond the grave rest in peace.

Another "more" of bus driving was that a lot of kids got an up close and personal experience with a fairly visible and – despite what you've just read – reasonably healthy transsexual, probably their first such experience – or, at least, the first of which they were aware. No one sets a place at the table for the invisible and the silent, and so, you've got to start speaking and being visible somewhere. I'd have rather started in the classroom, but that opportunity was not open to me.

Thinking that perhaps it would be easier to find a job teaching older children, I went to an information session at Sonoma State on getting a secondary credential. Teaching at the high school level would have allowed relationships to develop, and relationships are the key to changing attitudes, but several things discouraged me from pursuing it. In the process of researching an article on attitudes toward gays in the high schools a few years earlier, I had discovered that there were almost no "out" gay staff members in any high school in Sonoma County. The one person I managed to find was surly and uncooperative, as if the last thing he wanted to talk about was being gay. Of course, there had to be gay staff, but if they were afraid of coming out, in northern California of all places, what did that say about me, a transsexual, a queer among queers?

Even though by this time I knew they couldn't have fired me for being trans, proving it was why they hadn't hired me would be all but impossible.

My doubts about ever being hired were confirmed when a high school student came to me with a question. He was the last student on the bus, and when I pulled over at his stop, he turned before getting off and nervously said, "I want to ask you something, but I don't want you to get mad at me."

"Okay," I agreed.

"Just promise me you won't get mad at me for asking," he insisted.

"I promise that I will not get mad at whatever it is you want to ask me," I replied earnestly. Of course, by now, I knew what he was going to ask me, so I reached down and turned off the bus.

"Well some of the guys in the back of the bus were saying you used to be a man. Did you used to be a man?"

Without pause I said, "No, I was never a man."

"Okay," he said, and, seemingly satisfied, he got off the bus.

I, however, was not satisfied, because, while technically I could argue that I had never been a man but had only been doing an impersonation of one, it was not the whole truth. What concerned me most about this omission was the possible impression he might get that I was embarrassed or ashamed of being transgender, which, even if true was not the impression I wished to give.

I went to the Director of the Department of Transportation and told her what had happened and asked how the district wanted me to handle it. "If I was gay," I pointed out, "this would be easy. I could just say yes or no, but if I tell him I'm transgender, I'm going to have to say something about what that means."

"I'll talk to human resources," she said, and I trusted her.

The next day she told me that the head of human resources had expressed concern that if I talked to the student about being trans, the student might go home and talk to his family and it would turn into some sort of brouhaha.

"Well, yes, I know that's the concern," I agreed, "but surely they're teaching evolution in science, and that's controversial, and then, there's literature. Have you read

The Adventures of Tom Sawyer not to mention *Catcher in the Rye?*"

"I know, I know," she agreed.

"Should I talk to them," I offered.

"No, no, I'll handle it," she promised.

A couple of days went by, and I went back to her.

"Well, the head of human resources says he wants to talk to the superintendent," she said, rolling her eyes.

I should go in myself, I thought, but I was busy; I had this book to write. By then I had decided that "No, you can't talk to him," was not an answer I was willing to accept. Oh great, I thought, you're going to get fired again. This was definitely turning into a pattern.

After two weeks had gone by with no word, I decided, Screw this; I'm talking to the kid. They had their chance.

Fortuitously, he got off at the last stop, so as he was about to leave, I said, "C, will you stay for a minute. I want to talk to you."

"Why? What did I do?" he asked guiltily.

He was a cut up and therefore prone to getting in trouble.

"You're not in trouble," I assured him, "and you don't have to stay, but if you're willing, I'd like to talk to you for just a minute."

"Okay," he agreed.

"Remember you asked me if I had ever been a man a couple of weeks ago?"

"Yeah."

"Well, it's true, I was never a man, but I am transgender. Do you know what that means?"

"No," he frankly admitted.

"It means I was born with a male body but with a brain that told me I was a girl. Since that's not really okay, I spent a lot of my life pretending to be a man. When I couldn't stand doing that any more, I decided to come out and live my life as a woman. That's the...*fuller* truth."

"Oh. Okay," he said, and he turned to leave.

I was almost disappointed. I had prepared answers to a host of other questions, but none came. "Have a good weekend," I called after him.

"Yeah, you too," he replied.

I wondered if there would be fallout later. Would he talk to the other students, and then, would I be barraged with questions? Would he, in fact, talk to his parents, and they would make a stink? Then would I be in trouble for acting on my own? Would he start referring to me with male pronouns? Would he become belligerent? Would I have to put up with subtle ridicule, especially from the older boys? Would trouble spread to other venues? I waited.

Nothing happened. C did not change his behavior toward me. He called me "she" and "her." He continued to be a cut up. He was no more belligerent than usual, and nobody else changed either. If word spread around, I saw no evidence of it. Everything went right on as before, except – and maybe I imagined this –it seemed like the older boys were, if anything, more friendly.

It did confirm my suspicions, however, that even had I gotten the certification, they wouldn't have risked hiring me. Seems they weren't wild about being known as the school where the transsexual taught, either.

We're familiar with overt forms of prejudice and discrimination, the kind that says "I don't want to be known as the school where the transsexual works," but these are the easy kind. What the story of C illustrates is a hidden, more insidious form of prejudice that makes the victim's wounds seem self-inflicted. We don't go back for that degree, don't bother to fill out that application, don't try for that promotion or position because doing what it would take to qualify is expensive in time, energy and money and with no reasonable assurance that those in power will give us a fair chance, why take that risk? Why go to all that trouble and expense? And so we end up limiting ourselves and in so doing, shoulder not only the burdens of oppression but also the burden of guilt.

By the same token, when you've been told your entire life by the society in which you live that there's something wrong with you, that you are defective or depraved or damned, it's almost impossible not to, at least in part, believe it. And so, self doubt combines with the pervasive prejudice to form yet another barrier, a fence topped with concertina wire over which you must climb to enter the land which the privileged take for granted. It's possible to do, especially if laws or the kindness of others give you a hand up. I might have made it had others gone out of their way to encourage me or prod me or invite me, had I felt welcomed and wanted, but they did not and I was not.

So often in the long, dreary years of driving a bus, I wondered if I should've just stayed in the closet. Life would have been so much easier. Sometimes I wished to God I had. Yet why? Why should I have to deny who I am? It's not like coming out made me less qualified as a teacher or minister or anything else. In fact, there's every reason to believe I would have been better, much better.

Yet, isn't this always the cost of stigmatization, prejudice and discrimination? The gifts, the skills, the talents of those being victimized are lost, wasted, squandered? What they might have done – at least, in some sense – will forever remain undone. What they might have made will never be made, not in the same way. Who they might have been, they will never be. For every life denied, Life itself is denied, truncated, stunted, diminished. Think of what was lost and who we might be as a nation had we not wasted the lives, the talents, the skills, the intelligence of countless African Americans between the beginning of slavery and the election Barack Obama. What a horrible and senseless waste. I was just another victim in this long and tragic line, another in the legacy of ignorance and stupidity, and who wants to be part of that heritage?

But bus driving *did* allow me time and opportunity to write. Much of my contribution to 21st century literature was composed on a school bus, including the words you are presently reading.

With the perspective of years, I finally had to admit – albeit begrudgingly – that bus driving was a good place to finally and fully come out. While I so often wished I could have taught as Meredith, when our penury forced me into the job market, I was still so unsure of myself, unsure even of my right to *be* myself that the demands of teaching would have been hard to manage. Had I gotten my way and become a successful writer, even a marginally successful writer, I would have restricted the living of my days to very small circles of safety and acceptance. Bus driving forced me to get out there and live my life in the real world where I had to deal with the real ramifications of fear, guilt and shame, where I had to get smacked around emotionally, embarrassed and humiliated. I had to navigate territory I couldn't predict and into which I would never have willingly gone. A few times I might have actually been in real danger. But as Nietzsche said: what doesn't kill you makes you stronger. I quit caring so much about what others thought, because I had to. I also had to stop depending on other's approval for my right to be who I was. And while I hated the job, the people I worked with and the children I transported were wonderful; to them and for them, I shall forever be thankful.

When I moved from being in the professional class to being in the working class, from being at the top of the food chain to being lower down, from being one of the privileged to being one of the oppressed, I got my first real taste of what life is like for most American workers. I had no idea.

While as a teacher, dealing with neurotic parents and inept administrators was a pain in the ass, at least teaching was stimulating and challenging with lots of rewards, not the least of which was a decent sized pay check. As a bus driver, I still had to deal with ineptitude, but whereas school administrators have to reckon with the importance and power of teachers, bus drivers are about as valuable as lab rats. In the classroom, I had almost god-like power to control the behaviors of my students. In a school bus, where the only adult in charge was also trying to steer a ten ton vehicle safely through a gauntlet of traffic hazards, even normally well behaved children could turn into depraved miscreants. As a teacher I was given respect – half-hearted respect at times – but respect nonetheless. As a bus driver, I disappeared. Plus, there was the dehumanization. Mounting surveillance cameras in school buses might make sense, but then, why not in classrooms and for that matter, the district office? Shouldn't those getting the highest salaries be held most accountable? Why not have all school personnel subject to random drug tests? Physicals? (You can imagine how special getting a physical was for me.) We also received regular harassment from the California Highway Patrol officer in charge of school buses, whose favorite methods of dealing with drivers were bullying, threats and intimidation. Then there were the working conditions, especially the drivers' seats, which were seemingly engineered to promote permanent bodily injury, some of which I now suffer. Countless policies and procedures, rules and regulations touting safety were forced down our throats, while actual safety issues identified by the drivers themselves were routinely ignored. Of course, that's part of the cost for everyone living in an overpopulated, technologically sophisticated, secular society, but blue collar workers feel it in ways that the professional class would never tolerate. And all too readily workers just accept what is handed out to them. Sometimes they even support it, because that's what they've been told they deserve, and I, of all people, can appreciate how hard it is to question, much less defy, what you've been told you deserve. If it's hard for the privileged to see their privilege, it is equally hard for the oppressed to see their oppression – or recognize their oppressors.

In time, I came to be a proud member of the working class. There's a unique kind of camaraderie between those who do society's grunt work for little money and no recognition. Also, biblically speaking, I was in excellent company. Jesus was a carpenter, the disciples fishermen and the apostle Paul a tent maker. A bus driver would fit right in with that crowd.

Bus driving gave me a very real experience of what it feels like to truly be a nobody; to be nothing more than a function, an insignificant cog in the huge, public, corporate educational machine. Except for the few remarkable souls who, in spite of these conditions, are able to generate value and meaning from within, workers have no other significance than what they can perform and what they can consume. Our lives are as meaningless as the activities we spend our days doing.

This is what we in free-market, capitalist, corporate America have created for the working masses, and to cope with it, we eat too much and drink too much and smoke too much, and engage in all manner of stupid, self-destructive behaviors. We hear so much about the manifold ills of society on the news, but I contend that there is no obesity epidemic in this country. There is no epidemic of alcoholism or drug abuse or violence or crime or teen pregnancy. There is an epidemic of meaninglessness, of hopelessness, of boredom, of physical and spiritual poverty, of filling ourselves up and numbing ourselves down so we don't notice the pain of what we ourselves have created.

And not only created but continue to create day after meaningless day through our mindless loyalty to the corporate controllers who define our needs, dictate our wants and manipulate our addictions. They drive us like cattle until now, the numbed, dumbed-down herd of humanity teeters on the edge of an ecological disaster that to most feels about as real as Santa Claus.

What It Takes

Most books and articles about transsexuals deal with the predictable problems: the angst of trying to live a lie, the suicidal depression, the prequel of cross-dressing prior to finally coming out, invariably to the shock and dismay of colleagues, children, family, friends, et al, followed by divorce, the loss of job, culminating in the grand finale – sex reassignment surgery. The part that almost always gets left out is: Where do you find shoes to fit those feet?

It's not easy. In fact, the process of living a gender different than your sex is not to be undertaken by the faint of heart. Aside from having to survive the emotional hell, there are a host of practical barriers that must be bested some of which I have experienced, some of which I know via the testimony of others and some of which I can only imagine.

Before going any further, however, let me acknowledge that the information in this chapter will inevitably be inaccurate and outdated. Laws, policies, costs, etc. differ from place to place; costs for surgeries differ dramatically between the U.S. and say, Thailand. Getting the sex designation on a birth certificate changed in California is much easier than in other states, and in some states it is impossible altogether. Also, things are changing rapidly with regard to LGBT rights, especially in the medical community. Plus, I am speaking for myself and for my generation of transwomen, who bear about as much resemblance to the current generation of transwomen as a horse and buggy resembles a Porsche.

With that disclaimer, let's examine these issues more closely as they play out in the life of Gilbert, an imaginary, though otherwise healthy middle-aged man who decides to foreswear his former life and fulfill his lifelong dream of becoming Gilda, a vivacious, sexy, fun-loving gal.

Given that Gil is a sensible, responsible, intelligent man, you might expect him to seek some basic information about the perils and rewards that lie ahead – in other words, like any sane person setting out on a momentous and perilous journey, do some research, maybe even a cost/benefit analysis *before* commencing the conflagration of all his links, ties, connections and bonds. This, however, is not the way the psyche works, which is why we have all those wonderful and inscrutable fairytales, myths and legends – and why Gil is about to venture where few men have ever dared go.

The first place Gil begins is with that annoying, scratchy, telltale growth on his face. Concealing the average beard requires the administration of several layers of foundation, a term Gil, prior to casting his lot with the fairer sex, naively thought applied to the beginning stages of construction. A trip to the local drug store reveals that there are about six thousand different kinds, shades, brands and types of foundation.

Why, in the name of all that is sane and holy, women, who, after all, don't even have beards, would need such a dizzying array of choices is a mystery Gil has never pondered prior to this intensely disorienting, out of body experience as he frantically studies the array of containers, not sure which shade, brand, jar, tube, bottle or powder to buy. He begins to sweat profusely. Just standing in front of the cosmetics display feels as forbidden as using the women's restroom, trespassing on a military base, trying to pass through airport security wearing a cock ring.

His mind reels, his heart races, his eyes dart from side to side wondering if anyone notices him – a man – intently studying the cosmetics display undoubtedly wearing the same terror-stricken expression on his face a suicide bomber must display just before blowing himself to smithereens. At any moment, he expects someone to start screaming, "OH MY GOD! THERE'S A QUEER IN THE COSMETICS DEPARTMENT!" whereupon everyone will rush over to ogle and point just like in the recurring nightmares where he is walking down the street wearing only a bra, his man parts on full display. In desperation, he grabs a bottle and flees to another part of the store whereupon he buys several other things he doesn't actually need, shoestrings, Band-Aids, Maalox (which, come to think of it, he does need).

Then he decides to play it really safe and buy some condoms to show them just what sort of guy he really is. When Gil approaches the checkout (after first, making sure no one he knows is nearby) he pulls out his imaginary list and goes over it carefully in plain view of the clerk, so she can see that he is obviously buying the makeup for someone else.

At home, he rushes to the mirror, whereupon, after a maddening struggle to remove the bullet-proof plastic packaging, he slathers the gooey concoction on his cleanly shaven face fully expecting to see his disgustingly manly features magically transformed into the smooth, silky complexion of the glamorous girl on the package – that "Cover Girl look." Instead, what emerges is a powdery pale rendition of himself sporting a sort of weird geisha girl look except that the dark shadow of his beard is still clearly visible like a rain cloud shadowing his parade.

Standing back, he is forced to concede that his nose looks even bigger, if that's possible, and his square jaw has suddenly taken on the dimensions of a comic book superhero. Gil is crestfallen; his hopes dashed like so many eggs spilled onto the sidewalk. Forced by this depressing defeat to face the obvious futility of his quest, Gil makes a decision: next time he will get a darker shade.

If Gil is smart, before doing this at least a half-dozen times, he will buy a magazine or rent a video to try and learn about makeup before dropping another $40. Of course, nowadays, he could just log onto the Internet and get all kinds of help – anonymously, no less. (Transkids these days! They just don't know how good they have it! Why, when I was their age, I had to drive a hundred miles through hail, rain, sleet and snow just to find a decent pair of size 13 pumps!)

After struggling with it for some months, Gil finally decides his beard must go! First, he tries plucking it, but that takes frikkin' forever, and, yes, it's painful, but as they say at the gym: no pain, no gain. Next, he tries waxing it off. This excruciating depilatory process pegs the Ouch-o-Meter at several degrees beyond unbearable. Miraculously, however, he succeeds, and for over a week, he revels in his girlishly hairless face. It is wonderful beyond words, unbelievable, marvelous, fantastic – and so sadly, sadly temporary.

Emboldened by this flirtation with success, Gil decides to get serious and permanently remove the unsightly, stubborn growth. This requires driving to a nearby city where a sympathetic young woman in a nurse's uniform unleashes a swarm of killer bees on his face in what is deceptively called either laser hair removal or electrolysis, or, as in Gil's case, a sadistic mixture of both. After many, many hours paying to have his face attacked by killer bees, Gil's beard will no longer be visible *after* he shaves, but shave he will for the rest of his days. Beards are famously stubborn and female hormones have about the same effect on them as reason on a redneck. After spending anywhere from $5,000 -$10,000 to have the hair on his face mostly removed, Gil still has to contend with the growth on his chest, his arms, his hands, his knuckles and – if he is really unlucky – even his back – yuck! (Girls, of course, are supposed to shave their legs, so that's okay.)

As he struggles with how to get rid of facial and body hair, Gil likewise struggles with how to preserve the precious hair on his head, which he anxiously examines every day and on which he uses hair restoring products purchased on the internet supposedly derived from the intestinal juices of living sea urchins and that cost somewhere in the neighborhood of unspeakable. Hormones might help, but, unfortunately, by the time most MTFs get around to taking female hormones, their follicles are, as they say in Texas, fine as frog's hair split three ways. The only recourse is a wig.

While flipping through a magazine at the local hair salon where he gets "the man cut," Gil discovers an ad for mail-order wigs. Surreptitiously, he tears out the page and crams it into his "man bag." After an interminable seven day wait, the catalog finally arrives. Inside are a host of gorgeous wigs all being seductively modeled by…well, you know, models, the kind you might find in a Victoria's Secret catalog, the kind who could wear sack cloth and a gas mask and still look sexy. Gil does not take note of this. It doesn't matter. Even though it costs a couple of hundred dollars, Gil buys the long blonde wig, the hair every girl wants and about five on the entire planet actually have.

Waiting for it to arrive, Gil can hardly concentrate. He is worse than any kid waiting for Christmas; waiting for the day when his beautiful, long, blonde hair finally arrives, that ultimate symbol of femininity, promising to transform him instantly into the girl he has always dreamed of being.

Then, one day, without fanfare the UPS guy drops off a non-descript cardboard box in his drive. He carries it inside as if it contained a holy relic charmed with the power to banish evil from the world. With trembling hands, he opens it, peels away the tissue paper and, at last, feels the silky strands more precious than gold running through his trembling fingers. That most MTFs don't follow the advice of Job's counselors to "curse God and die" after trying on their first mail order wig proves that if love is blind, hope is even more so.

The wig, of course, looks stupid. For one thing, it makes his bushy black eyebrows look like the pelts of two small rodents pasted on his sloping forehead. His skin tone looks all wrong, like maybe his liver failed without telling him, turning his skin a sickly shade of yellow. His features look even larger, harder and squarer. For days, he tries to make it work, changing this, that and the other; he even takes scissors to it, all to no avail. Eventually, he gives up and throws the wig to his dog, who proceeds to make short work of it. If Gil is lucky, the third or fourth try will result in a short, simple, non-descript wig that actually looks somewhat believable if no one looks too closely.

When other men are trading in their aging wives for new, slimmer, bustier models who they parade around in their hot BMW convertibles, Gil decides to buy a one-way ticket to a place he has always dreamed of but never actually been. He cashes in his stocks, refinances the house, wipes out his savings account and makes a doctor's appointment. Soon people are taking X-rays of his face, calibrating the distances between his eyes, nose, lips and chin as they draw up plans like a cadre of eager engineers, to build a bridge across some yawning chasm – the chasm that separates Gil from Gilda. As a result, Gil will spend his life's savings to endure a series of complicated and painful medical procedures whereby his entire face will be removed, reshaped and replaced – more than once – and with absolutely no guarantees of success.

The evening before his first surgery, Gil sits alone in a hospital room. Other than the ubiquitous noises of the city filtering through his fifth floor window, all is quiet. Even the hallway is quiet, as if they have evacuated the floor in anticipation of his arrival. In the thick, sterile silence, Gil has one last chance to think about what he is about to do, to change his mind, to come to his senses and go back. But back to what? To being a man? Wouldn't that make all the other people in his life happy? "Oh, Gil, you're back! Let's throw a party. The prodigal son has returned!"

Amazingly, Gil is not even tempted. Not for an instant does he think of calling the whole thing off. He'd rather be dead than to continue living his life as a man, and death is something he has thought about many times. There is no going back. He knows people who have managed to stay in the closet and keep on living, but for some reason, he can't. He doesn't know why; he just can't.

Still, he is scared. Gil has lived long enough to hear his share of hospital horror stories. Things could go wrong, perhaps terribly wrong. Of course, the releases of liability he was required to sign didn't help. Gil promised in writing to hold blameless the hospital, the clinic, the doctors, nurses, anesthesiologist…hell, probably even the janitorial staff should something even as egregious as, say, a scalpel be left protruding through his right nostril.

He laughs at the absurdity of it all. But his fear is not like the fear one feels at the beginning of a perilous journey; it is more like the fear one feels awaiting a tumor extraction. It is dread more than fear, a dark and cold dread that when it's all over, nothing will really be different. Gil's life, Gil's family, Gil's job, Gil's friends, Gil's bills, Gil's problems will still be there. If only the surgeon could take his scalpel and remove his past like a tumor, like a mistaken, distorted, unwanted history, so that when Gilda walked out of that hospital, she would have before her a clean slate, an empty canvas, a smooth ball of clay with which she could shape and form a life of her own, for good or for ill and everything in between.

He wishes he could weep, but he has lived so long with the manly prohibition, he cannot summon the tears he knows are there. Besides, someone might hear him, although the hallway is as silent as a tomb. He is alone in the most profound sense, like the condemned are alone; loneliness amplified by the starkly sterile silence. He undresses and lays his clothes over the metal chair – Gil's clothes. He imagines the day when he will never again wear Gil's clothes. At least, that will be different. Finally, he crawls into bed sure he will be unable to sleep until the next thing he knows, the faithful little alarm clock calls him awake as dawn kisses the sky.

As they prep him for surgery, everyone is in a cheery mood, like removing, reshaping and replacing people's faces was the most fun job in the whole world. Even Gil begins to feel a little excited, though his stomach is as tight as a snare drum head. The nurse jokes with him. She calls him Gilda and says 'she' when she talks to the anesthesiologist about him. God, she is pretty. He would be happy if he could end up half as pretty as her.

The anesthesiologist asks Gil how "she" feels, then says something reassuring about the surgery. Gil isn't really listening. He feels numb; his psyche is hiding somewhere, and it has taken a goodly portion of his mind with it. He nods and smiles wanly at the anesthesiologist. The cute nurse comes back in; she gives Gil a shot. A few minutes later, the knots in his belly become butterflies and the butterflies turn into swallows. They are dipping and soaring, swooping and sailing, twirling and spinning. Now they could remove his head and what would he care?

When Gil awakens in the recovery room, his garish Adam's apple, an anatomical cruelty more visible even than shoulder hair, will be gone. A tracheal shave – the medical name for reducing the size of the Adam's apple – is one of the cheaper surgical remedies costing only about $1500. It mostly gets rid of the tell-tale bump, but, unfortunately, will do absolutely nothing to modulate the tenor of Gil's rich bass voice. Though he tries to alter it, he will never sound like a woman when he speaks or laughs or – hardest of all – when he must raise his voice above a girlishly demur whisper to do something like yell at his stupid dog when one day at the park the horny little bastard mounts someone's three-year-old when she bends over to get a ball. In fact, Gilda will be having a reasonably good day passing until she opens her mouth, whereupon the clerk will do that telltale double take, the person next to her in line will look up from *The National Inquirer* to shoot her that knowing glare, and the jig is up. No matter how hard she tries to alter it, Gilda's voice will regularly betray her like the bastard child of a wronged lover.

The surgeon will also try to soften Gil's ruggedly masculine features by removing the front of his skull, shaving his Neanderthal brow ridges and then reattaching it. Cost: $20,000. His prominent proboscis, appropriately sized for a man, will be reduced to more feminine proportions. Cost: $5,000. He will need to have his manly square jaw rounded. Cost: $8,000. When this has healed, his second surgery will include a face-lift to get rid of the excess skin, lest he end up resembling a basset hound, though not nearly as adorable. Cost: $10,000.

Gil will certainly want breasts – and not those cute little sensitive lumps that came up after four months of taking hormones. No, Gil wants real breasts; by god, he wants boobs! Cost: $6000. Then there are little incidentals like having his upper lip tweaked to show his front teeth – very girlish – his receding hairline closed (that is, if it hasn't already receded past the point of no return) his ears pinned. These costs are so minimal compared to the others they don't merit mentioning. (If you have to ask the price, Pumpkin, don't bother ordering from the menu.)

And that's only the money; there is also the pain. It is unbelievable. Even though prior to surgery, Gil had never actually wondered what it would feel like to have a professional weight lifter hit him in the head with a sledgehammer, after his forehead job, he thinks he probably knows. Just as the pain begins to subside, he realizes with horror, that his skin has been fastened with surgical steel staples that must be yanked out one by one without the benefit of anesthesia.

To fix his jaw, the surgeon makes an incision along the entire bottom of his mouth. For days afterward, Gil can hardly talk, he can barely swallow his own bloody spittle, because his entire lower jaw is packed with about a dozen rolls of gooey, bloody gauze. He will never fully regain feeling in it.

After nose surgery, his entire nasal passage, from the opening of his newly reduced nostrils – into which he can never again send an index finger probe – to the very back of his throat is filled with more snot and blood-soaked gauze. It begins to snake its way down the back of his throat several maddening days before the surgeon finally pulls it out foot by agonizing foot followed by enough blood to compensate for all those menstrual periods he missed out on. Afterward, he marvels that he endured something so ghastly and painful with hardly more than a gurgling whimper. Plus, he now has a new appreciation of just how true it was when his dad called him an airhead after he sees the pile of slimy, bloody gauze that was stuffed into the empty cavities inside his skull.

Recovery from breast implants and a tracheal shave are merely painful; nothing to write home about. Nor can this all happen with one surgery but, like they say about childbirth, by the time Gil was ready for the next one, he had mostly forgotten the agony of the last one. And through it all, lives the hope, the dream that once he is all done, Gilda will be the prettiest girl on the block.

If Gil is lucky, if his surgeon is extremely skilled, if he has no infections or complications, at the end of this long, expensive and painful ordeal Gil will finally get to see the former captain of the high school football team, prom king, president of his college student body, first lieutenant in the Air Force, salesman of the year, everyone's Prince Charming transformed into…Ta Dah! *not* Cinderella – more like one of her ugly stepsisters.

And still, clearly visible in the mirror between his legs, rendered flaccid by the hormones he gets illegally and which he takes at his peril, since female hormones are no lightweight drug and can and do cause blood clots, hangs his damned penis, still defiant even in defeat. To finally get rid of it, Gil has several sessions with his friendly neighborhood psychiatrist who declares, after taking about a thousand dollars of Gil's money, that Gil has Gender Identity Dysphoria. Once this qualified mental health professional deems Gil sufficiently crazy, he can be prescribed hormones legally. (What's wrong with this picture?) His health insurer might even pay for them – something I can assure you they will most certainly *not* do for any of the aforementioned procedures.

Once Gil manages to beg, borrow and steal the $20,000-$30,000 needed for Sex Reassignment Surgery, (the cost of Female to Male sexual reassignment surgery starts at about $40,000, though it is cheaper in foreign countries) a surgeon excavates a cavity up into his body between his legs, peels the skin off his penis, throws away the erectile muscle along with the unwanted testicles, lines the newly constructed cavity with this skin plus bits of the scrotum, fashions a clitoris from some of the more sensitive skin around the head of the penis and voila! Gil now has a vagina, and once it heals, it looks pretty damn good, too. There's still some work to do, like masturbating with dildos of ever increasing sizes to stretch this tissue… just in case Gil meets Mr. Wonderful – but then, Gil's not really into men. So exactly why was it he did all of this?

So now, some $100,000 later, he must surely be about there, but no, not really, because Gil will feel satisfied only when he has managed to go back in time and relive his life as the pretty little girl he was supposed to have been in the first place. Until that magically happens, he will always be looking for the next big thing, the right outfit, another surgical nip, tuck, pull, reduction; he will even wear a garment that, while it fits like a girdle, is padded to add pounds precisely where most women would kill to have them taken off. This process will continue as long as Gil's money holds out or until he finally achieves the weird and creepy Michael Jackson look.

All along the way, afterward and forevermore, there are a host of small but damaging indignities, too many to list, though here are a few:

- He must go to the Department of Motor Vehicles and get the sex designation on his driver's license changed – not too bad in northern California, but what about Mississippi?

- He has to get a legal name change, which requires a personal court appearance where everyone gets to render in hushed tones and not so discreet glances their judgments on his appearance and prospects.

- Same thing at the Social Security office.

- Armed with a court authorized name change, he begins the long and tedious process of getting his name and sex changed on his health, life, car, and homeowners insurance policies, the mortgage company, the bank, IRS, power company, phone company, cable company, and every other Tom, Dick and Harry he has ever done business with. In many of these places, he will get to look another human being in the eye and observe up close and personal their reaction when they discover he is not *really* a woman.

- In order to find a decent paying job, he will have to try and get his college transcripts reissued in his new name with his new gender. (As you might imagine, the little Baptist college I attended was not particularly sympathetic to this request.)

- Then, the job he finally manages to land requires – oh god – a physical! How will he handle this, especially if he didn't have the money needed for SRS? The list goes on and on, and Gilda will get mail for Gilbert for frickin' ever.

- And then, there is the problem of the bathroom. If she transitions on the job, where does Gilda pee now? (I knew an MTF who said her employer had no problem with her coming dressed as a woman just so long as she continued using the men's restroom. That's like telling a woman that during her menstrual cycle, she has to work in the basement and avoid contact with men, or like hiring a person in a wheel chair and telling him to never let the clients know he's a cripple. Or then there was the case when a female staff member sued her employer when an MTF was allowed to use the women's rest room.) Even with SRS, at 6'2" using the women's bathroom is unnerving, especially while traveling. Of course, she could always wear a diaper; that would be special.

- When her daughter does a semester abroad, Gilda wants to get a passport, but getting a passport requires having the sex designation on her birth certificate changed. Most states will not do that under any circumstances. And what will happen if she has a car wreck before SRS? In one incident years ago, a non-operative MTF was involved in a serious accident in Washington D.C. When the paramedics discovered the woman they were treating was male, they suspended treatment and the victim died. Of course, the victim's family sued, but a lot of good that did the deceased. And what will happen if she gets sick and has to be hospitalized? And, of course, for the rest of her life, Gilda will need to have her prostate checked, so that, no matter how much money she spends nor how much like a natural-born female she looks, Gilda will forever feel like a three-legged mutt in an Alabama trailer park.

Since Gilda wandered long enough in the darkness of denial to make the serious mistake of fathering children, she must now deal with the problems of parenthood, numerous as weeds in the garden.

- For starters, what do the kids call her? Dad? But if not Dad, what? Not Mom; that position is taken and jealously guarded by a fire-breathing dragon. They can call her Gilda, but then that requires they explain over and over again who Gilda is and what is precisely their relationship to her? As a result, now others suffer the same indignities she must – others she loves and who are not as prepared as Gilda and certainly not deserving.

- When her son gets into trouble, and Gilda is summoned to a conference with the vice principal, who does she go as? And, of course, when the vice principal invariably refers to Gilda as "he," the asshole might as well have picked up the old paddle they used back in the good old days and slapped her upside the head with it.

- And what if Gilda finds someone who will stick with her through all this? What about her? (I say "her" because the only people I know who have managed to do this are women.) Is she a lesbian now? Maybe she has no problem with lesbians, but at the same time is honest enough to know she's not one. What then? And what about *her* family? Even if her kids aren't overtly homophobic they still have trouble imagining their mother – the one who was married to their father all those years – as a lesbian, much less introducing her as such to their friends.

That's, of course, *if* Gilda has managed to find herself a life partner. But what if she hasn't? Who's gonna want her? Most Male-to-Female transsexuals I know are sexually attracted to straight women. The last time I checked, most straight women are attracted to men, and even if Gilda still has that thing dangling between her legs, it's useless after hormones, and even if it isn't, having sex with a penis is pretty hard on the new self-image she's trying to cultivate. (I have no idea how people required to wear wigs deal with sexual intimacy.) After SRS, maybe a lesbian will be open to a relationship – but not likely. Gay men are attracted to...well, you know, men, especially manly men, which Gilda definitely is not – not any more, at least.

Maybe you read *Transsister Radio* in which the main character, an MTF, runs off in the end with a formerly transphobic straight man. Who knows where author Chris Bohjalian did the research he claims to have done, but to suggest that there are men out there who would enter into a romantic relationship with a transsexual seems about as likely as me becoming governor of California – though, considering that The Terminator was governor of California when I first composed this piece, maybe that's not so far-fetched after all.) Still, let's face it, Gilda's prospects for finding a date on Saturday night diminished dramatically when she stepped out of that closet all dressed up with nowhere to go.

And when Gilda's eighty-three year old mom gets sick and needs help, again, who does Gilda go as? Maybe her mother loves her no matter what, but at eighty-three is she really going to be able to embrace Gilda as her long-lost daughter? So poor Gilda's in for another ass whuppin'. Then when her mom dies, and Gilda's religious fundamentalist older brother contests Gilda's right to inheritance, because, after all, the will says "My son, Gilbert," what then?

Gilda will forever be second-guessing why people do what they do.

Does her best friend no longer call because he can't deal with the new Gil?

Did she not get invited to the party?

Was the clerk rude?

Was her neighbor unfriendly?

Do her children never have friends over?

Did she get passed over for the raise?

Was her application rejected because…?

Then when Gilda finally gets a job as a woman – invariably for less pay, usually *much* less pay – the worrying isn't over. Now that Gilda is finally out of the closet, Gil is in.

What's going to happen if they find out?

Will they think she deceived them?

Will they understand that she really is a woman even though she was born male?

Even when she succeeds at passing as a woman, she is reluctant to form friendships, because real friendships require self-disclosure, and what is Gilda going to do, totally fabricate a past she never had?

So do you get it? There is no escape. The one immutable sin is that Gilda was born with a dick, and she will *never* have the luxury of thinking of herself as an ordinary woman. She will *never* be a citizen in the nation of women; she will, at best, be an immigrant and often, an illegal one at that.

While all of this does not apply to every transsexual, especially not now, I promise it is not an exaggeration for many and not at all an exaggeration for transwomen of my generation. In fact, it is just the tip of the proverbial iceberg. These are just the major issues, the ones I came up with without even trying. There are countless others that must be dealt with day in and day out.

So who would choose this?

Why would anyone with a modicum of sanity choose to live this way?

Why not just stay in the closet and suffer quietly and thereby, maintain at least a shred of dignity, albeit, undeserved?

What is it that compels us?

Most transsexuals will tell you that they came out of the closet when they simply could no longer stand living inside it, which, when all is said and done, is probably the best reason for coming out, the moral being: stay in the closet as long as you can.

Usually depression is credited as the driving force for leaving the closet. Talk about out of the frying pan and into the fire! Depression outside the closet can be just as intense as it was inside, except before, the MTF was depressed about the life she couldn't have; now she's depressed about the life she has.

Coming out of the closet is the ultimate *dis*illusioning experience. In Gil's fantasies he imagined it would feel like getting on a plane in the Arctic and stepping off in the Bahamas, Gilda in an adorable little sundress, her long, lustrous hair catching the tropical breeze, the warm water lapping at her tiny sandal-clad feet.

Instead, the plane dumps her in a vast, trackless desert. The rocks cut her feet, the spiny plants torment her, the sun is searing, the night's cold and lonely. There is no food and precious little water. Nothing in her life has prepared her for how to live in this new, alien environment, how to negotiate the time when she is a freak of nature, neither male nor female, man nor woman. Still, like most transfolk who've made it this far, Gilda is a survivor – she begins to wander.

Since she is lucky enough to live near a large metropolitan area, there is a community of gays and lesbians, who, out of the goodness of their queerly large hearts, take Gilda in and offer her comfort, support and acceptance. The transgender community owes an enormous debt of gratitude to the gay and lesbian community who have so generously adopted our cause as their own and allowed us to reap where they have sown and to share in the spoils of victory few of us fought to win.

Over time, Gilda likewise discovers that the desert is not so empty as she first imagined. There are springs that flow in hidden places where orchids grow and exotic birds flit among lush vegetation. Though it is a postage stamp of the land she originally imagined, it is nonetheless just as wonderful as she imagined.

Over time, she realizes that the desert is full of incredible things, and, because it is a desert, Gilda cherishes them all the more. Things most women take totally for granted, like being referred to as "she" and "her," are to Gilda like gifts of chocolate and roses.

Her dresser fills with feminine garments, in her closet hang dresses and skirts, and they're all Gilda's, not her mother's or her sister's or her friend's sister's or her ex's – they're Gilda's!

She is received into the company of women – perhaps one of the greatest gifts any MTF can be given. They even talk about "woman" things in her presence.

People acknowledge her differently even though she'd be hard pressed to say exactly how.

A man in the checkout line strikes up a conversation with her and later, she realizes he was flirting – okay, so he was twenty years older, but hey! it was a guy, and he was flirting – with *her!*

And slowly, ever so slowly, Gilda begins to release the illusions and to live life as a desert-dweller; creatures know and admired more for their strength, endurance, and ingenuity than for their beauty.

UUP

At sixty, I have this dream:

A beautiful young woman walks into the room. She is tall and thin and wears a long, silky, sleeveless dress. I am sitting looking up at her. As she talks, she pulls down one shoulder of the dress, revealing that she has no breast. As she continues speaking in words that make no sense, I realize she is a boy. She walks to the window and pulls apart the curtain to look out. I ask where she works, thinking that her job possibly prevents her from coming out, since I can see no other reason why she wouldn't; she is such a beautiful woman. She walks back toward me speaking her incomprehensible language.

Awake, I go back into the dream, and ask the beautiful young woman who she is. Without hesitation she answers, "I am your longing." Instantly, I am filled with the old, familiar ache that I have known since the inception of consciousness. Her language is incomprehensible because there are no words to express this agony of hopeless longing.

As dawn insinuates itself through the blanket of northern California fog, I decide to go for a walk. Sitting on my dresser, waiting to be cleaned is a 357 magnum pistol Jan's sister lent us for camping trips to remote places. Four of us from the bus yard went out to a ranch a couple of days ago for some target shooting, something I hadn't done in years. Couldn't hit a damn thing with it.

I pick up the pistol. It is empty I know. I have checked it at least three times since putting it there. I am scrupulously careful about such things. Beside it in a small pouch are seven bullets. "One pull," I say out loud to no one.

I pull back the hammer. It locks into place with a series of cold, crisp clicks. Cocked and ready, all it needs is a bullet. "One pull of this trigger, and this agony will end," I speak into the emptiness. I admire its finely honed, stainless precision. It could all be over with just one pull. The struggle and the failure. The boredom of bus driving. The loneliness. The unending frustration of never seeing in the mirror the person I feel inside. Never hearing a woman's voice speak or sing or laugh when it comes out of my mouth. The agony of impossible longing. All over. Just one bullet and a faint squeeze of the trigger.

I touch the barrel to a point just above my right ear, the right front parietal lobe of the cerebral cortex, the area of the brain associated with body image and the spot most likely responsible for the lifelong disconnect between my brain and my body. "A bullet could fix that I bet."

Coco, our year old calico kitten jumps onto the bed and looks up at me with her huge bright eyes. Coco exudes life like a sparkler. "Hey Mom, what ya doin?" she seems to ask. I lower the gun. "Nothing, Honey." I stroke her small head. "I'm just going out for a walk." I release the hammer and put the gun back on the dresser.

I think about it as I walk. I could end this pain; that is true, but with the cessation of mine, the pain of others would begin. I think first of Lia. I always think first of Lia; I'm not sure why. It's not because I love her more than her brother. I think it's because she is the youngest, and that's just what we do as parents. And maybe it's because she's a girl, or maybe it's because she and I are so much alike. Whatever the reason, Caleb is a quick second. Haven't I caused them enough pain, asked more of them than any parent has the right to ask of her children? Would I burden them with this as well? I cannot even consider such a thing.

It seems I am destined – or doomed – or called – to live on this razor's edge, neither man nor woman, but flesh all the same and thus, capable of being sliced open. Living in a no man's land, essentially alone, not because I want to be, not out of some pathological self-pity, alone because that's the way of it for those of us who have no pronoun. It's just the way of it, and I know now there is neither shame nor escape.

To have our illusions dissed is a good thing, Gordon used to say. (Gordon was pastor of Church of the Savior when I was there.) And so, some seven years after I came out, I entered what might be called a period of great awakening – that often didn't feel so great.

It began with the Unitarian Universalist fellowship of Petaluma, more conveniently known as UUP. (Unitarian Universalism is a kind of interfaith, not-very-religious religious organization located on the political and social left. If you take a traditional protestant church, replace all references to God with "The Divine," remove Jesus entirely, and edit the Bible down to about four pages, but keep most of the liturgical trappings – Sunday morning worship, church building, minister, hymnals, offering, prayers-by-another-name, and fellowship – you have a UU church.)

Since moving to California from Maryland over fifteen years earlier, I had longed for and looked for a spiritual community to replace Dayspring with no luck. I had tried UUP probably a year earlier, but found it rather uninspiring. For some reason, I returned, and this time something moved inside me. Partly I was just lonely and desperate for some sort of community. It also helped that as soon as I walked through the door, I knew UUP was one of those rare places of refuge where my identity as a transsexual was neither a mystery nor mattered. It was a friendly space and much closer to home than the Castro. It was also a small congregation averaging about thirty worshipers on a Sunday morning; similar to what I had known at Dayspring, plus they were exceedingly kind to the strange stranger in their midst.

After attending a few months, I joined, and shortly thereafter, they invited me to give a talk customary for new members entitled "This I Believe." It was the first time I had ever preached as Meredith, and I discovered a voice that, while frustratingly un-girl like, was, nonetheless, mine.

People loved it, and it left me hungry to do more; quite a surprise, since, as Hank, I had never enjoyed preaching nor considered myself very good at it. As Meredith, however, I discovered not only a new and different experience of something I had done without enjoyment as Hank, but a new and different experience of myself – a foretelling of what was to come. So in order to get to know these people better, I signed up for the annual Memorial Day church-wide retreat.

While I had many times been in groups of all women, the church-wide retreat was the first time I had ever been invited into a gathering reserved exclusively for women, the church women's group. The significance of this was diminished in large part when it became obvious that a disgruntled church member whose cause it was to discredit gender based groups wanted to use me as her case in point, since, as she pointed out, I was not genetically qualified to be in the women's group, and yet, I was welcome. Philosophically, I tended to share her misgivings about groups based on gender. Still, I was not about to question being allowed into the very place I had dreamed of going since second grade when I watched with such aching longing the Brownies disappear into the inner sanctum of the Girl Scout hut.

As it turned out, the meeting was rather boring. Nor did I hear anything profound or unique by virtue of its being exclusively women. For some people it might be easier to be in your own skin in like gendered groups, but it doesn't change the fact that it's still the same old skin with all the same old scars, wounds and blemishes.

What *did* have a significant and life-altering impact on me was when, some weeks after the church-wide retreat, a woman came up to me and asked casually, "You are coming on the women's retreat with us, aren't you?" Had she not been standing right in front of me, I would have doubted that I heard her right. I mean, it was one thing to go to a meeting so someone with an axe to grind could use me as show and tell, but to actually be invited on the women's retreat, simply because I was, you know, *a woman,* was about as likely as, say…walking on water.

A women's retreat was a different thing all together. It would involve bedrooms and sleeping, sharing bathrooms and changing clothes, things I had never done with women as a woman, except for Jan who, as my partner, didn't count. For my entire life, I'd been telling myself – with virtually the entire human family backing me up – that because I was born male I could never be a woman. Yet here these people were inviting me on the women's retreat, because to them I *was* a woman – and as far as I could tell, they weren't even breaking a sweat!

Of course, I didn't go. Just being invited was more than I could have hoped for. Why spoil it? It was too good to be true anyway, and I wasn't about to put my entire version of reality into the hands of a small group of obviously misguided women, however kind, loving and well-meaning they might be. It would only be a matter of time before they saw what was so painfully obvious to me: that I was about as much like one of them as was an orangutan.

The things we tell ourselves are not, as we believe, information; they are acts of creation. By defining ourselves in a certain way, we create what is and is not possible, who we can and cannot be and what we can and cannot do. From such beliefs, we can assemble entire inner dwellings in which we live out our lives in cold, windowless rooms dark with despair and drafty with depression. Then when someone knocks on the door and we finally have the courage to open it, and they invite us out to play, we find ourselves oddly reluctant. Isn't this what we always wanted? Isn't this what we've been dreaming of doing, sitting huddled in our dark hovel staring out dirty windows at all the beautiful and lucky people living lives we can never have? So what's the problem? Why not race out into the sunlight, arms thrown open, singing and dancing? What's the reticence? Seems it's just hard to leave home, even if home is a hovel. Strange creatures we are.

I went on the next women's retreat, and when the speaking stone came around the circle of women to me, I held it and wept. It was indeed too good to be true, but it was true nonetheless.

Forbidden Love

It was the next retreat, however, that I remember best.

I had gotten through the first retreat without somehow exposing myself as the impostcr, the fake, the fraud I surely was, but then, they insisted I come on the next one. What the hell was wrong with these people? Hadn't they gotten the memo?

I signed up and paid the fee, but then at the last minute got cold feet. I mean, why not stop while I was ahead? Why run the risk of a humiliating disaster waiting to happen? Surely it was only a matter of time before they came to their senses, plus I had a perfect out: Cimarron had a hoof abscess.

This potentially serious condition required a visit from the vet, after which the hoof had to be soaked twice daily in Epsom salt, then carefully wrapped to keep dirt out as well as the oral administration of antibiotics. On a horse, especially one prone to hysteria, this is no small task. By the time the retreat rolled around, Cimarron's hoof was well on its way to being healed, but still, how could I go and leave Jan to do this difficult and dangerous task by herself?

In truth, I felt a lot safer doctoring a twelve hundred pound nervous nellie's rear hoof with which he could have easily cracked my skull or sent me sailing across the pasture like he had already done the rubber boot in which we had unsuccessfully tried to soak it than I was in spending the weekend with a group of perfectly lovely women. I had just finished the morning treatment and had almost talked myself out of going when Jodi called.

Prior to this I did not know Jodi well. She, her husband Phil, and their two children, Griffin and Phoebe, were active members of the church, so I knew who she was, and I liked her. In addition to being an overall nice person, she seemed particularly interested in making sure I knew I was welcome. Her call touched and moved me; they wanted me to come; they *wanted* me! It also played on my pleaser: how could I disappoint them? And so, I went.

I fell in love with Jodi.

It was such an incredibly surprising thing, impossible really – or so I thought. For one thing I was almost sixty years old. Almost sixty year olds do not fall in love, especially if their libido has been all but obliterated by the miracle of modern medicine. It can't happen. It's scientifically impossible. Not only that, I didn't want it, and I sure as hell wasn't looking for it. It was the farthest thing from my mind, especially with a woman and a straight, married mother of two young children at that. It took me an entire day to figure out what these strange, though vaguely familiar feelings were playing around in my heart like a swarm of butterflies. And then, in a sudden flash of realization, I got it: I had a crush on Jodi.

It started like this: The most distinctive activity on the UUP Women's Retreat is the sharing circle. After T, the originator, organizer and facilitator of the group, lights a candle and shares a reading, a smooth stone about the size of a woman's palm is passed around the circle. The person with the stone is free to share whatever they like without interruption or response and when they are finished, they pass the stone to the next person and so it goes. It is an exercise in carefully crafted control and safety, which, given the way I've done my life and the fact that I'm ADHD is kind of boring, but hey, I'm on the women's retreat; I'm not complaining.

It is Saturday morning. I have slept on a cot in the game room – alone. OK, that's suspicious, but hey, they invited me on the Women's Retreat; beggars can't be choosers. I am the last person to join the circle. Sitting on the floor hurts my back, but all the seats are taken, except there is this one large overstuffed chair capable of accommodating two people of standard girth who are really comfortable being really close. Jodi is in the chair. Without a second's thought, without reservation or hesitation, I plop my skinny butt in the chair next to hers, and she readily makes way.

This audacious act was not just remarkable; it was unthinkable. As I said earlier, I was still horribly insecure about my place in this circle, about whether or not I belonged, about my right to be there after all those perfidious years impersonating a man. With all that guilt and shame and insecurity, the last thing I would have expected of myself – or anyone else in that state – was that I would boldly and with such flagrancy project myself uninvited into another's physical space, and yet, that's precisely what I did. When I squeezed my body into the chair next to Jodi's and our hands spontaneously entwined, it was so out of the realm of the reasonable, so inexplicable and so wonderful that theologically is the only way I can make sense of it.

Then again, maybe the way from having nowhere to sit to snuggled beside the person who would become my Companion on the Way had been prepared by Jodi herself who had for some time been praying for a special friend, someone with whom she could share her deepest spiritual thoughts, feelings and longings, and God, that divine kidder, sent me.

The months that followed the women's retreat could be characterized in several ways:

I am a high school girl who has fallen madly in love with her classmate. I can't stop thinking about her. All I want is to be with her. I am utterly and completely smitten. I am pathetic. It is like running with a mug full of soup; my feelings are sloshing everywhere and making a terrible mess. I swing from intense highs to dramatic lows. I write bad poetry and worse, I send it. I am almost sixty fucking years old! What the hell is wrong with me? Have I completely taken leave of my senses? Well, yes, it seems I have.

And poor Jodi. She must have wondered what in heaven's name she had stumbled into, what sort of cruel joke the gods were playing on her sending me in response to her prayers. She thought she'd found this wise, older woman, schooled and scarred in things of the Spirit. And here she was in her mid-forties, a wife and mother of two young children, dealing with an angst ridden, love struck, goofy-eyed teenage lesbian. Why she chose to endure this period in our relationship is beyond me; maybe it was for the sheer entertainment value.

The best thing I can say about this time is that one of my oldest prayers was answered: I finally got the chance to feel what it's like to be a teenage girl, a teenage lesbian as it turns out, who falls in love with her beautiful but very straight classmate. It's awful; it's dreadful; it hurts like hell, and my heart goes out to all those young lesbians who've done the same. As K.D. Lang sings, "Go with it, stay with it, but be prepared to bleed."

Fortunately this phase passed before I spiked my hair or dyed it blue or got a tattoo. What emerged as the dominant force in our relationship was far more wonderful than any adolescent romance I might have imagined. In fact, it is impossible to imagine any form of love making so satisfying to me as what Jodi and I shared on a regular basis "lying together in God's green pastures, having our souls restored beside still waters and following the meandering paths of righteousness for the sake of nothing more and nothing less than to know the name of the Divine." (Psalm 23, shamelessly adapted for my parochial purposes.)

Not since Dayspring, some fifteen years earlier, had I had someone with whom I could share my love of and lifelong commitment to things of the Spirit. As a teacher, I'd been able to integrate spirituality somewhat into my work with children, plus, at the end of an exhausting day of

186

teaching, I felt good about what I had done, but that was over and gone now. For the past six years I'd been getting up at 4:30 a.m. to drive a school bus for what felt like wasted hours of meaningless drudgery. As a result, I was spiritually famished, and Jodi was a banquet. Being with her was like feasting, but this was not the feasting of someone who has known only privation. At Church of the Savior, I had tasted the best, eaten until I was full and then eaten some more, and not just on holidays, but virtually every day there was rich and wonderful spiritual fare to be had for the taking. With the death of the farm and the move to California, I had sacrificed all of that, and in the long, hungry years that followed, I sucked on dried memories to stave off the pangs of hunger. That is reason enough for a little obsession.

While I had managed to get through the initial infatuation and obsession with Jodi, the feelings of attraction persisted, waxing and waning in response to hormones, to how things were going between Jan and me, to how often I got to see Jodi, to how the sun shone in her hair when we walked, to the adorable earnestness on her face when she was trying hard to describe some wonderful realization she'd had while picking up the kids, to those brown eyes in which I would sometimes find myself swimming, to the smell of her when we embraced, to those rare and wonderful times on women's retreats when I got to lie in bed next to her, listening to her read Mary Oliver, the words falling from her lips like kisses. It was impossible not to want her in such times, and that wanting, though neither the biggest nor best of what we shared, also served.

It served one Sunday at worship early in our relationship not long after the providential women's retreat when Jodi made a point of inviting me to a women's group meeting the next week. She suggested I drive to her house and we walk the few blocks to where the monthly meeting was held. I intuitively felt suspicious about this; something was up, but I wasn't about to turn down an opportunity to be with Jodi. It was only later that I learned that the theme of the discussion that night was childhood, and everyone was to bring a photo of themselves at about age 12. (Jodi swears she knew nothing about this when she invited me.)

Ironically enough, a couple of weeks earlier, my mom had sent me a box of old photos thinking it was time to pass on some of the family antiquities. In the collection was – you guessed it – a lovely photo of twelve-year-old Hank. The Staffwork of Omnipotence was at it again.

As the stone made its way slowly around the circle, each woman placed her childhood photo in the center and shared about that time in her life. Finally the stone came to me and to the collection of photos of little girls, the likes of which I had always wanted to be, I added the photo of twelve year-old Hank.

They were fascinated. They picked up the photo and studied it intently, looking for signs of the terrible angst that must have been hidden in the face of that young boy. *Surely this will do it,* I thought. This irrefutable, undeniable, black and white proof of who and what I was would surely push their acceptance beyond the limits of good will, political correctness, and even Unitarian Universalist tradition and bragging rights. Of course, they wouldn't be mean about it. They might not even do it consciously. Without noticing, they'd just start avoiding me and forgetting to invite me and gradually, I would be excluded.

Walking home, I told Jodi how hard it had been to share the photo, how anxious I had felt all day about the meeting. She stopped, reached over and took my hand in hers, looked into my eyes with those soft, loving, brown eyes of hers, so earnest and full of compassion and spoke words that rang in me like the peal of bells, "Mer, we want all of you, all of you," she repeated.

What does one do in the seconds that follow news that will change their life forever? If someone had walked up to me and said, "You have won the lottery," even those five words would not have rocked my world as much as the ones Jodi spoke so tenderly that fateful evening. Had I known to, I might have wept for joy, cried out in pain that I had waited so long to hear this invocation, lifted my voice in shouts of grateful jubilation that I had heard them at last – and from someone so lovely as this. I might have fallen on my knees and kissed the feet of the bearer of such good tidings. I might have knelt and pledged lifelong fealty to her. As it was, I did nothing of the sort. We just turned and kept on walking, as if nothing more than a few words had passed between friends, as if those few words had not somehow been transformed into the Word itself, like the atoms of carbon in a lump of coal rearranging themselves into a diamond.

Perhaps some of the import of these words might have swept over me in the moment, like a fragrant whisper blown from the lips of God, but at the time, I barely felt it. Only later would I realize what had happened that night, and what those words would come to mean, what I could do because of them, who I could become and what I could let go of.

I don't remember the rest of the evening, what else was said, our parting, driving home. I do remember those words – we want all of you – echoing over and over again in my mind, cracking the rock of my reality, loosing the rubble, and starting an avalanche that would completely remake the landscape of my life.

For about a year, Jodi, another woman from the church and I met weekly in a spiritual support group. One winter we decided to go on a weekend retreat to Jodi's family's cabin in the Sierras. When the other person dropped out, Jodi and I decided to go anyway.

It was the first time we had ever gone away just the two of us overnight, and Jan was beside herself. I insisted that just like with friends in the past, I had every right to go away with Jodi. Jan's take on it, however, was that since she and I lived in what, for all practical purposes, was a lesbian relationship my going away with Jodi, a woman for whom I clearly had feelings, was tantamount to Jodi's husband going away on some romantic weekend tryst with another woman. How did I think Jodi would feel about that?

Reasonable as her argument was, it didn't matter. I was convinced that this relationship had been given, that it was a gift from God, and that something important was going on in it, something vital and essential to my own unfolding. Any sexual attraction was merely fuel for the fire, fire in which shame, fear, and self loathing might finally be burned away, and the possibility of that outcome was worth almost any risk.

In addition to talking virtually nonstop about spiritual stuff, being with someone who was my physical equal – and more – was reminiscent of the old adventures I'd enjoyed with Paul. We had hardly trucked our stuff to the cabin through knee deep snow when Jodi pounced on me like a kitten, and I found myself in the clutches of a younger, stronger adversary.

Something similar happened the next day when we went snowshoeing. I had imagined snowshoes would allow me to scuttle over the surface of the snow like a wood rat. With snow shoes, however, instead of sinking up to my knees, I sank to just below my knees. Nor did I scuttle. I staggered, stumbled, shuffled, and eventually ended up tagging along after Jodi like an old dog, quite literally following in her footsteps.

At one point when we were in the middle of what in summer was a man-made lake, I climbed up on a snow covered boulder to get a better view of the surrounding mountains. Jodi was below me, looking shoreward to the forested slopes of a nearby ridge. I don't know what it was about the way she was standing, about her stance, but I knew in that moment that I was witnessing something special, though at the time I could not have said what. I felt so blessed to see her this way, in this time of her blossoming, of coming into her power, of discovering her gifts, and I prayed with all my heart that I would do nothing to violate this incredibly precious relationship I had been so graciously given.

Over the course of time, Jodi's and my relationship would go through periods of frequent and intense contact followed by periods of absence and detachment. These oscillations were controlled mainly by Jodi's busy schedule, her children, her commitments to family, friends, school, church, and almost surely an understandable need to get away from my brooding intensity and neediness. Often I ended up feeling like a piece of flotsam bobbing around on the tides of Jodi's hectic life.

In the beginning I would make excuses for her. She was, after all, the mother of two young children who gave an extraordinary amount of time to their school. Sometimes I would remind myself that this was my karma finally catching up to me. How many women had been attracted to Hank who, though for very different reasons, was likewise, totally unavailable and distracted? In the early days I would often feel really hurt and mad and betrayed and forsaken and heartbroken and like, you know, totally sixteen. And then, my parental self would chime in, saying that this was, after all, for the best. I was relying too much on Jodi for companionship. Pulling back was good. I had lived without her before, and I could certainly do so again. In fact, I wasn't so sure I actually wanted to see her again. Come to think of it, I was over her. I had just had a moment of temporary insanity, that's all. She wasn't really that special anyway. Well, yeah she was, but hey, she wasn't available, and I was tired of just being another thing she had to juggle and find room for.

And then, she would be back, ready to take up where we'd left off, and out would come the sun!

One of my hopes had always been that we would someday work together, and lots of our long ranging conversations were about what we might do, what we might create or build with one another. One idea was called the Center for Spiritual Practice. CSP would provide opportunities for people to explore various spiritual practices, help them find a practice suitable for them, and then, support them in their commitment to it while holding them accountable in agreed upon ways.

It was a lovely idea. It gave me hope that I might, after all, be able to do something worthwhile despite bus driving. It was also time to be with Jodi in ways I loved, and the mission appealed to me and seemed worthy.

Then one day while we were eating lunch together at her house, she took a deep breath as if steeling herself to do something difficult, looked me in the eye and said, "We're not going to work together. I'm going to go my own way."

There had been signs this was coming. The nature of our weekly time had changed from inner work to mostly talking. We hadn't gone away together, even for a day, in a long time. I quit going to the women's retreats. They were mostly about hanging out, eating and socializing, and I resented that Jodi kept going rather than devote those two precious weekends a year to the work we had once done and that I wanted us to keep on doing. As I withdrew from UUP, partly because I repeatedly found it hostile to Christianity, Jodi became more involved.

Each step Jodi withdrew from me to do her own thing, I withdrew another from her. Our weekly meetings changed into weekly walks, which changed into regular get-togethers, which changed into occasional get-togethers.

Dream work and energy work and healing work turned into theological conversations, which sometimes devolved into arguments. There were exceptions, some of them notable, but that was the trajectory.

Looking back now I see that there were always fundamental differences between us that would inevitably send us in different directions.

I was terribly lonely for a spiritual community, while Jodi had more community than she could manage. My life was empty and bereft, while Jodi's was full to overflowing. Jodi lived a charmed existence, idealized by others and almost universally loved and admired. I lived daily with the fact that I was a queer.

One day, standing on the cliffs overlooking the ocean, the waves breaking on the rocks below us, the sea birds swooping and calling, Caleb, home from college, asked me this question: "If you could choose, which would you have, gills or feathers?" meaning, which would I want most to do, swim in the deeps or soar to the heights? With only a second's pause, I answered, "gills."

"Yeah, me too," he said.

That seems to me to describe the fundamental difference between Jodi and me. She is a person of light and air. She is a feather person. Feathers are not made for swimming. She needed to soar.

Griffin and Phoebe

What I didn't expect was the effect Jodi's children, Griffin and Phoebe would have on me.

When I first met them, Griffin would have been about seven and Phoebe, five. Now it's true, I'm pretty good with kids. I like them; I'm comfortable with them and probably most importantly, I'm genuinely interested in them. They're kind of fascinating if you take the time to notice. But I often present children, especially young children, with an unusual – and sometime, disturbing – dilemma.

One of the first things children do in order to make sense of the world and its occupants is to sort the multiplicity of things into meaningful categories. Fifteen month old step grandson, Donnie, knows and can name two categories that are especially important to him: "cat" and "hot," and in time, he will learn that individual cats have names and that not everything that glows is hot. Two of the earliest and most important categories children learn are "mommy" and "daddy" with their correlatives, "man" and "woman," "boy" and "girl," and from that point on, they are conscripted into society's obsession with drawing and redrawing the lines of distinction between these binaries. What people like me do, though not intentionally and certainly not maliciously, is mess with these heretofore, reliable categories, and that can be downright disorienting, if not a little scary.

For example: from time to time after I left teaching, Jan would have me into her classroom of 6-8 year olds to help out with science and math. One day at the midmorning snack break after I had presented a science lesson, one of the older girls came over to me and very politely said, "I don't mean to be rude, but are you a boy or a girl?" Now mind you, I was wearing a skirt and blouse, my hair was fixed and I had on makeup, but this perspicacious little kid was no fool; she could spot a wolf in sheep's clothing. It was such an open, honest and genuine question, I had to laugh. "I'm a woman," I assured her. "OK," she responded, turned and went back to her snack.

Of course, Griffin and Phoebe took their cues from Jodi and Phil as well as other adults around them who accepted me as a woman and addressed me as such. Still, that didn't fully explain it. After all, there were plenty of other things their parents expected of them that they did not feel particularly obliged to comply with, especially feisty little Phoebe.

I know they must have gotten queries from their friends about the tall strange looking woman in their house. What did they say? How did they answer? But if my presence ever made them uncomfortable, I never saw it. No doubt Phil and Jodi ran a lot of interference on my behalf; that would be like them, but there was something particularly and peculiarly radical in the way Griffin and Phoebe just accepted me.

Of course, they knew. What exactly they knew and when exactly they knew it, I don't know, but I know that they knew I was transgender. Gradually, over time, their simple, unassuming acceptance came to have a special quality. It was so pure, so natural, so uncontaminated. They weren't accepting and addressing me as a woman to be politically correct, or to demonstrate and validate their views and values, or to try and correct society's prejudice and injustice. They harbored no unconscious doubts about my legitimacy as a woman that needed to be concealed, denied, or atoned for. They just accepted me for who I was, and there was nothing I needed to do or even *could* do to earn it. To them, I was just Meredith, a woman friend of the family, nothing more and nothing less. It was perhaps one of the only places where I got a sense of what it would be like just to be a woman, not a transwoman, not a special woman, not a faux woman – just a woman, and, interestingly enough, sometimes I wanted to be more.

The Freak and the Cripple redux

Amidst all the sunshine and love, the relationship with Jodi was exposing what I had known inchoately when I first penned those words years earlier describing Jan's and my relationship as the fairy tale of *The Freak and the Cripple*. I intuited then that such a relationship was fraught with peril, though, at the time, I assumed it was because having someone as your one and only left you terribly vulnerable to their loss. It never dawned on me that the real weakness, the real danger, the fatal flaw was the implicit requirement that I stay a freak and Jan remain a cripple.

Thanks to Jodi, her family and the people of UUP, being a freak was an image of myself I was rapidly discarding like a bird in molt, and even as much as I needed to stop seeing myself that way, I also needed Jan to stop playing the role of the cripple. I had witnessed her at work in a classroom of 6-8 year-olds where she was a competent, capable, strong, wise, playful, compassionate teacher. That's the Jan I wanted, but that's not the Jan I got.

The Jan I got revered me, completely turned over her power to me, tried in every way possible to please me, even though I made abundantly clear, I didn't want to be pleased. What I longed for was someone who felt free to disagree with me, challenge me and call me on my stuff. I wanted someone who I could butt heads with intellectually, who would make me think. Jan simply would not do that, not because she lacked the intelligence, but because she couldn't/wouldn't stop giving herself away long enough to occupy her own body and know her own mind. In order to have a relationship with a person, there has got to be a person there, and a person was not who I was getting. I kept getting a distorted reflection of myself, and while I understood the origins of that in her terrible childhood and felt sympathetic, I was done with it.

On top of that, due to a lifetime of neglect and abuse, Jan's body fell prey to illnesses and injuries that made it all but impossible for us to do together the kinds of things we had done before, particularly our adventures on horseback. Putting her horse Cimarron down when his arthritis permanently crippled him turned out to be more than just the sad loss of a dear, old friend. It marked the end of the life we had known and shared together, the life by and through which we had known and loved one another.

I am old enough now to know that every relationship has its fault zones, those places buried beneath layers of crusty unconsciousness where the plates of pathology and dysfunction rub up against each other. Yet deeper still, closer to the very core of what it means to be human, is a longing to shape and form ourselves into an ever more perfect image of who we are in the white-hot center of God's Love meant to be. The tensions between this longing for authenticity and our resistance, rebellion and fear (aka "sin") grow, until the plates eventually slip, shaking everything on the surface so violently that sometimes decade's worth of carefully constructed edifices built on lies and illusions are torn down and cast into ruins.

While Jodi might have innocently caused Jan's and my plates to suddenly shift when she took my precious stone with the word "Freak" meticulously carved on it and unceremoniously hurled it into the sea, the fault lines had been there from the beginning, and the tension had been building for years, at least in me. So, like people dwelling in different hemispheres, as the sun rose on my spring, for Jan, the cold darkness of winter began. As I sang hymns of celebration and renewal, Jan sank into jealousy, despair and bitterness. The life we had built together that had seemed so inviolable, so eternal, so perfect was crumbling all around us, and once begun, there was no stopping it. At her insistence, we separated, and I moved into the out building where the children had partied and Caleb and Dustin had once lived.

For Jan, the problem was simply "You've fallen in love with someone else." It became her mantra. Distilling my relationship with Jodi into this apodictic eight word phrase maximized both my guilt and her innocence, relieved her of the taxing effort of introspection, was guaranteed to garner truck loads of sympathy from friends and family, and was endowed with sufficient cultural currency to support her inner Victim in the manner to which it had become accustomed. All that with the added bonus that it was an indictment I could not entirely deny.

How do you explain that a relationship between people who find each other enormously attractive can be passionate and yet not sexual? And who would ever believe that a conversation about God (of all things) could be a form of love making more satisfying than sex? Yet, that was the only defense I had. While Jodi and I loved each other, we weren't lovers. For one thing, Jodi was about the straightest person I knew; there wasn't a lesbian bone in her body, and I had no functioning male equipment. Yet, even if I had and she had been willing, having sex with a woman as a man would have been the last thing in the world I wanted, especially by that time. Jan knew that, and she admitted that she knew that. She knew, or said she knew, we weren't having sex, but it didn't matter; for her, these were mere distinctions without a difference.

What I *had* done was betray the promise I made at our marriage that we would be each other's one and only forever. To that I plead guilty. When I made that promise, I never imagined that there would ever be others who could love and accept me as Jan did. Perhaps Jan felt the same, and as a result, felt protective and possessive of me. She had done what others could not and would not, and as a result, had bragging rights she wasn't interested in sharing.

In time, living apart began to reflect, not so much estrangement as preference. Jan had always longed for but never had a place of her own, a place where she could keep the hours she preferred, decorate the way she liked, come and go as she wished. And what the kids called "the barn," little more than a spacious, well appointed shack, was perfect for me. Now Jan and I check in with each other every morning and evening, know the other's schedule, make sure the lights are on if the other is out after dark, eat together frequently, watch movies, share all expenses, divvy up chores and generally, take pleasure and comfort in each other's nearness. When we are forced by physical and/or financial necessities to leave this ratty little piece of property, it's impossible to imagine being separated.

The real irony is the love that set me free, in its own way, and in its own time, did the same for Jan. A marriage was shattered; but from the remains, two lives emerged reborn, neither freak nor cripple, and into the Mystery that can sponsor that, I will gladly entrust my future.

The Sea and Me

While Jodi had become the central character in the unfolding of my life, she was not the only one. She wasn't even present on the women's retreat when I performed what turned out to be an important and dramatic ritual of my own making.

Driven by the undeniable changes happening to my body as a result of age, one of the things I resolved to do in my 60th year was a rite of passage wherein I would acknowledge and accept the ending of my youth and embrace the commencement of old age with its inevitable *dénouement*.

I knew it would involve water, probably the ocean, the womb from which all life originally sprang, and that during this ritual, I would make some sort of prayer. As with rituals I had done in the past, this one would be sealed through immersion beneath the surface, symbolizing death to the old and reemergence, symbolizing resurrection to the new. However, unlike times in the past when I had prayed I might one day become the person I most truly felt I was, this time, I would be accepting a loss I did not want to suffer and a journey I did not want to make.

As I mused on what this would look like, it occurred to me that this ritual needed to be done with others. I needed witnesses, and this led like the needle of a compass to the women's retreat. Though I already knew Jodi would not be on this particular retreat, others who I trusted would be, especially Leslie, who I knew from past experience would make an excellent witness.

The house in which we were staying was also conveniently located near the beach, facilitating the logistical imperative that I have a warm refuge nearby once I emerged from the frigid Northern California waters, and afterward, there would be ample time and space to reflect on the experience both alone and with others. It was ideal.

In the weeks prior to the rite, I formulated three prayers I wanted to make:

1. I rededicate myself to lifelong service of God.
2. Throughout old age, I want a heart ready to love and able to be broken.
3. I want to face my death with unfailing courage.

These prayers would be made in the water, each followed by immersion.

From the beginning, this rite frightened me. The vast, dark, powerful ocean is, in and of itself, frightening, especially in Northern California where it is deceptively rough and dangerously cold to an unprotected body, and I would be wearing no wet suit. I was afraid that once I was under in death I would not be able to come back up. I was afraid of great white sharks who ply these waters. I poo pooed these obviously irrational concerns. I mean, how likely was it I would be attacked by a shark? Or what would hold me under the water against my will? And while, yes, the water was breathtakingly cold and rough, I was an excellent swimmer, and besides that, it was a bay into which I would be wading and not the ocean itself. Still, the anxiety persisted.

During the Saturday morning meeting, I shared with the others what I intended to do and invited them to join Leslie and T in witnessing if they wanted. Afterward, I went downstairs to change, and as soon as I entered the bedroom and saw the candle Leslie, Jodi and I always lit at our weekly meetings, I began to cry. I did not want to do this. I did not want to take my warm, tender body into that cold, powerful ocean. I did not want to surrender my youth, especially not now, just as I was beginning to find an expression of the person I had always longed to be. I did not want to grow old and suffer the inevitable and ignominious decline and decay of my body and mind. Oh God, I did not want any part of this.

Leslie came into the room and held me as I sobbed, assuring me that I did not have to go through with this. I could change my mind; no one would think less of me. But once the emotions passed, I felt ready. There was, after all, no turning back from what the ritual symbolized, no changing my mind about getting old, no avoiding the ultimate and final outcome and so, I resolved to do this thing, this fittingly painful and frightening rite of passage. I would die to my youth and be reborn to my death.

Down the steep hill to the beach I walked between Leslie and T, singing that little piece of Verdi's *Te Deum* that I remembered from when the college chorale sang it with the New Orleans symphony. It's in Latin, so I have no idea what the words actually mean, but sung on my journey to the sea, they sounded like a lament – or a dirge.

Once there, I handed my protective coat to the person nearest me and waded straight away into the water, fearing that if I hesitated, I might yet lose my resolve. Immediately I felt the pull of powerful currents, invisible from shore, threatening to take my feet out from under me. I struggled forward until the waves struck my body full on with unexpected force, knocking me back despite pushing into them with all my might. One after another they came and each I met full on, only to find my forward progress cut in half as if they were trying to prohibit – or to prove – my intent.

I no longer had any idea of why I was there. All thinking stopped. I had no sensation of being cold. Finally, I dove under an oncoming wave and began to swim. Once beyond the breakers, I stopped swimming and to my surprise, found the bottom within reach. Barely able to stand, I remembered why I had come. I started to make a prayer, but no sooner had I opened my mouth to speak, than salt water poured in. "Be quiet," the Sea seemed to say, "and listen." I ducked a wave about to break on me and began to swim further out.

Suddenly I felt the sandy floor begin to rise beneath me until I was standing in water hardly up to my knees, though I was considerably farther from shore. Then I saw it, a large green wave forming in the distance, sucking into itself the water from around my legs. As it advanced, I watched it rise higher and higher. This is what I had come for. This would be my baptism. Soon it would crash right on top of me – and I was not afraid.

When it broke, I was thrown head over heels and swept back into deeper water but closer to shore. When I came up, I wasn't sure what to do next. Was it over? Had I done what I had come to do? Something said, "Go back," and so, I began to swim.

About half way, I realized how tired I was. I tried my best to ride the waves, but they swept past me, forcing me to fight the back flow. I was growing weaker by the second – and terribly cold. Numb with cold and exhaustion, I finally found the bottom. When I tried to stand my legs were so weak the waves easily knocked me over, and I had to fight not to be sucked back out.

Walking was virtually impossible, so, with what strength remained, I swam until the water was quite shallow and the shore only a dozen yards away. Still, when I tried to stand, my legs threatened not to hold me. I knew the others could easily get out to me, but I didn't want them thinking I was just being dramatic.

Finally I managed to stagger onto the beach into the welcoming towels and arms of my friends. I had no idea who was there. I only recall leaning on Leslie going back up the hill and her telling me to sit down when I thought I was going to throw up. It was then I realized how much salt water I had swallowed and how terribly cold I was. Back at the house, I went straight away into the hot shower where I stood light-headed and shivering. With the steaming water revitalizing my frigid body, I began to realize the power of what had just happened. Plus, I had the distinct impression the Sea had said something to me, though I didn't know or couldn't remember what.

After I fully returned to the land of the living, others shared with me how powerful it had been to witness, and I wished I had considered them more in the preparation.

When I awoke the next morning, Leslie still sleeping beside me in the bed, I suddenly knew what the Sea had said. It said, "Okay."

Into the Valley of the Shadow

I had been out of the closet for over ten years when my spry, little 86 year-old mother living in Georgia was diagnosed with advanced pancreatic cancer and had, at most, a few months to live.

The last time I visited her had been about three years earlier when I went out to help after she had shoulder replacement surgery. Though we did not see one another often – I had not the money and she had not the inclination to fly – we talked regularly on the phone.

Mom and I had never been really close. She was about as opposite to one of those overprotective smother-mothers as you could get, and, perhaps as a result, I was about as independent as they come, even as a small child.

Mother tells that before I started school, I would often play outside in my sandbox for hours all alone and perfectly happy. I'd come in to eat, take a nap and then, go back outside. I have no recollection of ever sitting in my mother's lap, of her ever reading to me, or of us cuddling. About all I can remember of anything that resembles intimacy between us was when she would come in at night to say my prayers with me.

She beat me a few times, but it was, after all, the 50's when parents – especially Southern parents – took quite literally the old proverb "spare the rod, spoil the child." The most memorable beating I ever got from her was when, in second grade, I called the teacher a witch. I can still see that woman's face. She was old and mean and cruel – the very picture of everything evil I had ever seen or heard about witches.

The provocation for my intemperate accusation was her mistreatment of a classmate. As I recall, I told her she was a witch in front of the entire class, without any fear and perhaps, without malice, like a small child might innocently walk up and smack a junk-yard dog on its nose to get it to stop barking. The teacher, as you might imagine, did not take kindly to this observation, however astute and well deserved it might have been.

The school called Mom. Mom came and got me and once home, took me into the bedroom, told me to pull down my pants and proceeded to beat the hell out of me with one of Dad's belts. It hurt something fierce, and I screamed bloody murder.

I'm pretty sure Mom felt bad about it later. She as much as told me so when I was well into adulthood. She was just following the old rule common in her day that "if you get in trouble at school, you get in trouble at home." Something made her change her mind, though, and she repented. I readily forgave her. We have all blindly obeyed bad rules at one time or another, and every parent stands in need of forgiveness.

In preparation for the difficult journey back into the hostile lands of the rural South to say my final good-bye to Mom, I decided to take a walk out to the coast with Strider, my horse. I called Jodi the day before to tell her my plans, and she asked if there was anything I needed. I said she could come with me, but as I anticipated, she wasn't available. She had just come back from several weeks at her family cabin, and she wanted to attend worship at UUP that morning. It didn't really matter. Having had no serious contact in weeks, I was already feeling disconnected from her.

Saturday evening as Jan and I were having our customary drinks and smoke, I told her my plan for the morrow. I hadn't considered asking Jan, because I assumed with her bum knee and ankle she couldn't hike that far, but she volunteered to go anyway and serve as my witness. By then, I had come to appreciate the importance of a witness in such times, so we decided to take the shortest route to the coast rather than the most scenic, which Jan was confident she could walk.

As we made our way westward toward that great expanse of ocean, I saw the road on which we walked as symbolic of that portion of the journey I would make with Mom – the final portion for her. At the ocean our journey together would end, and there, I would symbolically release her.

Along the way, Strider would sometimes stop to graze, and I would feast my eyes on the incredible beauty of this planet on which I have been blessed to live out my life. I wept in both gratitude and sorrow and wondered what I might do or say, once there, that would help Mom in her final days.

Strider was a great companion, not pushy or piggy. A few times as he grazed, I just leaned against his soft, warm, fragrant body and let him support me, a magnificent equine incarnation of God's loving support. Jan was there witnessing, vigilant and silent, keeping her distance. I talked to her some, but she simply listened and made no reply.

Finally, we reached the place where I would release Mom. Jan took Strider and I walked to the edge of the cliff high above the vast, mysterious sea, the perfect metaphor for death. There I imagined letting her go and watched as her small body walked out into that vast, blue expanse. It was terribly painful; though when it was done, I felt better, almost ready.

By the time I arrived in Georgia, Mom was already actively detaching herself from this realm, loosening the ties of love and obligation that might hold her. She was already well on the way, and I was probably more of a nuisance than a comfort to her. Still, there were things to be done. There were all the papers to go through annunciating how she wished to be treated, what she wanted and didn't want in terms of medical interventions and what to do with her precious little body once she had vacated it.

Then there was the obituary that Greg none too subtly suggested I write, since I was, after all, the writer. I had never written an obituary, so while Mom and I watched an episode of the Gilmore Girls, I read through that day's obits in the local newspaper. (Amy, my younger sister, suggested that my appreciation of this ultimate TV Chick Flick, would incontrovertibly validate my credentials as a real woman. Ah, yet another miserable failure.)

Early the next morning as I set to my loathsome literary task, I had described mother as a "devoted friend," and was searching for a different adjective to go with "mother." What kind of mother was she, I pondered? I thought about Amy and me and all we had required of her over the years, and the word that sprang immediately to mind was "longsuffering." I would have had it that way had she not objected when I read it to her. "You cain't put that," she drawled, laughing. "I knew you'd edit out all the fun parts," I replied in mock annoyance.

There were other light and funny moments like that, quite a few considering the grim circumstances. But then, there were others that were not at all light or funny. One morning as I sat at the computer composing an email to my older brother who hadn't spoken to me in ten years explaining why Mom was refusing further treatments, I heard her out on the patio fussing at her cat Sophie for harassing her precious birds. I don't know what it was about that moment. Maybe it was knowing that soon poor, innocent, unsuspecting Sophie would never hear that scolding little voice again or get her food heated up in the microwave and delivered to her like she was a cat in pharaoh's court. Or maybe it was knowing that I too would never hear her melodic southern twang on my answering machine. (Oh God, why didn't I save at least one of those messages?), would never again talk to her on the phone about the birds visiting her feeder. Or maybe it was the terrible finality of it all that crushed me under the weight of unbearable grief, even as it does now, all this time later. I got up from the computer, went outside, sat down next to her, took her small hand in mine and croaked through my tears, "You know, this is the last time we'll be together." She looked me dead in the eye and without any hint of emotion said, "I know. I've thought about that."

That cold, calculated response and the news that she had all but eliminated me from her will was perhaps her way of saying, even unconsciously, how she really felt about me as Meredith. If I had continued pretending to be her dutiful son, I have no doubt it would have been different, and I was reminded once again of what it has cost to just be me.

I went to help Mom navigate the final passage of her life, but as it turned out, she didn't need my help. She made her way across on her own. She died just the way she lived: with stoic forthrightness and calm resolution.

After she was gone, a friend and I rode her horses out the same trail where I had some three weeks earlier done the preparation ritual with Strider and Jan. As we rode along the cliff several stories above the ocean, the morning fog wafted lazily above us in patches, riding an imperceptible breeze. Only the emerald waves split the uncommon stillness with their clean, rhythmic assault on the virginous sand.

In these circumstances, a horse is a wonderful – if not somewhat irreverent – metaphor for God. He willingly bears us upon his strong back sure-footedly mounting the obstacles, finding The Way through the tangled thickets of our unruly thoughts and emotions, carrying us back to the primordial soup from which He originally lured all life where we might stand before Life's greatest final mystery and be reminded of what we would like to forget – that there is no path that does not lead to this place. Those who go before us give to us a parting gift in calling us here; for it is in their footsteps that we follow. Making the long, painful journey to the edge of that Mystery helps prepare us for that day when we too must step across the dreaded threshold between this life and whatever is next. In my sorrow, I was grateful to Mom yet again.

There were only a few tears this time, and as I stood looking out over the ocean toward a horizon hidden in the blanket of concealing fog, I said my final good-bye. In the billowing grayness, I felt like I could see her, young and strong and beautiful, laughing and smiling as if in reunion with old friends I could not see. In my imagination, she turned toward me and said, *I love you*, and with that, she was gone. It is a sad and jubilant final image of her that has returned many times. May it always be so.

I didn't go back to the old Mississippi home for her internment next to Dad. It bothers me how my absence might have been interpreted – that there was something wrong with me, that I no longer belong even to my family, that I was too embarrassed or ashamed to be seen. It especially irked me that my older brother probably felt vindicated in his rejection. After all, Marsha, my ex-wife was there, so where was the queer? Back in California where it belonged with the fags and the dykes, back in Sodom and Gomorrah.

As it was, on the day and at the time when Mom's body was being buried, I was speaking to a class at the junior college. It's the fourth year I've spoken to this class about racism and homophobia (transphobia in my case). Having grown up trans in Mississippi during the Civil Rights struggle, I am uniquely qualified to address these topics. Given what happened in the class, it seems to me I was where I needed to be, otherwise, I wouldn't have heard what a student said.

At the end of my hour-long presentation, the teacher went around the circle and had each student report something they had gotten from my talk. A tall, handsome young man smiled and said, "I was on the high school basketball and track teams, and you were sometimes our bus driver. We always loved it when you drove. We all knew (meaning that they all knew I was transsexual), but I swear no one ever ripped on you. I promise they didn't," he repeated, as if even he too found this a bit incredulous.

His words reminded me of what I already knew: that my very presence in these kid's lives – even as a lowly bus driver – was making an important statement. That just by showing up, I was educating them, that by being out and visible in all my queer glory, I was possibly making it a little easier and safer for some gay or transgender teen to be who God in his glory and infinite good humor made them to be. I hope so, because that would make it worth the cost.

The Adder's Elixir

In a *New Yorker* cartoon two bearded, robed men are on a road. One has a walking staff and is following an arrow pointing the way to "TRUTH." The other is sitting beside the road with several jugs of rot-gut marked XX and XXX. The one with the jugs of whiskey says to the one following the way to Truth, "I'll be here on your way back."

As best I could discern it, I had followed the way of Truth. I had put aside my perfidious, though highly successful impersonation of a man, come out of the closet, and begun to live my life as the person I had been created to be, and where had it gotten me? Stuck driving a school bus, bored out of my mind, frustrated, angry, lonely and depressed. My children were grown, my students were gone, the horses were gone, sex was gone, the marriage...well, not gone but going, and as a writer, I was a complete failure. To the problems of no passion, no meaning, no excitement, no sex, no reason to keep on living, I found a quick and easy solution: alcohol. It was fun in a bottle; and it *was* fun. For about six years, drinking became the one thing I looked forward to, the one thing I could count on to give me a couple of hours of happiness at the end of an otherwise unbearable day.

I figure it was inevitable. I was a writer, after all; being a drunk was part of the *noblesse oblige* of the profession. I also came from a long line of notorious drunks; it was a family tradition. On top of that I was a queer. Alcohol abuse is rampant in the queer community, and I wasn't just your run of the mill gay queer; I was a trannie, a queer among queers. I wasn't just destined; I was entitled.

In the days before Jodi came along, alcohol also magically restored Jan's and my relationship. Drinking together we felt giddy and sexy and close again. We giggled and joked and teased and roughhoused like a couple of horny teenagers. After that first brandybeer, I felt good for the first time all day. By the second, I was feeling no pain.

It wasn't joy; I knew that. It wasn't even real happiness. Drinking didn't restore meaning or purpose to my life. But meaning and purpose were nothing more than painful memories now, empty places that alcohol filled like a rattlesnake coiling itself into the empty, abandoned den of a family of field mice it has consumed.

Alcohol occupied that place in me where once a thriving colony of children had lived. It made a home inside me, and every evening at about five, its fangs would begin to drip their terrible and wonderful venom that made me feel so good.

Of course, I didn't plan on becoming addicted. Such a thing never occurred to me, though why it didn't I can't imagine now. As I said, alcoholism was rife in my family. My grandfather had abandoned his family when Dad was still in high school. Having seen firsthand the devastating effects of alcoholism, Dad never had so much as a drop of liquor in our house when I was growing up. Consequently, I never had any experience with alcohol, so when I became a liberal, free thinking, enlightened adult, I chalked my parents' abstinence up to their being old-fashioned, Baptist teetotalers. Since I did not subscribe to their version of fundamentalist religion, I saw no reason to abstain from an occasional drink.

For many years I drank moderately or not at all. When the kids came along, I learned quickly that even one beer sent my patience, never abundant, in the wrong direction, so I never touched it when they were around. That's why when they started to drink at an early age, I wasn't overly concerned. Oh sure, I thought, they'll experiment, but eventually, they'll grow out of it and be the wiser. This turned out to be true, though not without some harrowingly close calls that had I known about at the time, would have made me think twice about my laissez-faire attitude toward alcohol.

Even at its worst, my drinking never got completely out of control. I never drove after I started drinking; though I drove hung-over plenty of times. I never drank during the day. During the day I planned. I timed my eating, so that by the time my afternoon run was over, my stomach would be empty and ready to receive the full effect of the adder's elixir.

I wasn't an addict, though; or so I told myself, and to demonstrate that, I'd come home and before I had anything to drink, I'd do whatever chores needed to be done. Animals would be fed (though not cared for), garbage taken out, supper hastily started; sometimes I'd wait a full hour before I made my first brandybeer. After that, it was all downhill.

Eventually, I'd eat, though the next morning I could never remember what. We'd put on a movie, which I also could never remember the next day, during which I'd pass out on the couch. At about eight, Jan, who never drank as heavily as I did, would wake me up. I'd floss and brush my teeth, and fall into bed where I'd be asleep almost before my head hit the pillow. I'd wake up the next morning at 4:30 feeling like shit and resolve that tonight I wouldn't drink. I'd get myself ready, go to work and by the time my afternoon run was over, I'd be right back where I had been 24 hours earlier. I did that for about six years, three of which I was actively trying to stop on my own.

In time, I managed to get the drinking down. Sometimes I'd go for days, maybe even a week without a drink, which I'd take as evidence that I was finally back in control. Under the sway of this illusion, I'd "pick up" again, as they say in AA, and the cycle would begin all over.

About the time I had really begun to make some headway toward defeating the addiction on my own, I had this dream:

I have just gotten out of this yucky swimming pool full of green algae, when I notice that I have a large grasshopper and two worm-like creatures with sharp claws attached to my right thumb. They don't really bother me, but when I try to remove one, its grip tightens painfully. In a mild panic, I grab it, and to my horror, it begins to burrow under my skin. I try to grab it, but it manages to disappear under the skin of my thumb. Frantically, I grasp it underneath the skin and start squeezing. I manage to pop it and squeeze its squashed body out the hole where it entered. The other one is still attached firmly to my thumb, so I decide to go to the hospital for help getting it off.

It was one of the creepiest dreams I have ever had, and instantly, I knew it was about my addiction. I kept trying to get rid of it myself – with some success – but as I did so, it attached itself even more firmly, worming its way under my skin. The meaning of the dream was clear: I needed help.

Where do you go to get help with alcoholism? The only place I knew was Alcoholics Anonymous, so I went online and found a schedule of meetings in Petaluma.

Oh God, I didn't want to go. I was doing so good quitting on my own, did I really need to do this? It was just a dream, after all.

The morning before the noon meeting that I had decided to attend, I began negotiating with myself: "If I get drunk again, I'll go to AA," I resolved.

Having made this reasonable sounding decision, I heard a calm, confident voice reply "Okay. You've said that before, but go ahead; that's fine; you already know what's going to happen. You're just delaying it."

"Shit!" I responded. The truth was patently clear. I knew what I had to do; so, sick at the thought of it, I attended the noon meeting of Alcoholics Anonymous at the Alano Club.

I walked in knowing virtually nothing. Could you just walk into a meeting? Did you need to talk to someone first? Get permission? Be screened? I found someone who looked like they were in charge and asked, "Are you in charge?"

A dapper man with graying hair and a thin mustache looked at me suspiciously and replied, "I'm the moderator for this meeting."

"Well, is it okay if I attend?" I asked tremulously.

"Well, yes, this is an open meeting." he replied coolly. "Are you a visitor?"

"No," I answered in surprise. "I'm an alcoholic."

His face lit up like a ray of sun had just found its way through a window and lit on him. "Oh!" he exclaimed. He reached out and eagerly took my hand. "I'm Scott, and I'm an alcoholic," he effused.

"Hi, my name's Meredith," I supplied. I almost added, "and I'm an alcoholic," since I knew that's what they said in AA, but I left that out, since that's what I'd just told him.

"Yes, of course you can come. Have a seat."

And so I attended my first meeting of AA.

As I rushed out early to get back in time for my afternoon run, I was intercepted by several people who interpreted my hasty departure as me making a run for it. One gave me the *Big Book of Alcoholics Anonymous,* and in it several people wrote their names and numbers for me to call if I needed help. I was moved to tears.

During the first few months, I attended the noon meeting several times a week. It was fascinating, though attendance did not diminish my desire to drink as I hoped and as they claimed. I did, however, add to the strategies I had already come up with to keep from drinking when the witching hour of 5:00 rolled around.

Much of what I heard at the meetings and read in the *Big Book* didn't really apply to me; for instance I was never a social drinker. In fact, being with other people was one of the few times I didn't over drink. Even on weekends and holidays, I didn't drink during the day. Compared to the stories I read and heard, I wondered if the little I consumed even counted. Would they throw me out if they found out what a lightweight I was? No one ever asked, and I didn't tell. It didn't matter, anyway; I was an alcoholic, and I knew it.

It also didn't matter how little I drank, because with an active case of Hepatitis B, any alcohol was too much alcohol. I think I picked up HBV back in grad school when I was exploring the possibility that I was gay. Considering the time and the person with whom I was doing this exploring, I'm lucky I didn't end up with AIDS. Still, having HBV from such a young age makes me a good candidate for liver cancer, even without the alcohol.

What surprised me was the religious part of AA. Not that there *was* a religious part; I knew that, and I had no problem with it. I just didn't expect people to be so serious about it – and so open. Virtually all my friends were liberals. They might talk about "spiritual" things but rarely did they use the "G" word, and then, they usually referred to God as "The Divine." It is, after all, so much more tasteful. Plus, all the liberals I knew were professionals; they were at the top of society's food chain. For them, God was optional, icing on the cake, tasteful decoration, bling.

Not so with the people in Alcoholics Anonymous. They had seen their lives go to shit, and even if they had managed to claw their way back up the social food chain, they were never the same again. They could not and did not want to forget where they had been and what they had done, and who they had become. Time and time again, I heard guys, and I'm talking about manly guys, tough guys, guys big enough to pick me up and break me in two like a stick, praise and credit God with saving them from a life of wretchedness, despair, debauchery, and death. And there was no ambivalence, no equivocation, no disclaimers, no euphemisms – God, the Almighty, Creator of heaven and earth, had saved them. Hallelujah! Praise be! It was downright refreshing.

The theology – when I bothered to notice – was usually simplistic, even pietistic; yet it seemed remarkably functional despite that. I hadn't realized what a privileged lot I hung out with until I started attending AA, and I felt a kind of kinship with them that was only partly due to my drinking problem. They had become outsiders in their own way. They had made choices, though different in kind and quality from mine, which cost them just as dearly. They had been beaten, had failed, had lost almost everything and everybody, and then they had fought their way back, but not to where they had been before, and not unchanged or unscathed. They were different people, like me, and like me, they could never go back. And through it all, they counted themselves better for it. Though still screwed up, they had reached beyond themselves, had been touched by something – or Someone – and had been transformed by it into a terrible and wondrous likeness of...well, "The Divine." In AA, I found a spiritual community that finally felt real.

Speakers would time and again exhort we new comers to "do the program," which meant to get a sponsor and submit one's self entirely to his or her direction. But by then, I had begun to write again. I wasn't willing to turn over what little time I had to write to someone who would most likely want me to attend meetings, do service work and report in regularly.

If plotted on a graph, my recovery would not have been a straight line that went invariably onward and upward. I relapsed. After a period of sobriety, I'd tell myself that I could drink moderately; that there was no reason to be a fundamentalist about this, and so, I'd "pick back up." As an alcoholic, I, of course, never had "a" drink. I would have at least two, or whatever it took to get me high, and then, I'd always want more, though I wouldn't always have more. Sometimes the craving would roll over my resistance like a bulldozer rolls over a daffodil, especially if I'd had a really bad day, or a really good day, or if it was Friday and virtually everybody I knew was going home to toast the blessed weekend with a drink.

The worst part of this was that once I "picked up" again, I was invariable drawn back into conversation with my inner alcoholic. "Wow, that was fun last night," she'd observe cheerily. "And we didn't drink too much, did we? Just a couple of glasses of wine, that's all. That's well within the range of what's acceptable. Maybe tonight on the way home, you could pick up another bottle. Just one. Don't get any more," she would caution, as if my well-being was her sole concern, "that way you won't be tempted."

If I gave in to this, once in the wine aisle, she'd invariably point out – always in feigned surprise, "Wow, look at how much cheaper those big bottles of wine are. They could last for a couple of nights at least. And man, look at that brandy. Doesn't that brandy look good? You know, if you have the brandy with water, it doesn't taste so good; that way you won't be tempted to drink too much, plus the water keeps you hydrated so you don't get such a bad hangover. And it's cheaper than the wine; more bang for the buck, you know." Oh, she was a veritable fountain of information once she got going and so *reasonable* and *persuasive*. It got tiring. I had better things to do than have long conversations with my inner addict, and if I gave that girl an ounce, she would invariable want the bottle. It was just easier to quit.

I still regret not getting a sponsor, since doing "the program" was a prerequisite for moderating a meeting, and

I think it would have been cool to have had a transsexual lead an AA meeting.

Eventually I quit going to meetings so I could spend every available minute writing. I miss it, though. I miss the people. I miss the stories that so often moved me to tears. I miss being part of something real, something dirty and soiled and bloody with the struggle and sorrow of life; yet also, so full of redemption and hope. It was a community worthy of the name, clear about its mission and committed without ambivalence or equivocation to recovery. That is so rare now in a world where nothing is ever definite, where all statements must conform to the prevailing views of political correctness, and where the one commitment we can unequivocally make that will never subject us to error or offense is to never make an unequivocal commitment.

I love having my life back now, my evenings back. I could regret all the time I lost, time in which I might have been writing, or all the money I spent. Strangely, though, I don't. I feel like alcoholism and AA were places I needed to go, steps on the journey. Being an alcoholic and being part of AA allowed me to finally let go of the sad old need to "make something of myself." Adding "alcoholic" to the list of other disappointments and failures finally made it possible for me to lay that burden down; add it to the altar piled so high with broken dreams and abject failures, and in so doing, finally find some rest for my soul.

Never a Woman

Through it all remained the haunting suspicion that when all was said and done, I would never be a woman – *could* never be a woman. People could address me as a woman, accept me as a woman, welcome me into their company as a woman. I could dress like a woman, style my hair like a woman, wear makeup, alter my voice, change my mannerisms and it wouldn't matter; I would never be a woman, not really.

Sometimes this doubt would morph into a terrible fear. What if this had all been a terrible mistake? What if it *was* some sort of fetish or sexual compulsion that had gotten completely out of hand? What if this life-long desire to be a woman was due to some childhood trauma that had I taken the time and trouble to work through might have dissipated, leaving me free to live a normal, successful, happy life as a man? What if it was some insane, twisted attempt to win the love and affection of my father who had always wanted a daughter? What if…What if…

When thus assailed, I would suspect that my doubts about ever being a woman were due to persistent shame. After all, I didn't deserve to be a woman; hadn't earned it, hadn't won it fair and square. I was unworthy, unfit, unqualified. Maybe it had something to do with never having had sex reassignment surgery. How can you ever live comfortably and confidently as a woman with a penis? How can you ever hope to be fully free of shame?

Usually when I was just out there living life as it had to be lived, I thought little or nothing of it. Then someone would refer to me as "she" or "her", and it would be there again, winking at me, as if to say, "You didn't deserve that." Though I loved that they referred to me that way, because I suspected I didn't deserve it, I could never completely take it in. It was like getting gifts of fine chocolate that, much as I wanted to, I couldn't give myself permission to eat.

If a male stranger greeted me as a woman or opened a door for me or performed some small, chivalrous act, I would feel an initial rush of glee, and in that split second between happiness and the fear of being read, I would taste it, taste the sweet richness of being the woman I knew myself to be, yet could not be.

When someone who knew me performed such an act, I would always feel a mixture of surprise, delight, and something between embarrassment and gratitude. They didn't have to; I didn't expect them to; I didn't deserve it; and yet, they did it all the same. It must be similar to what an abused person feels at every unexpected act of kindness.

Yet nothing I told myself, no amount of acceptance from others, nothing I did to try and improve my presentation as a woman, made the nagging doubt go away. *You aren't really a woman*, a voice would suspire like the fabled serpent in the garden, *and you never will be*.

As Jodi's daughter, Phoebe, approached thirteen, Jodi said she was thinking about getting together a group of woman to go away with Phoebe for some sort of ritual welcoming her into womanhood. In the telling of it to me, it was clear that she included me in this company of women. I just smiled, looked down, and shook my head. "Surely you're not still questioning if you qualify," she asked with mild incredulity.

In Wendell Berry's novel, *The Memories of Old Jack*, there is a scene in which several of the women have gathered at the Feltner place to prepare the noon meal for the men who are out harvesting the tobacco. Old Jack, who is increasingly lost in his memories and therefore, absent from the present, has been invited to the meal. When he fails to show up, Hannah Coulter, who is pregnant with her third child, volunteers to walk into town and get him.

She finds him in Jayber's barber shop, and as they walk back arm in arm, she revels in the vision of herself in his eyes. "She is sturdily accompanied by his knowledge that she is whole. In his gaze she feels herself to be, not just physically, but historically a woman; one among generations bearing into mystery the dark seed. She feels herself completed by that, as she could not be completed by the desire of a younger man."

When I read these words, it was like finally understanding the lyrics of a song I'd been hearing from childhood. Nothing I could ever do, and nothing anyone else could do would make it possible for me to be a woman historically. I could never be "one among generations bearing into mystery the dark seed." This is what I always knew, though vaguely, inchoately: I could no more be a woman than I could change history.

From birth we are forced to find our place in the binary – and most do. We are either male *or* female, boy *or* girl, man *or* woman. If we have the temerity to question or resist, we are pressured, lectured, taunted, teased, humiliated, threatened, and eventually tortured into compliance. Yet, as it turns out (and as we should have known it would turn out given the predictably unpredictable nature of Nature) the binaries of sex and gender are about as stable, predictable, dependable and enforceable as the binaries of right and wrong, good and bad.

But if I did not belong historically to the generations of women, to whom *did* I belong? Not men; that was for sure. Not even gay men or lesbians, who were, after all, still as solidly part of the binary as their straight counterparts, sans the rights. Did I then, as I so often felt, belong nowhere and to no one? Just as there was no pronoun for me, was there likewise no place where I belonged, no community, no family, no fellowship?

The poet Adrienne Rich says, "When someone with authority describes the world and you are not in it, there is a moment of psychic disequilibrium, as if you looked into a mirror and saw nothing." We can leave people like me out of history just like we left out – and in many places, still *are* leaving out – gay and lesbian people. In so doing we can preserve the narrative of the status quo with its illusion of binary stability, but it will not make us go away. All it will do is exclude, stigmatize and torture innocent people, until one day we wake up to discover that among the outcast is someone we love.

Nor will it do to make exceptions. It's easy to accept the transgender media darlings, since they conform in virtually every way to society's idealized images of what it means to be a woman or what it means to be a man. If you look the part and sound the part and play the part, society will make an exception for you. They'll even hold you up as a poster child to their tolerance, since everybody loves a beautiful poster child, and all the more so if she – or he – is sexy.

Nor, I fear, will it do to *be* an exception. Coming out early enough in life, makes it possible to delay the onset of puberty until a person is old enough to fully transition, making them almost completely unreadable. The same is true for most female-to-male transsexuals once they begin taking testosterone. I worked for a year with an FTM and never recognized him as trans until he finally came out to me. While these people have little or no trouble successfully fitting into the binary, I'm not so sure it's going to work for them. While yes, they will see in the pages of history an external manifestation of themselves, internally, they will know differently; they will know themselves to be exceptions. This conflict between external acceptance and internal awareness will, I fear, in time, become intolerable and unworkable.

Of course, I *do* belong to a history and to a lineage of people. They once lived among and had a place within the societies of the continent's indigenous inhabitants. Sometimes they were called two-spirits. Most were destroyed by a culture that did not and does not recognize or value them. Those who managed to survive did so by becoming invisible. They do not exist in the pages of history. In the mirror of time, they are but shadows. From this lineage and from this history, I am therefore separated by vast time and space. While I am glad to belong to this heritage, this people – even proud – it grieves me and it has damaged me that I am thus separated from the generations of my kind, bearing into mystery the dark seed of our being, our knowing, our wisdom.

Now I have become an elder, though to whom I do not know. I know other transsexuals, of course, but all of them seem as committed to the binary as those lucky enough to be born into its conformity. Most are doing their best to pass as one or the other, and the young are enjoying a level of success I could scarcely imagine.

With this knowledge, not entirely new but newly known, I went back in my imagination to the gathering of women who might prepare Phoebe for her womanhood. The image made me smile, for I did have a place there, though, again, not the place of a woman. As women, they could offer her instruction in things I knew only second hand, things they knew by the experience and the bond of generations of women; things I had, at best, merely observed or read about.

Yet, I had things to offer her, too. I certainly had a perspective on men that her other counselors would not, the main one being a greater sympathy. While I was intimately aware of men's tendency to think with their reproductive appendage, I also knew what it felt like to be a horny young buck running hard on high octane testosterone. It's like having a locomotive in your loins, and while I do not suggest that this should be an excuse for bad behavior, it should stir in a girl, if not sympathy, then a healthy dose of fear.

But the main contribution I would bring to her out of the legacy of my life and my kind would be that she hold lightly and view skeptically society's fidelity to the fixed. Just when you think you've got it figured out, when it all seems in order and put away neat, that's when Nature or God or your best friend or your partner or your child or even your own self will throw you a curve ball the likes of which you have never seen. I knew a minister who liked to say "God's middle name is Surprise." Life is never orderly or predictable or manageable (despite your mother's most valiant attempts to make it so); it's always free. If you wish to live in harmony with Life, you should strive to be the same.

In fact, view with the greatest suspicion that which the society holds most sacred. Short of a miracle, this will always be the best policy.

Finding, embracing and living your True Self – the self you were fashioned in the loving heart and hand and mind of God to be – is the real work of your lifetime; there really is no other work. Though many other things will occupy you, many of which will be worthy, they will all in time work together for the glory of your unique unfolding.

There are impediments to the liberation of your True Self, and these will test you; some will bruise you; others will wound you; a few will break you. But as the poet, Mr. Berry, says, "it is the impeded stream that sings." If freedom isn't free, the blood that is shed in the liberation of your True Self will most often be your own – except when it is the blood of those you hold most dear.

Don't be fooled; being put on a pedestal, however ornate, only makes you a better target. Don't accept it however generous it might seem or good it might feel.

Always insist on being your own flesh and blood human person, standing gladly on feet of clay.

Though you must define yourself in relation to others, never let others define you for yourself.

Find a people you can make your own; a fellowship of belonging, especially with other women, and when you find it, count it more precious than gold. In like manner, find a place on earth in which you can labor and to which you can be faithful; for in the end, what matters most is that which we have served.

Try your best to find a man who is your equal. Don't settle for too little no matter how pretty he is and how much in need of your saving graces.

On these matters, I speak with the authority of age and as one who has suffered, and yet, has endured – perhaps, even thrived.

And while I am at it, and since I am one in whom both male and female live, to Griffin I offer these words:

If a woman offers you her love on the condition of your improvement, run away, for you are destined to be the fulfillment of her disappointment.

Never seek power. Accept power only in the knowledge that it is love's opposite; that with an increase in power comes the diminution of love.

Just because you don't have a womb, does not mean you cannot create life. Just because you cannot suckle, does not mean you cannot nurture. To create and nurture is just as much your right – and your responsibility – as it is a woman's.

Cultivate the warm camaraderie of men. Insist on it if you must. It will be your refuge.

Marrying the woman you fall in lust with (though you will not call it that) will be to build a marriage on the terms of your ruin. Every man wants the princess – until he has her.

You do not exist to make money and provide for your family. You exist to become your True Self. In faithfulness to this, you will be faithful to all.

The Man in my Life

I am blessed to live 45 minutes away from one of the most beautiful places on earth, Point Reyes National Seashore. For some twenty years, I have hiked and ridden the trails of Point Reyes, so I know the park intimately and love it dearly. While I can still hike – and do – after ours were gone, I missed being out on the trails with a horse; so when I found out I could volunteer in the park, I contacted Harold, the manager of the Morgan Horse Ranch, to see if I could volunteer there. After checking me out and determining that I knew my way around a horse and had some skill at managing the beast, Harold bestowed upon me a shirt and cap emblazoned with the National Park Service volunteer emblem and sent me out to muck.

I never minded mucking. Unlike the shit you get from your boss or your spouse or your parents or your children, horse shit is just plain, old, ordinary shit. It doesn't even stink. I especially enjoyed mucking surrounded by such natural beauty, alone with my thoughts and in the excellent company of horses. As a volunteer, I mucked all year round and in all conditions, in heat that drenched my shirt and stained my cap with sweat, in the cool, damp cocoon of fog and even in the rain, the wind lashing my face and assaulting my duster, seeking out the seams through which it would eventually seep, driving me for refuge into the fragrant barn with the horses and hay.

I saw wonderful things out mucking, some no less magical for being so ordinary: the aerial acrobatics of mating hawks, their cries ringing out over the valley, the frolicking of young deer, the raucous laughter of acorn woodpeckers. One morning I saw two bobcats in a dramatic territorial standoff in the dead tree pasture. I saw a badger sitting on the edge of his cavernous den, belligerently staring at me, as if daring me to throw manure down his carefully excavated front door. I saw the bloody remains of a recently killed deer, but killed by what? A bobcat? Are bobcats big enough to bring down an adult deer? Or could it have been a lion? And if so, was it lying there in the poison oak thicket, eyeing me as I examined the leftovers of its supper, armed only with a mucking rake?

I got to go out alone on horseback, patrolling the trails that wound through dense forests of towering firs, majestic bays, oaks, maples and some of the largest alders I have ever seen. Allowing my horse to graze, I would pick berries in their season, salmon berries, service berries, huckleberries, and if I was lucky enough to score one, native blackberries, small but incredibly sweet. I assisted visitors who were lost, called in on my two-way radio if they had questions I couldn't answer or if they needed assistance. I cleared trails and picked up trash. All with a beautiful, well trained horse that I didn't have to feed, shoe or pay vet bills for.

Because I enjoy work for its own sake, before long I had established myself as a regular ranch hand. After several months of going out almost every Saturday, when a new fence had to be built, I eagerly agreed to help.

The winter came early that year with drenching rains that rendered the ground unsuitable for the use of a tractor – not that Harold had much use for tractors. He sent two other volunteers and me out to dig post holes the old fashioned way – with posthole diggers.

Digging a hole with a posthole digger is hard enough in the best of conditions. In an almost constant drizzle, clad in cumbersome rain gear, it was especially tough. The rain also rendered the clay through which we were digging heavy, wet and sticky, so that it clung to the metal blades of our diggers like dirty taffy. Once we lifted the goop out of the ground, we then had to bang it several times on an old post laid on the ground to dislodge it, thereby forcing us to lift the clay not just once but several times. It was grueling physical labor, some of the hardest I have ever done.

At the end of one of those days, trudging back across the pasture between the curious horses, aching from head to toe, a post hole digger over one shoulder, a heavy, steel digging bar in the other hand, my boots soaked, my leather work chaps covered with mud, my volunteer shirt filthy, my gloves sodden, my hair dripping, it came to me that I was completely happy. In fact, had I not hurt so bad, I'd have been downright blissful. I had to laugh. All those years I had longed to be a Victoria's Secret model, and here I was in love with a version of me that fully embraced the man in my life. Who would have thunk it? And with that, another gear dropped into place, and I was finally at home in my own skin.

Choosing a Name

For some reason, I, rather than my older brother, Richard, was named after my father, making me Henry Grady Guest, III. Since Richard was rightfully due it by virtue of being the first-born son, I don't think he ever forgave me; though I, of course, had no say in the matter; and had I, it would have been the last name in the world I would have chosen. Since Dad was called Henry or H.G., they called me Hank. I never liked the name. It wasn't me. I'd have preferred something like Sam, since I could have at least imagined that it was short for Samantha. Even Bobby could be a girl's name, but Hank was a guy's name through and through.

Like a lot of transfolk, I first explored names that sounded a little like Hank. Hannah was one such name, and I liked it. If you ever have a trans friend or family member, one of the best things you can do for them is help them find the right name. It's hard to know if a name's going to work until you've heard someone else use it on you, and even then, you usually have to hear it more than once and wear it around for a while like a new pair of shoes.

A name has to fit, and not just for you. It also needs to fit for the people with whom you share your life. Kimmie Sue may be a perfectly wonderful name to your way of thinking, but you don't want to suffer the sight of people almost choking every time they try to call you that.

Most transsexuals start off being very self-conscious about their name. In many ways your name is like your face; it's how people know you; it's how they recognize you. It's who you are to them, and so it's hard to ask them to call you something different. Your new name will *re*-define you and not just in the minds of others – in your own as well. Meredith not only feels like who I *am* now; it feels like who I always was. It's even hard to remember that people once called me something else.

As it became obvious that I was actually going to go through with this, I began to search in earnest for a name that both fit me and had meaning. Since I knew this would be hardest on my family, especially my mother who must have had some part in choosing the old name I was about to discard, I turned over a few family stones, and that's where I found it. My dad, who had been dead for many years by this time, had some cousins who were farmers in Mississippi. I never knew them very well, and from something Mom said, I don't think he liked them a lot. Their last name was Meredith, and I immediately liked it. I liked that the Meredith's were people of the land, because that's how I saw myself, as a person of the land. I liked the sound of it, the way it rolled off the tongue. By choosing Meredith as my name, I also chose to identify with my family of origin. It was a way of saying, you might reject me, but I want it known that I am not rejecting you.

Meredith is not a perfect name for an MTF. It's not like Sue or Annie or Lisa, which are unambiguously female. Meredith is androgynous, so it doesn't automatically identify me as a woman. It's also sort of long, so it's a lot to ask people to say, though I love the shortened form of it that my kids came up with – Mer. There's something intimate about it, and it's often interesting who uses the shortened form and who doesn't. Another drawback to Meredith is that it's almost impossible for my Spanish-speaking friends to say. But the version they eventually come up with, the way they bend and fold the syllables is truly endearing and adorable. So in choosing Meredith I got to declare my allegiance to my family, identify myself in an important way and have a name that embraced both masculine and feminine. Pretty good for a name.

What It Means

Depending on the source and era of your information, as well as the generosity of your spirit, you might think of me in one of several ways.

You might consider me living proof that God does have a sense of humor – and a wicked one at that. My personal favorite.

Since the belief that a person's sex determines their gender is nothing short of canonical, most people see male-to-female transsexuals as men who want to be women. For much of my life, this is also the way I saw it; I was a boy who wanted to be a girl. This is understandable, since it's virtually impossible to recognize that a belief so fundamental to everyone's way of thinking as the alignment of sex and gender is an assumption rather than an undeniable, irrefutable, incontrovertible, capital "T" Truth. That's why nothing I did stopped me from wanting to be a woman, because the assumption that, because I was male, I was also a man was fundamentally flawed. It was flawed in precisely the same way, prior to Copernicus, astronomers were unable to explain the strange movements of the planets, because their fundamental, commonly held, intuitively reasonable, incontrovertible belief that the earth was the center of the universe was actually an assumption, which, as it turns out, was wrong.

Even the psychiatric community falls victim to the assumption when it labels me a man with Gender Identity Dysphoria (GID). But I am not a man with a psychological problem; I am a woman with a physical problem, and eventually, I got to the place where I could no longer stand living a lie. (Of course, it didn't help that I did such a stellar impersonation of a man. I should get the Oscar for Best Actress Playing a Male Lead, though, come to think of it, I don't think there is such an award. Pity.)

Besides growing up doing all the boy things, further evidence of my manliness was the kind of relationships I had with men. When I lived at Dayspring, I had several particularly close friendships with men, one of whom rented a room in a house just up the road from me. Paul was an avid outdoorsman, who, like me, found solace in field, forest and moving water, but, unlike me, was a serious hunter and fisherman. He could tie a trout fly that – I swear – was about three molecules big, and then with great skill and precision, deliver it like a tasty hors d'oeuvre to some wily trout in Big Hunting Creek.

Meanwhile, a safe distance upstream so as not to endanger other terrestrial life forms, I was wildly flailing about with my fly rod armed with a wooly bugger I had managed to piece together that was so bulky when it invariably caught me in the back of my head on the forecast, I risked giving myself a concussion. You could almost hear fish guffaws whenever my fly smacked the water with the ease and grace of a cannonball, which was not really as often as you might suppose, since I had an uncanny knack at hooking trees, bushes, sticks, logs, rocks and, with alarming frequency, myself.

Despite the difference in age and skill, ours was a quick and easy friendship, the kind I think men are particularly good at forming with one another. It's not just that Paul and I did classically manly things like canoe, camp, hunt and fish with one another, it's that we did them so easily and naturally. It was camaraderie, what my dictionary tells me is the kind of friendship usually enjoyed between men, though, interestingly enough, the origin of the word is feminine.

Virtually every summer we would spend several days canoeing and fishing on the Shenandoah River in West Virginia where we sometimes caught so many fish we got tired of reeling them in. We'd keep only enough for the evening meal while the rest we allowed to slip off our debarbed hooks with only so much as a moment's grateful admiration.

If the summer sun got too hot, we'd just roll out of the canoe into the river's cool embrace. Even though Paul was a dozen years my junior, he was far more knowledgeable about the outdoors than me. We'd spy some rather small, seemingly unremarkable bird on the river's bank and after a few seconds of careful observation, Paul would pronounce it a Louisiana water thrush or some such thing, an identification Mr. Audubon's field guide would invariably confirm. Outfitted with goggles and snorkel, Paul would crawl around for half an hour in two-foot deep water carefully turning over one stone after another examining the miniscule creatures living beneath them.

We had this one particularly silly thing we did; it's embarrassing to mention, really. Paul, again like me, went through a period of fundamentalist fervor in his early 20s. He accepted Jesus into his heart, received the gift of tongues, praised the Lord, cast out the Devil, and memorized the Roman Road to Salvation – the whole nine yards. Fortunately, he got over it before committing nearly as many atrocities as I did during my similar flirtation with theocratic insanity. In long, calm stretches of the river when we tired of catching fish, we'd do a raucous and irreverent impersonation of my favorite evangelist, Rev. Rectal Roberts, the imaginary brother of Oral Roberts – the actual name of a traveling revival preacher popular in Mississippi during my teens.

As the figment of my rather sick imagination, Rectal, without warning, would call out, "Brotha Paul, I feel the Spirit movin' me," whereupon Rectal would thrust his open hand skyward as if ready to catch a fly ball from heaven.

"Hallelujah, Praise the Lord," Paul would shout back, never breaking the rhythm of his cast and retrieve.

"Yes, Brotha Paul, I feel it movin' deep down inside me like a mighty wind."

"Preach on, Brotha!"

"Whatcha gotta do when the Spirit calls?"

"Ya gotta shout!" Paul would yell, scaring up shore birds on either bank of the broad river.

"Yes indeed, and sometimes, Brotha Paul, ya gotta shit. I'm headin' toward yonder bank, cause I got ta cast out a demon."

Whereupon we'd canoe to the bank, I'd find a suitably private spot, preferably with some large sycamore leaves handy and proceed to…well, shit.

Stupid, I know, and puerile in just the sort of way you'd expect from a couple of guys out fishing, and to make matters worse, we were stone cold sober. We never took so much as a can of beer on those trips, which, I suppose looking back, wasn't very manly of us, but Paul, to my knowledge, never touched a drop of liquor.

What I'm saying is that, in addition to everything else, I had these wonderful relationships with men as a man. And it's not like I was faking it either, not like I consciously thought, "Gee golly, I'd better act like a man or else people are going to catch on." No, it was all very genuine and very dear and very sweet. Nor was Paul the only man with whom I had a similarly close friendship; his was just the most emblematically male and why it's so damn confusing to everyone – even me at times – when I claim that I was never a man.

Still, I think several justifications can be offered as to why I engaged in shamelessly male behavior and enjoyed the camaraderie of men most women are denied. First, you have to remember that I was raised almost exclusively in the company of men, and not just any men – southern men! This, in and of itself, should absolve me of a multitude of sins. You wouldn't expect a child raised by baboons not to act a bit apish, would you?

Also, as much as I loved my men friends and enjoyed our unique camaraderie, it was in the company of women that I felt most at home; it was in the company of women, I felt like I was amongst my kin and kind. It's a bit like living in the country versus living in the city.

When I worked at the coffee shop in San Francisco's Castro's district during the first year or so after I came out, the Castro was the only place where I felt really safe. When I stepped off the metro train at the Castro station, I quit holding my breath waiting for something bad to happen. My politics, my values, my way of thinking and looking at the world, my very identity itself are much more in keeping with San Francisco than Hicksville, Wyoming. While I enjoy, love and appreciate the city, the truth is, my soul is much more at home in Hicksville than lovely, liberal San Francisco. The country is where I belong, just like being a woman is where I belong.

Also, I loved my time with Paul, partly because I simply loved Paul, and I, like a lot of other women, loved the kind of man he was, though for me, *unlike* a lot of other women, there was no sexual attraction in our love. I also loved the outdoors, and that is certainly not a man thing, though for too many reasons, women are often denied the opportunities I was afforded.

Some people will think that my desire to be a woman is really about the sexual turn on that comes with dressing in women's clothing, that it's really just some sort of sexual fetish. In other words, I am what used to be called a transvestite, a pejorative term no longer used in polite conversation. I'll admit that one of the first visible signs that something was not quite on the button was my early obsession with wearing women's clothing. My senior year of college after my dad died, I repeatedly broke into the college speech and drama department in the wee hours of the mornings to don my favorite evening wear, a lavender satin antebellum gown that was ridiculously small and then, either parade around the darkened building like a ghost or else sit on the green room couch trying to memorize Greek verb tenses. It's a tragic, pathetic, embarrassing memory, and now, wearing women's clothing is no more erotic to me than it is to any other woman. Still, you've got to admit: women's clothing is certainly more sensual, sexy and just plain interesting than men's, which usually rival unsalted boiled zucchini for sheer erotic delight.

While there may be fetishistic overtones to transsexuality, especially prior to coming out, the notion that it's a fetish is discounted for one simple reason. Soon after a male begins taking female hormones, sexual desire – along with the male sex organ itself – dry up like a plump, juicy grape in the hot desert sun. Given that a fetish derives its power from sexual desire, when the desire diminishes, so too should the behavior associated with the fetish; yet that is decidedly not the case with me or with any other transsexual I know. What diminished for me was not the desire to live my life as a woman, but the anxiety, the anger and the angst of trying to live as a man.

A few people think I'm a female impersonator. Now, technically, this is true. If it's true that I once impersonated being a man even though I was really a woman, now I impersonate being female even though anatomically I am male. But, let's face it, tens of thousands of dollars in painful, bloody surgery is a little over the top for someone who simply wants a show business career caricaturing females. Still, God knows, even after all that surgery, I wish I looked half as good as some of those drag queens.

To make things even more complicated, transsexuality often gets mixed up with sexual orientation.

If sex is considered the one reliable fixed point by which we know and are known, if it is the lodestar of identity and virtually everything else about us is up for grabs, then the orientation of our attraction, like the needle of a compass, should be similarly predictable. According to this line of thinking, if a man is sexually attracted to other men, then, at least on some level, he must want to be a woman. While there might be some obscure shred of logic to this belief, I'd be willing to lay money that most gay men – even the wonderfully effeminate ones – do not want their beloved dicks turned inside out and reconfigured into vaginas; nor do lesbians, even the very butch ones, want their clitorises refashioned into permanently attached dildos – though about that I am not as certain.

When people know that I am a Male-to-Female transsexual and that my partner is a woman, they often lurch from simple confusion to outright incredulity. So what does that make me? A lesbian? And why in heaven's name would I go to all the expense and trouble to try and become female if I am sexually attracted to females? It makes no sense. And for that matter, what does it make my partner who started out in a relationship with a guy named Hank? If a Queer is someone who is gay, lesbian, transgender or bisexual, it seems at one time or other, I have been something of them all.

Like a lot of people, I initially confused being transsexual with being gay. If I wanted to be a woman, then surely I had some attraction to men that for some reason had become so repressed as to be unrecognizable. So, following that line of reasoning, I had a few sexual encounters with men that began when I was in graduate school. They were okay; nothing to write home about. (Now there's a letter to spark the imagination. Dear Mom, Had sex with a nice man last night. He was sweet, but I didn't really like the flavor. Your loving son, Hank.)

Many years after I was living in California, I had a couple of encounters with a man I had known years earlier. By this time, I knew I wasn't a gay man, but somehow I fantasized that, as a woman, I might have a long-term romantic relationship with this man who I cared for a great deal. Even though he likewise cared for me, he very clearly had no interest in romance, though he was only too glad to let me give him a little oral pleasure, something it seems, his wife was unwilling to do. For my part, I gladly complied; if for no other reason than to lie with someone stronger than me, and to savor, if just for a few hours, the delicious illusion of love with which so many women deceive themselves.

Ergo: transsexuality and sexual orientation are two different things. Maybe they're related like water that falls from the sky as rain and water that shoots from the earth in a geyser are both water, they, nonetheless, come from entirely different sources. Plus sexual orientation of every kind is confusing. Who can make any sense of it? By what logic can you explain the nature of attraction, even your own – especially your own? Sex – homosexual, heterosexual, whateversexual – is an enigma wrapped in a mystery enclosed in a conundrum – and that's just for "normal" people.

Transsexuality, on the other hand, is really quite simple.

One day on my job as a school bus driver for handicapped kids, I picked up Stephen from the high school. Because of a serious birth defect, Stephen cannot walk, though his other faculties seem reasonably well in order, given that he is, after all, a teenage boy. Standing near him, also waiting for a ride, though not from me, was a lovely young woman. Her long, dark hair, her beautiful olive complexion, the contours of her female body made her a walking incarnation of classic feminine beauty. There they were, just the two of them, not five feet apart, but slouched in his wheel chair like an oversized frog, Stephen had about as much chance of wooing this girl as he had of marrying that Bimbo Barbie pop star he adores. Looking at him, hopelessly stuck in that damaged body for the rest of his days, I realized the similarity of our predicaments and the kinship of our torment. I had as much chance of being like that girl as he had of taking her to the prom, though there the similarity ends. While no one would deny Stephen a medical remedy, should one be found, that might one day allow him to dance at his prom, the same is not true for me. While teams of medical experts work to find a cure for Stephen, transsexuals remain stigmatized, and the relatively simple procedures that might offer at least some chance for a happy life are far beyond most of our financial means. Yet, the unique signature of longing that Stephen and others like him feel is what convinces me that being transsexual is, at bottom, a birth defect just as real and just as painful as Stephen's.

Having said that, I do not think the same is true for homosexuality, and here's why. In a perfect world where people are – in the stirring words of Dr. King – judged by "the content of their character, not the color of their skin" or, in this case, the nature of their love, gay men and lesbian women would not want to be straight. In a perfect world, they would simply love persons of like sex openly and freely, just like hetero couples do today. However, in a perfect world where transsexuals were accepted, even honored, I and others like me would still willingly go through the bloody, painful, risky medical procedures to try and craft a body that as nearly matched our gender as possible – just, in a perfect world, insurance would pay for it. In other words, even in the best of all possible worlds, I still want to look into a mirror and see me, not some man.

No doubt it's the same for someone confined to a wheelchair. If the world was totally wheelchair friendly, if wheelchair bound people were admired, respected and adored, even if there were lots of hot studs and babes flying around in souped-up wheelchairs, given the chance, it's impossible to imagine someone choosing to remain cripple.

That's why it's fitting that when my bus filled with the maimed, the halt, the blind, the c.p. and spinabifida kids, the autistics and Down's, unbeknownst to them, the driver was also a member of the family of the infirm.

Being the Change

I have spoken to enough groups, had enough conversations, endured enough misapplications of pronouns to know that most people find the whole topic of transsexuality terribly confusing. Okay, it's confusing, but so is the theory of relativity, but because Einstein wasn't intimidated by it, we have put people on the moon and one day may travel to distant galaxies. For that matter, my computer's confusing, but if I ever took the time to understand the damn thing, I would undoubtedly be amazed at all the things I could do with it other than just type. And don't get me started on cell phones, whose multitude of indecipherable capabilities make the sending and receiving of calls a mere afterthought.

Likewise, if it sounds preposterous to suggest that sex does not define gender, that being a man might not depend on being male and that being a woman might not depend on being female, let's not forget that at one time it sounded preposterous – as well as blasphemous – to suggest that the earth was not the center of the universe and convincing people otherwise proved no small task.

Maybe if we faced into this confusion, explored it, embraced it…hell, just allowed it to be without stigmatization or prejudice, we might discover – as my favorite therapist was fond of saying – that confusion is the beginning of understanding.

Religious fundamentalists (with whom the vast majority of Christians should not be confused) keep talking about a "gay agenda." Perhaps the real problem with the "gay agenda" is *not* that it is a risible figment of their paranoid delusions but that we have been too timid, too needy for approval, too awash in the shame and guilt they have heaped upon us to rise up and give flesh to their worst fears. And what is their worst fear? Is it that we will seduce the unwary into our silken beds of happy abomination? If so, I think they have seriously underestimated the true magnitude of the threat. The prospect of *verboten* love is the least of their worries, and, at some level, I think they know it. Just as the civil rights struggle established not only the legal rights of African-American people but also, discredited racism's place in society's Story, equal rights for lesbian, gay, bisexual and transgender people will eventually herald an end to heterocentrism and its thuggish bodyguard, homophobia.

Heterocentrism, the assumption that heterosexuality is the center of the relational universe and that everyone is, wants to be, or should be heterosexual is one of those fundamental operating assumptions that might have had survival value back in the days when knuckles were aids in ambulation but now persists in the dark recesses of our vestigial consciousness atrophied by evolution but clung to nonetheless, like the ashes of a long-dead ancestor, too old to remember why they are too important to forget. Just as eliminating racism has expanded the menu of possible relationships we might enjoy to include people of other races, so the end of heterocentrism will likewise expand relational opportunities to include, not only people of the same sex, but of the same sex but opposite gender or the same gender but opposite sex, or, over the course of a lifetime, a veritable smorgasbord of possibilities. Suddenly the menu gets much more interesting.

Still, equal rights for LGBT people *do* threaten the status quo more than Civil Rights, because while civil rights changed laws and attitudes (at least, in those with moral I.Q.s above 50), LGBT rights threaten to redefine our most basic relationships and, at least to some degree, identity itself.

While this sounds radical, I am not the first to suggest that we need to expand the ways we think of ourselves and each other. The great psychologist Carl Jung talked about the powerful unseen forces of the Masculine and the Feminine and how these two great forces exert a tremendous influence on the unconscious doings of us all in ways both great and small.

When we ascribe dominance of each to the corresponding sex – Masculine to males and Feminine to females as implied by the very language we use – we accept the dogma of the old order: that these eternal spiritual forces must be coerced to conform to our frail physiology, thereby fixing their eternal separation. But as Jung said, both Masculine and Feminine forces live conjointly in each of us irrespective of our gender: Feminine as well as Masculine in men and Masculine as well as Feminine in women. Denial of either results in fundamental imbalances that have destructive consequences at a variety of levels and in a variety of ways often as hidden and delayed as those brought on by chemical imbalances in the body. These imbalances, if not righted, can and will lead to pathology.

This pathological imbalance is perpetuated through countless, rarely even noticed restrictions and prohibitions placed on boys and men, restrictions and prohibitions about what they can and cannot do, what they can and cannot wear, how they can and cannot walk, how they must speak, even the words they are permitted to use. I know, because I've been there. While these restrictions and prohibitions can seem trivial, even laughable, each and every one is a nick, a cut, a slice, paring away from boys and men their essential Feminine.

And in a masculine dominated system like ours the Feminine is essentially exiled, though not to some distant land or, even as suggested in certain myths, to the underworld. That would be a mercy. No, the mass marketers have found a better place for her, a more useful place. Situated atop an ornate pedestal, sexualized images of her stand seductively on display, exploiting the addictive qualities of desire in the service of the addictive qualities of greed.

Born into the lineage of this sexualized ideal of the Feminine, girls are told through countless images and media messages that their sexuality, their beauty, and desirability are the sum total of their identities. Even those who resist are not unaffected. Even I'm not unaffected; for the ultimate affirmation of my womanhood is to be found attractive by a man.

While a male-controlled, Masculine-dominated culture like ours might allow a few females of a certain type to exercise the preferred Masculine, the Feminine in men – especially visible manifestations of it – are strictly forbidden and brutally enforced. On any given day on school playgrounds and campuses throughout this country, you can witness boys brutally wielding the club of homophobia against each other through insults, taunts, slurs and threats, only the most egregious of which are ever challenged by school officials and those only because of court decisions that have cost school districts millions of dollars due to their unwillingness to protect gay or gay perceived students.

Sundered at an early age from their Feminine, men, in an attempt not to lose her entirely, project this vital part of themselves onto women, the only socially authorized bearers of the Feminine. They then proceed to objectify, idolize, mistreat, adore, detest, lust after and hate women, since, being objects of projection rather than flesh and blood humans, little real relationship is possible. The opposite is also true for women, though usually not to the same degree.

Even though society pays an exorbitant price for maintaining such an imbalance, there is a generalized acceptance of it, presumably for fear that allowing an unauthorized union of the Masculine and Feminine might abrogate some immutable law of nature, setting loose a kind of atomic relational fusion, resulting in...well, who knows? An outbreak of peace. An epidemic of uncontrolled and uncontrollable cooperation. The creation of a society in which a cup of love is more valuable than a barrel of power – or money. A world where rivers run so clean that on warm, summer days they're full of naked little kids having fun. In other words, chaos!

Hysterical Chicken Littles, furthermore, predict that allowing the Feminine to flourish in men will emasculate, humiliate and depose them from their god-given thrones of power. It will turn them into sissies – girlish men unfit for warriors or mates, plus it might even make them objects of desire for other men, whereupon the sky will surely crash down on our wicked heads. But freeing the Feminine in men will not make them sissies. Nor will it make them gay – unless, by that you mean really, really happy. No, allowing men to embrace their Feminine and women to embrace their Masculine will release us all from the constant need to deny and repress these vital parts of our personalities, and then, project them onto each other with disastrous results. Embracing the sundered parts of ourselves, particularly the Feminine in men, will free us finally to know our true selves, the selves we were lovingly made in the image of God to be.

Yet, the old order benefits in one particularly powerful way from maintaining a macho ideal of manliness; one we have been mystifyingly slow to recognize. Driven by the specter of homophobia, which demands men prove their manliness, our armies are filled with impressionable and often desperate young men. These young men, few of whom are gay, are the real victims of homophobia, because with it, they are driven to perform the senseless acts of violence necessary to promote our nation's corporately determined national agenda. If men, in what might well be the underlying message of the old fairy tales, were ever to find their bewitched inner princess and then, muster the courage necessary to kiss her, they would find themselves freed from this insanity and pathology that demands they slaughter and be slaughtered upon the altar to the patriotic gods of war.

Of course, the ultimate pathology of the old imbalance is the war we are waging on the ultimate expression of the Great Feminine – Mother Earth. We are like a virus multiplying uncontrollably that will stop only when the host upon whom we live dies as a result of our ceaseless aggression. We cannot even enact simple laws, such as building into the price of gasoline the environmental costs of burning it. Corporations continue to exploit labor around the globe so we can consume with ever greater appetites at ever lower prices the blood, sweat and tear stained commodities bought and sold by corporate vampires like Wal-Mart despite the horrendous wake-up call September 11 should have been about the hatred such exploitation breeds. Over and over and over again we convert beautiful places into strip malls and pretentious plastic-sided houses seemingly unaware that as we do so the very things that make life worth living are dying all around us with cries we cannot hear over the ceaseless din of our televisions. What will stop this insanity, this madness, this hell-bent rush toward mass suicide? Nothing less than a restoration of balance between the forces of the Masculine and the forces of the Feminine, a balance that reinstates the Feminine to a position of equal power and authority. Otherwise, beautifully enshrined on her ornate pedestal, she will one day stand over our ravaged planet like a forlorn megalith.

Gandhi said, "Be the change you wish to see in the world." The change I wish to see is the unfettered expression of the Masculine *and* Feminine in both men and women. I want us to authorize females to celebrate their Feminine even as they recover the Masculine power they were forced to relinquish for the specious rewards of domestication promised by the patriarchs. And for males, I want us to validate a potent masculinity liberated from the oppression of machismo even as we invite men to experience, explore and express their Feminine – flamboyantly if they wish – without fear, shame or guilt. So liberated, men will be free to take their place in the ancient lineage and fulfill their role – not of warriors – but of husbands, guardians and stewards of the earth and her inhabitants.

As a result, heterocentrism must be replaced by a richer, larger, more inclusive paradigm and homophobia cast onto the dung heap along with racism, sexism and all the other forms of hatred by which the old order seeks to perpetuate itself. In so doing, we will invariably discredit the god of fundamentalism and expose him for what he is: nothing more than a pig in lipstick masquerading as the God of Scripture, who, by contrast, always stood with the outcast, the oppressed, the poor – the queer – and never on the side of the privileged and the powerful.

That we with our rainbow flag and our subversive loves could be the ones who, in the words of the prophet Isaiah, "loose the bonds of injustice, undo the thongs of the yoke, and allow the oppressed to go free," strikes me as an irony so wondrous as to only be Divine and a threat to the current order far greater than their imagined "gay agenda."

As I play my little part in being the change I wish to see, I am painfully aware of just how weak, fearful, and flawed I am and how hopelessly absurd it is to claim that I am anything other than just another poor soul trying to claw some scrap of meaning out of my otherwise brief existence. And yet, I am convinced that – for reasons of their own – the Powers of Creation throughout time have used the likes of me; have used the likes of you, to work their will, to speak their Word, to touch the world with hope and redeem for good the very worst that we can do. Evidence to the contrary notwithstanding, I believe I am a piece of that redemption, and I believe that you can be a piece of that redemption, and that together we can be the change we wish to see; we can be the change that allows us all to freely be the people we were lovingly made in the image of God to be.

And that's my story, and I'm stickin' to it.

Appendix

Coming out Letter – January 1, 1998

Dear Friends and Family,

In the year I turn 50, I've resolved to tell a story, a love story, a tragedy, an expose, a confession, a comedy, a story some would just as soon not hear and honestly, I'd just as soon not tell. But it is a story that has finally burned its way out of me, and I am compelled to tell it nonetheless.

In my late twenties a big thing was moving through the religious circles of which I was then a part called the healing of memories. It was a version of current trends in the forbidden lands of psychotherapy sanitized for fundamentalist consumption. In it, the leader got us into a hypnotic state (though, of course, it wasn't called that) and had us go back to the earliest memory we could find that needed healing. Over 20 years later, what returned is still clear and unhealed. In the memory, I was very young, no older than two. I was standing before the closed door of a closet. When I opened the door, the only garment hanging inside was a small, blue print dress with white lace circling the collar and edging the sleeves. It was mine.

I did not choose wanting to be a girl. It came unbidden with the territory. And I did not hate being a boy. In fact, I mostly enjoyed it. I played football with reckless abandon and for the sheer delight of its brutal intimacy. I hunted and fished, swam fearlessly in the snake-infested waters of my Mississippi home and camped where there weren't even pit toilets. As an adult, I have loved the camaraderie of men and their uncomplicated friendships. I learned how to fight in some of the final struggles for Civil Rights in the South and managed to lose two well paying careers as a result of my combativeness. I have done the man thing well.

And I always envied the girls. I listened to them talk of slumber parties and ached to be included. I dreamed of being tucked into bed wearing the long, soft, flannel gown embroidered with pink roses I looked at time and again in the J.C. Penny catalog, and I longed to have dark, curly hair that fell about my shoulders or bounced behind me in a ponytail. Deep inside me lived a yearning forbidden and unspoken, a dream I only recently awoke to and found like an undelivered Christmas toy.

Probably the most complicated part of changing my gender is what it means to the other people in my life, especially my partner and two children, Caleb, 17 and Lia, just turning 15. So what's happened to their dad? Is he gone, dead, transformed into another mom? And in public, addressing the person wearing the skirt as 'Dad' certainly attracts attention, but calling me anything else feels weird. And what do you do with the pronouns? We haven't worked it all out yet. This is poorly charted territory, and we're making our way along as best we can, together.

And then there's finding a job as a woman. In the powerful little book *Ishmael*, Daniel Quinn observes that every culture has a story. This story continuously plays in the background, so ubiquitous as to be unnoticed, providing the unquestioned assumptions upon which we base the countless mundane as well as life changing decisions that are our daily fare. The story defines us and everything around us; it assigns our roles and predetermines our choices. We may not like the story; we may even rebel, but eventually we are forced to comply, because disobedience draws a simple and effective punishment: we are not fed. The story can be changed but not without great sacrifice and struggle. In most places, my tribe, queer folk, are not yet accepted within this society's story and are allowed to eat only if we agree to be invisible and often the silent objects of ridicule and scorn. (When was the last time you saw two men walking down the street holding hands or two women romantically kissing in a restaurant? It isn't because we aren't there; we just want to be fed.) God knows, I'd be invisible too if I could. I'd love to just pass as another woman, but the fickle whims of genetics or perhaps wicked, divine humor has rendered that almost impossible. I am either out there in all my glory or hiding in the closet, and it seems I have lost the damn key, and the door somehow locked behind me. Maybe if I get hungry enough, or if I can't feed my children, I'll find it again. But I am now an open and visible member of my tribe and once again in a struggle for civil rights, but this time, my own. Rights are not granted to the unknown and the invisible, and that is part of what compels me to come out. I regret I waited so long; I'm glad I waited no longer.

As you might guess, I'm compounding the confusion by changing my name to Meredith. The Meredith's were part of my father's family who I hardly knew. They were farmers, and the most wonderful work I ever did was farming on a Christian community in Maryland before moving to California. So, to honor my love for the land and as a way of staying connected to my family of origin, I chose the name. Besides, I just like it. You will honor me to use it, though I will certainly understand if you forget.

So, when we next meet, by chance or design, I'm more likely to be the one wearing the dress. It may be a little awkward at first, but if we can keep our sense of humor, respect each other even if we don't necessarily understand and try to keep an open mind, it will work out, more easily than you might think.

But this one thing I know: That memory is finally being healed.

Love,
Meredith

255

Timeline

The Mississippi Period – birth to 33 years old
(with 3 years in Kentucky for seminary and afterward a year working in Big Bend National Park, Texas)

I was born in Clarksdale, Mississippi, some thirty miles east of Old Man River and sixty miles south of Memphis, Tennessee, home of The King – Elvis – who, personally, I couldn't stand. I went from 1st through 12th grades in Mississippi public schools and never had a Black classmate, since those were the days of "separate but equal" education of the races. I can even remember "white" and "colored" drinking fountains and bathrooms at the Greyhound bus station. I wish I could say that I, or at least, someone in my family recognized the terrible injustice of that ridiculous system and opposed it, but I can't. Prejudice and discrimination were as much a part of the air I breathed as DDT, though far and away more toxic.

When Dad, in a vain attempt to make something of himself, bit off more than he could chew on a large commercial construction project and went broke, Greg, my younger brother by seven years, Mom, Dad and I moved to Gulfport, Mississippi where Dad went to work for a construction company. Richard, my older brother by seven years, was married and living in Texas. Amy, seven years younger than Greg, was born while I was in high school in Gulfport, giving her the rare distinction of being younger than her nephews, Richard's sons. So the birth order of my siblings and me goes as follows: Richard, me, Greg and Amy, each separated by about seven years.

After high school, because I fancied I had been called by God into "fulltime Christian service" and was, according to those whose opinions I valued, destined to becoming a mighty Christian evangelist in the lineage of Billy Graham, I attended a small Southern Baptist college some 30 miles north of Gulfport to pursue a theological education. Midway through my senior year, Dad died suddenly, and my life quickly began to unravel.

With the help of Graham Hales, the chaplain at the University of Southern Mississippi and a dear friend, I managed to avoid getting drafted and shipped off to Vietnam. I enrolled in USM ostensibly to get a Masters degree in philosophy while receiving free therapy from the psychology department. To my chagrin I never finished the degree, though, in truth, I didn't deserve it. I had no idea what most of those philosophers were talking about, except, of course, Plato who anyone can understand and everyone should read. Oddly enough, I completely understood Alfred North Whitehead who everyone else seemed to struggle with. I read his cosmology, *Process and Reality* like it was a romance novel, and in some ways, at least for me, it was.

Despite the psychology department's best efforts to make me a normal man, after a year of therapy and graduate study, I went off to the Southern Baptist Theological Seminary in Louisville, Kentucky, still a queer. In three years I managed to get my Master of Divinity degree which prepared me for the pastorate, but, as my childhood minister had predicted, ruined me for being an evangelist – thank God.

Still, you have to appreciate the lost opportunity for scandal. Unlike Jimmy Bakker whose televangelistic empire collapsed when he was convicted of nothing more than run-of-the-mill fraud and conspiracy, I, on the other hand, offered the prospect of a scandal worthy of the name. Can't you just see the headline splashed across the cover of the trashy supermarket tabloid? "Highly Regarded Televangelist Rev. Henry Guest Secretly a Transvestite!" Below the headline would be a photo, all six-foot, two of me gasping in horror into the camera's flash seductively clad in a tight, leather mini skirt, frilly top with big, fake boobs, bigger hair, fishnets and stilettos. Now *that* would be a memoir.

As it was, my final year in seminary I married a lovely, young southern belle, Marsha Lynn Walters. We had been dating for over three years, and she had no idea that I wanted to be…well, *her*. My entire life I've fallen in love with women I've wanted to be – or at least, be like. In a way, it's a compliment to them, since the kind of woman I always wanted to be was kind and loving and pretty and yes, sexy, though in a wholesome, natural sort of way, and smart – don't forget smart. You can't accuse me of setting the bar too low.

After a year of being the Christian minister in Big Bend National Park, we moved back to Mississippi. When Marsha completed her Master's Degree, we moved to Wiggins, Mississippi where I was the assistant minister in charge of youth at the First Baptist Church. It was during this period that I did two things that would change my life forever for the better. I got into group therapy and started attending retreats at Dayspring, the rural Maryland retreat center of Church of the Savior.

CofS was a progressive Christian church headquartered in Washington DC that was founded by Gordon Cosby in the late '40s. It was (and still is) a peace and justice church, anti-war and otherwise socially and politically progressive.

We were in Wiggins for about two and a half years when I moved up the career ladder to the associate minister position at Northminster Baptist Church in Jackson, Mississippi, the state capitol. There I worked with the renowned Dr. John Claypool who, after about a year, fired me when, in his absence, I seriously pissed off some of the most powerful members of the church.

After I was fired from Northminster, we had to sell our house and move into a single room of the private Montessori school where Marsha taught. The school met in a large, rambling house on the bank of a manmade lake surrounded by a small forest of hardwoods. The room where we lived was glass on three sides. I did some of my best bird watching lying in bed early in the mornings before we got up for work.

I worked as the school cook, janitor and after-school Daycare provider. Every day with the help of rotating groups of 4-6 graders, we prepared a hot lunch for the school's 60 students and staff. Our favorite was pizza. We made the dough from scratch every time. Best pizza I've ever eaten.

After school I organized games for the kids who stayed for Daycare. A favorite was Frisbee football. It was played like regular touch football, except with a Frisbee. The teams were always the same – boys vs. girls. I, of course, played on the girls' team. Not because I was out about being a girl; that would be decades later. I played on the girl's team because they were at a cultural disadvantage; no one had ever taught them how to play football – Frisbee or otherwise. They were girls, for god's sake! Why did they need to know how to play football!?

I was determined to change that, and to some degree I think I did. We never beat the boys, but we had a great time trying.

The Maryland Period – 33 years to 40 years old

After a year at the Montessori school, we moved to Dayspring Farm, the retreat and church renewal center of CofS. I went to work on the farm while Marsha taught 4-6 graders at a Montessori school in Silver Spring. When she was out on maternity leave with Caleb, our firstborn, I substituted for her. It didn't take long to realize that putting me in a classroom was like throwing a duck in water; I just instinctively knew what to do. The director, alert to my skills and thrilled at the prospect of having a male elementary teacher, offered to pay for my Montessori training. Driven by the financial demands of children, I quit the farm and became a credentialed elementary Montessori teacher where I taught 4-6 graders in a classroom adjoining Marsha's. Two and a half years after Caleb's birth, Lia was born.

The California Period – 40 years old to the present

When Lia was two and Caleb five, the farming operation of which I was still very much a part went belly up. Marsha and I had always nursed a fantasy of living out West, so when I found teaching jobs for us both at two different Montessori schools, we packed up and moved to Petaluma, California, some thirty miles north of San Francisco. It makes sense that I would have chosen to live near San Francisco, since it was without doubt the best places in the entire country to come out as a transsexual. But for such a propitious choice I have to give credit to the Staffwork of Omnipotence whose choreographic capabilities are consistently misunderstood and seriously underrated.

We hadn't been in Petaluma six months before Thom and Marsha fell in love. I was glad for them. Now, I could be out from under the burden of at least one male identifier: husband. Even though I hated Petaluma from the start and pined for Dayspring like a lost lover, I stayed. Eventually Marsha and I set up different households and shared equally the care of our two beloved children.

With the coveted place of my own and every other week to myself, I finally had the space and time to begin working in earnest with the life-long, all-consuming desire to be a woman. It is about this journey that I have written.

- 1948 – born in Clarksdale, Mississippi

- 1962 – moved to Gulfport, Mississippi where I attended high school
- 1966 – graduated from Gulfport High School
- 1970 – graduated from William Carey College with a BA in religion and philosophy
- 1970/71 – did a year of study at the University of Southern Mississippi in philosophy while getting therapy from a psychology grad student.
- 1971/74 – went to the Southern Baptist Theological Seminary in Louisville, Kentucky
- 1974 – married Marsha Walters
- 74/75 – worked for a year in Big Bend National Park with Christian Ministries in the National Parks
- 1975 – worked for Caruthers construction company in Cleveland, Mississippi while Marsha got her MA from Delta State
- December 1975 – began at First Baptist Church, Wiggins, Mississippi
- 1976 – started group therapy
- October 15, 1976 – began my association with Church of the Savior headquartered in Washington DC
- 1978 – went to Northminster Baptist Church in Jackson, Mississippi
- 1980 – was fired from Northminster and worked for a year at a Montessori school.
- 1981 – moved to Dayspring Retreat Farm near Germantown, Maryland
- 1983 – Caleb was born
- 1985 – Lia was born
- 1987 – left Dayspring for California